The Qumran Text of Samuel and Josephus

HARVARD SEMITIC MUSEUM

HARVARD SEMITIC MONOGRAPHS

edited by
Frank Moore Cross, Jr.

Number 19
THE QUMRAN TEXT OF SAMUEL AND JOSEPHUS
by
Eugene Charles Ulrich, Jr.

Eugene Charles Ulrich, Jr.

THE QUMRAN TEXT
OF SAMUEL
AND JOSEPHUS

Scholars Press

Distributed by
Scholars Press
PO Box 5207
Missoula, Montana 59806

THE QUMRAN TEXT OF SAMUEL AND JOSEPHUS
Eugene Charles Ulrich, Jr.

Library of Congress Cataloging in Publication Data

Ulrich, Eugene Charles, 1938–
    The Qumran text of Samuel and Josephus.

    (Harvard Semitic monographs ; no. 19 ISSN
0073–0637)
        Bibliography: p.
        Includes index.
        1. Bible. O.T. Samuel—Criticism, Textual—History.
2. Josephus, Flavius. I. Title. II. Series.
BS1325.2.U45   222'.4'06   78-15254
ISBN 0-89130-256-5

Printed in the United States of America
1 2 3 4 5
Edwards Brothers, Inc.
Ann Arbor, MI 48104

C O N T E N T S

To my Mother and Father

first and most revered

teachers

PREFACE

This volume presents my doctoral dissertation in essentially unrevised form. It appears unrevised because thus can it more quickly make available the treasures of this remarkable scroll, because critique from the scholarly community will spark the best revision, and because definitive revision will be in order after the complete edition of 4QSam^a in the *Discoveries in the Judaean Desert*. Effort has been made to remove errors that persisted to the dissertation stage, and one entry originally omitted has been restored, thanks to a query from Professor P. A. H. de Boer.

Several people have contributed to the progress of this work, and it is a pleasant reminiscence to express my gratitude to them.

Professor Frank Moore Cross inspired me and this study. He kindled my curiosity for Qumran, alerted me to the importance of Josephus, and offered both the use of the 4QSam^a photographs and generous, patient discussion as the task moved forward. I make frequent reference in my commentary to his "Notes." It is a bit unfair to include them in a published format, but they served a past purpose in distinguishing my original work from his previous observations and a future purpose in alluding to commentary to appear in revised form in the *DJD* volume.

Professor Dr. Dr. Robert Hanhart of Göttingen graciously welcomed me to the Septuaginta Unternehmen and to his seminar. He and the Theological Faculty at Göttingen, especially Professor Walther Zimmerli and his family, could not have made my wife and me feel more at home.

Professor Hanhart and Professor John W. Wevers of Toronto offered their time to read and make suggestions for various parts of this study. Valuable critique came also from my readers, Professor John Strugnell giving insight into assessment of Josephan manuscript evidence and into clues hidden in Old Latin readings, and Professor Paul Hanson clarifying the logic and consistency of the argument.

Père Pierre Benoit of the Ecole Biblique et Archéologique kindly admitted me to the Scrollery for examination of the 4QSam^a scroll, and Hannah Katzenstein and her staff at the Rockefeller Museum provided friendly assistance.

The Sheldon and Pfeiffer Funds supported my Göttingen and Jerusalem study, and the loyal, late Professor G. Ernest Wright, with Professor Cross, helped me procure those grants.

The Notre Dame Theology Department, as *removens prohibens*, helped greatly by making allowances for the completion of this work.

A special prize goes to Miss Carol Cross. She courageously agreed to type the manuscript and did so with stellar competence, cheer, and care--once for the dissertation and yet again for the publication.

Saving the most pleasant till last, I thank Mary Virginia. Though my dissertation put a dent in her career, her thoughtfulness, creativity, and efficiency turned a dissertation home into a happy home. In addition to support and happiness, she gave me Megan and Laura, my two most delightful antidotes to concentration, and, finally, freedom for comradeship with the ghosts of Josephus and that nameless Qumran scribe.

Eugene Charles Ulrich, Jr.
University of Notre Dame
April 4, 1978

x

ABBREVIATIONS AND SIGLA

𝒜̸	Armenian version
ALQ	Cross, *The Ancient Library of Qumran*
Ant.	Josephus, *Jewish Antiquities*
Ap.	Josephus, *Against Apion*
Armc	Aramaic (language)
BANE	Cross, "The Development of the Jewish Scripts" in *The Bible and the Ancient Near East*, ed. G. Ernest Wright, pp. 170-264
BASOR	Cross, "A New Qumran...," *BASOR* 132 (1953) 15-26
B-M	*The O.T. in Greek*, ed. Brooke, McLean, and Thackeray (usually Vol. II, Part I: *I-II Samuel*)
₵̸	Coptic version
C	Chronicles
C^{MG}	M, G of Chronicles
DA	Barthélemy, *Les Devanciers d'Aquila*
de	*deest*: the ms is lacking at this point
Driver	Driver, *Notes on the Hebrew...*
𝐸̸	Ethiopic version
ed	in the text of the critical edition
Field	Field, *Origenis Hexaplorum ... Fragmenta*
G	the majority Greek text (normally S unless specified)
G_2	revised Greek text
G^{SC}	Greek text of S, C
G^h	later Greek text influenced by α' σ' ϑ' or G^o
Gk	Greek (language)
GKC	Gesenius' *Grammar*
G^o	text of Origen's fifth column ("Septuaginta")
G^V	hypothetic Vorlage of the G text
hab	*habet*
Hb	Hebrew (language)
H-P	*Vetus Testamentum graecum cum variis lectionibus*, ed. Holmes and Parsons
HTR	Cross, "The History...," *HTR* 57 (1964) 281-299
J	(1) Josephus; (2) Niese text of *Ant.* V-VII
JBL	Cross, "The Oldest Manuscripts...," *JBL* 74 (1955) 147-172

K	Kings
Kenn	Kennicott
KR	the *kaige* recension
L	(1) the ms group boc_2e_2; (2) Lucianic recension
L_2	late, post-hexaplaric stratum of L
Lexicon	Thackeray and Marcus, *A Lexicon to Josephus*
Loeb	Loeb edition of *Ant.*, ed. Thackeray and Marcus
LXX	"Septuagint," the majority text of the Greek version, recension unspecified
M	(1) Massoretic text; (2) Massoretic text of Samuel, ed. Kittel, 14th ed.
M^{SC}	Massoretic text of S, C
mg	in the margin of the ms
ms(s)	manuscript(s)
n.	note, footnote
NAB	*New American Bible* "Textual Notes"
Notes	Cross, unpublished notes on $4QSam^{a,b,c}$ (see Preface)
OG	Old Greek translation in contrast to later recensions
OL	Old Latin version
$OL^{bsv,etc.}$	editions of OL fragments (cf. B-M, *I-II Samuel*, p. vii)
om	omit
om 4Q	4Q is extant but leaves out the reading
omn	*omnes*: all Greek mss
P	Peshitta
pL	proto-Lucian, the early stratum of L
Ps^{MG}	M, G of Psalms
rell	*reliqui*: the rest of the Gk mss
Rgn	Gk version of 1-2 S (1-2 Rgn) and 1-2 K (3-4 Rgn)
2 Rgn	Gk version of 2 S 1--1 K 2:11
RSV	Revised Standard Version
$\mathcal{S}$	Syriac version
$\mathcal{S}^a$	Ambrosian Codex of the Peshitta
$\mathcal{S}$-ap-Barh	Syh as in Schlesinger (cf. B-M, p. viii)
$\mathcal{S}^b$	Syh as in *Barhebraeus' Scholia on the O.T.*, ed. Sprengling and Graham
$\mathcal{S}^j$	Syriac version of Jacob of Edessa (= Peshitta revised after Gk mss; cf. B-M, p. viii)
$\mathcal{S}^m$	Syh of Barhebraeus attested in Masius (cf. B-M, p. viii)

S	Samuel
S^{MG}	M, G of Samuel
SAYP	Cross, *Studies in Ancient Yahwistic Poetry*
Seb	*Sebîr*: preferred reading
sin nom	*sine nomine*: a marginal reading without attestation of source
Syh	Syro-hexaplar version (largely lost for 1-2 S)
Syrc	Syriac (language)
T	Targum
trp	*transpone(ndum)*, *-it*: (to be) placed in reversed order
txt	in the text of the ms
V	Vorlage (e.g., $4Q^V$ = the Vorlage of 4Q)
vac	*vacat*: the ms is extant but uninscribed at this point
Vann.	Vannutelli, *Libri synoptici*...
vid	*ut videtur*: so it seems from the evidence
Vita	Josephus, *Vita*
Well.	Wellhausen, *Der Text der Bücher Samuelis*
x	times

4Q	4QSam^a
4QSam^a	fragments of the S scroll, Cave 4 Qumran, first half of the first century B.C.
4QSam^{b,c}	similarly, (b) third century, and (c) early first century B.C. scrolls
V VI VII	book V, VI, VII of *Ant.* The Arabic numeral following is the marginal section number in the Niese and Loeb editions.

α	1 Rgn
ββ	2 Rgn 1:1--9:13 (11:1 for Thackeray and Barthélemy)
βγ	2 Rgn 10:1 (11:2 for Th. and B.)--3 Rgn 2:11
γγ	3 Rgn 2:12--21:43
γδ	3 Rgn 22:1--4 Rgn 24:25
βδ	βγ and γδ together

α'	third column of the Hexapla (Aquila)
ϑ'	sixth column of the Hexapla (Theodotion, though in βδ it is L, not Theodotion)
ο'	fifth column of the Hexapla ("70": Origen's reconstruction of the "original LXX")

σ'	fourth column of the Hexapla (Symmachus)
οι γ'	the three (= α' σ' ϑ')
οι λ	the other (λοιποι) translators
+	other mss in addition (e.g., MN+ = MNcdfpx)
++	many or most mss in addition (e.g., MNcdfghipqvwz^{mg} a$_2$b$_2$)
*	(1) hypothetical form (2) original writing of the scribe
a	corrections by the same or an approximately contemporary hand (e.g., B^a)
b	corrections by a later hand
=	the mss cited agree
≠	the mss cited disagree
~	J is paraphrasing, therefore no judgment can be made concerning his Vorlage
>	becomes, changes into
<	is derived from, develops from

INTRODUCTION

The pert Jerusalem tourist agent was persistently curious
to know why I was so eager to trek out to Qumran. Finally with
all the transparently camouflaged enthusiasm of the stereotyped
dissertationist, I replied, "Well, I'm also writing an analysis
of one of the Scrolls." "Oh, no! not another one!" was her de-
flating *Punkt* to that conversation.

But one need not resort to Aristotle's παντες ανθρωποι του
ειδεναι ορεγονται φυσει in order to justify the study of any
human artifact thousands of years old--especially when it is a
written document, and most especially when it is a biblical
manuscript.

On September 4, 1972, at the Los Angeles Congress, the International Organization for Septuagint and Cognate Studies
held a symposium precisely on "The Methodology of Textual Criticism in Jewish Greek Scriptures, with Special Attention to the
Problems in Samuel-Kings."[1]   .

The reasons warranting text-critical attention to the
Books of Samuel are neither new or unpublicized: The Massoretic text of Samuel is "incomplete and difficult,"[2] the Septuagint of Samuel reflects "many interesting Hebrew readings,
very often superior to the MT,"[3] and a recently-discovered
Hebrew text of Samuel 2000 years old "stands in the same general tradition as the Hebrew text upon which the Septuagint was
based,"[4] thus authenticating the critical use of the Septuagint

---

1. The working drafts of the papers delivered at this
symposium are available in *1972 Proceedings: IOSCS and Pseudepigrapha*, ed. Robert A. Kraft (Missoula: Scholars Press, 1972).

2. Harry M. Orlinsky, "The Textual Criticism of the Old
Testament," *The Bible and the Ancient Near East*, ed. G. Ernest
Wright (Garden City, N.Y., 1965), p. 150.

3. Emanuel Tov, "The State of the Question: Problems and
Proposed Solutions," *1972 Proceedings*, p. 3.

4. Frank M. Cross, "A New Qumran Biblical Fragment related to the Original Hebrew Underlying the Septuagint," *BASOR*

for reconstruction of the archaic Hebrew text of Samuel.

The connection of Josephus with a textual study of the books of Samuel may be less obvious, but it is not of less significance: "With the books of Samuel..., Josephus becomes a witness of first-rate importance for the text of the Greek Bible."[5] Josephus, indeed, proves to be a witness of high significance to the Hebrew text of Samuel as well, preserving at least four genuine Samuel readings which were preserved by no other witness until 4QSam[a] was recovered.[6] His reputation as "unscriptural"[7] must therefore be partly reevaluated. And because Josephus' Greek account shows striking similarities with the Hebrew fragments from Qumran, the Lucianic (or, due to the first-century date of Josephus, the proto-Lucianic) text also needs fresh examination[8] as the possible bridge between the Hebrew Samuel and the Greek *Antiquities*.

Purpose

The purpose of this study of 4QSam[a], then, is to determine its relationship to the Massoretic, Septuagintal, and Josephan texts of Samuel. What new data does 4QSam[a] offer concerning the ancient text of Samuel? What does it tell us about the early history of the Septuagint and the postulated "early

---

132 (1953) 23. (Cross's article is hereafter cited as BASOR.) See also now H. M. Orlinsky, "The Septuagint as Holy Writ and the Philosophy of the Translators," *HUCA* 46 (1975) 89-114, esp. the final paragraph.

5. Henry St J. Thackeray, "Notes on the Evidence of Josephus," *The Old Testament in Greek*, ed. A. E. Brooke, N. McLean, and H. St J. Thackeray, Vol. II, Part I (London, 1927), p. ix. (Hereafter cited as B-M.)

6. For discussion of these readings, see below, pp. 165-173.

7. See, for example, Josephus, *Jewish Antiquities*, Vol. V, tr. H. St J. Thackeray and Ralph Marcus (Cambridge, Mass., 1934), pp. 201 note c, 330 note a, 433 note a, etc.

8. The dependence of J on the Lucianic text was first proposed by A. Mez in 1895 but "refuted" by A. Rahlfs in 1911. See below, pp. 22-27 and 250-252.

stratum" of the Lucianic text? What clues does it yield concerning the problem of the text tradition and language of Josephus' Vorlage? Concomitantly, it is necessary to state what does not lie
within the confines of our aims. First, this is not an "edition" of 4QSam^a. That task is beyond the scope of this work
and will be supplied by the *Discoveries in the Judaean Desert*
volume in preparation by Professor Frank Cross with the collaboration of the present author. The analyses here presented
were made independently and from a different starting-point.
In practice, however, for this present study many stages of the
work for an edition had to be worked out in varying degrees of
roughness, but it is foreseen that numerous adjustments will
prove necessary in light of a completely worked-out edition.

Secondly, it cannot be claimed that this is a systematic
study of the Old Greek or proto-Lucianic text. A necessary
prerequisite for that achievement is a thorough and comprehensive work such as the Göttingen critical edition of 1-4 Kingdoms. Nonetheless, the present study will attempt to isolate
and treat in a preliminary fashion material which may be useful
for such a systematic study. Analysis of the Greek version at
points where the pre-Christian 4QSam^a presents readings at variance with the Massoretic Text should illuminate some part of
the early history of the Greek text and provide some criteria
for judging authentic readings, early readings, expansions,
conflations, and so forth.

Thirdly, this is not a comprehensive study of Josephus'
Antiquities. We will not be examining his work as a history,
nor his trustworthiness as a historian, his perceptive and cre-
ative powers as a narrator, his hermeneutical stance and theological framework, or even his diverse sources as a historian.
Our attention will focus only on those points at which his narrative intersects with the contents of the fragmentary 4QSam^a,
and only insofar as he repeats Samuel readings actually attested
in our biblical manuscripts.

Finally, our study will not include the more fragmentary
mss 4QSam^b and 4QSam^c, but for unity of focus and usefulness of
results it will confine itself to the single larger scroll,
4QSam^a. It follows that the results of this study apply

properly only to those sections of the Samuel text for which
4QSam[a] is extant.[9] But, because the characteristics of the
scroll and its patterns of textual affiliation are quite consistent where the fragments are extant, the applicability of
our results to all of 1-2 Samuel should enjoy a high degree of
probability.

The purpose of this study, then, is to describe the textual nature of the major Samuel Scroll from Qumran, and to
chart its relationship to the Massoretic Text, to the various
forms of the Greek Version, and to the narrative of Josephus'
Jewish Antiquities. The hypothesis, suggested by Cross[10]--
that Josephus used a Greek Bible reflecting a Hebrew Vorlage
close to 4QSam[a]--will be tested in detail.

Presuppositions

A presupposition of the present study is the theory of recensional development in the Greek text of Samuel-Kings orig-
inated by Père D. Barthélemy and amplified by Cross. A pellu-
cid exposition of this hypothesis is enunciated by James D.
Shenkel in *Chronology and Recensional Development in the Greek
Text of Kings*, pp. 5-21, to which the reader is referred.[11]
Here it is necessary to mention only four main points.

First, the majority of Greek manuscripts, including and
especially B, display basically the Old Greek translation of
approximately the second century B.C. predominantly for 1 S 1--
2 S 9 and then the *kaige* recension of approximately the turn of
the era predominantly for 2 S 10--1 K 2:11. The majority Greek
text will be designated G in general, but where it is possible
and useful to distinguish, the designations OG and KR will be
used. "The *kaige* recension" may prove to be a yet more complex
phenomenon (see chapters I D. and VII A.).

Secondly, the Lucianic text family in Samuel is composed

---

9. See the List of 4QSam[a] Fragments on p. 271.

10. F. M. Cross, "The History of the Biblical Text in the
Light of Discoveries in the Judaean Desert," *HTR* 57 (1964) 292.
(This article is hereafter cited as HTR.)

11. See also now Cross, "The Evolution of a Theory of
Local Texts," *1972 Proceedings*, pp. 108-126.

of at least two strata. An early stratum, designated pL, is
early enough to influence New Testament writers, the *Vetus
Itala*, Josephus, Justin Martyr, and others. A late stratum,
designated L_2, dates from approximately the time of Lucian, the
presbyter and martyr of the late third and early fourth centuries (d. 311/2), but at any rate it is late enough to be considerably influenced by the hexaplaric recension.[12] Whether
the early stratum is further divided into an original Greek
translation and an early proto-Lucianic revision of OG will be
discussed below.[13]

Thirdly, the various components (G^h) of the hexaplaric
text, and specifically Origen's attempted reconstruction of the
LXX (G^o), are generally the OG corrected toward the developing
Massoretic text.

Fourthly, with the destruction of Qumran and especially
the adoption of the Massoretic text in the second half of the
first century A.D., the Hebrew texttype displayed by 4QSam[a] was
no longer directly influential after the end of that century.

It should be stressed that the theory of recensional development is being presupposed here as a working hypothesis; it
is not being presumed as a priori true or as pronounced true by
the judgment of scholars in consensus. The data, moreover, are
so presented that they should be useful irrespective of the
hypothesis. The alternative to building upon some form of this
hypothesis is to admit an array of unrelated and sporadically
corrected/corrupted manuscripts or text traditions. There is,
however, sufficient evidence,[14] not necessarily to prove incon-
trovertibly the details of that hypothesis, but to indicate
that the patterns of variants are defined enough now to warrant
and even demand that it be rigorously tested. This volume is
both a partial test of that hypothesis and an effort to build a

---

12. See the carefully worked dissertation of Sebastian
Brock, "The Recensions of the Septuagint Version of I Samuel"
(D.Phil. dissertation, Oxford University, 1966). It is unfor-
tunate that most of the present study was completed by the time
I learned of this work and was able to obtain a copy.

13. Pp. 32-33 and 257-259.

14. See pp. 33-36 below.

broader base for testing.

With regard to results, though formulae will be used, it is understood that they are only a Procrustean means for categorizing and systematizing data. The comparative importance and strength of the results will lie not in the formulae, but in the readings and analyses themselves. Furthermore, individual readings--no matter how striking--do not of themselves yield certitude. Rather, what we should hope for is a type of inductive probability: since there is a certain amount of mixing of readings observable in all texts, the usefulness of this investigation will depend upon the isolation of significant patterns (formulae), but even more upon the frequency of examples which clearly incarnate those formulae.

Methods and Outline

The investigation will take the following shape. Those segments, and only those, of 1-2 Samuel will be examined where 4QSam^a is extant and diverges from the Massoretic Text or from the Greek version (hereafter, 4Q, M, and G, respectively). An attempt has been made to include all the instances of the latter as well, since emphasis only on the former could occasion a distorted view of 4Q's extensive agreement with M. 4Q variations from M, however, are rather clearly discernible, whereas 4Q variations from the Greek are at times difficult to isolate.

There are three classes of 4Q material which will not be included: (1) proper names as such, (2) purely orthographic variants, and (3) readings too fragmentary or nebulous to produce any result. Otherwise, all 4Q divergences from M and as many as detectable from G are included.

Each of the divergent readings will consist of a line-up of the mss relevant for that reading (4Q M T P G L G^h OL for Samuel, followed by parallels from Chronicles or Psalms, and finally by J).[15] 4Q, M, and G will always be listed; when other versions are not extant or not helpful for the point under discussion, they will be omitted. Similarly, not all variants (especially within G) are given, but all those *are* given

_____

15. Cf. the List of Abbreviations on pp. **xi-xiv** and the discussion of Texts and Editions on pp. 9-14.

that may have a bearing on the point under discussion. It will
be assumed that the reader is armed with M, the Brooke-McLean-
Thackeray critical edition of Samuel, and the *Antiquities*.
A commentary on the reading will be appended, including
the following where appropriate: (1) citation of comment by
other critics (such as Wellhausen, Driver, Barthélemy, Cross,
or the "Textual Notes" of the *New American Bible*); (2) discussion of 4Q palaeography, spacing, reconstruction; (3) explanation of the stages of development of the several variants,
where possible; and (4) a formula categorizing the reading, preceded by an indication of the relative strength of the reading.

Rather than being presented simply seriatim, the analyses
of the variant readings will be grouped qualitatively into
categories, to assist the reader in assessing the overall significance of the readings.[16] The categories will be in accord
with the theory of recensional development discussed above.

After a survey (Chapter I) of the history of the problem,
Chapter II will present readings in which 4Q agrees with G
against M. Chapter III will present readings in which 4Q
agrees with L against the combined M G. Again, in accord with
the stated presuppositions--namely, that there is a qualitative
change in the Greek text at 2 S 10, and that the Lucianic text
in βγ (2 S 10--24) is a more consistent witness to the OG than
the majority of Greek uncials and minuscules--part A in each of
the two chapters will contain the readings from α ββ, and part
B will contain the readings from βγ. The readings will be further subdivided into plus, minus, and variant readings (relative to M as the traditional basis). Several of the more

---

16. The qualitative categorization of the readings does
not have as its purpose to impose the writer's presuppositions
or conclusions on the reader, but rather to assist in gaining
focus on the data--data which span not a single, continuous
spectrum but a series of fragmented spectra along multiple axes.
The reader is asked to question critically (1) whether each individual reading is correctly categorized, (2) whether the category itself is validated by the sum of the readings included,
and (3) whether the contents of the divisions of categories
support or discredit the theories upon which this study is based.

striking examples from each type of reading will introduce
their respective sections in order to elucidate the significance of the section as a whole and to illuminate the significance of readings where the evidence may be fragmentary, nebulous, etc.

Chapter IV will then present and evaluate evidence contrary to the alleged 4Q = OG/pL agreement; it will be subdivided into 4Q combinations of M + G, readings in agreement
with neither M nor G where those two differ, readings in disagreement with the combined M G witness, and readings in agreement with M against G.

Chapter V will consider the evidence of Chronicles in
those Samuel-Chronicles parallels for which 4Q is extant.[17] The
Hebrew text of C is a witness to the Hebrew text of S in early
post-exilic Judah. It thus provides an added control on the
ancient Hebrew text of S.

Chapter VI will list the Josephus evidence. The text of J
has been checked for all parallels with the 4QSam[a] material.
Understandably, many of the 4Q divergences were so minute as
not to be reflected by J, and many were simply passed over by
him as unimportant for his narrative. These have, accordingly,
remained tacitly unrecorded or been explicitly marked "om." J
has often paraphrased the content in such a way that his evidence is partially or totally ambiguous. In such instances,
the reference has been noted and marked "˜"; his evidence has
been omitted or listed nonetheless, as considered appropriate.
Where J does recount the detail in a given reading, his witness
has already been listed in chapters II-V. Chapter VI will then
pull together that evidence so that the reader may review it
systematically. It will be introduced in part A by the dramatic readings which exhibit agreement of J and 4Q alone, followed by other patterns of J-4Q agreement. Part B will examine
the textual affiliation of J in those readings in which J disagrees with 4Q.

The evidence presented in chapters II-VI, grouped qualitatively according to categories of readings, presents an

---

17. See the List of Chronicles Parallels to Samuel and
4QSam[a], p. 273.

atomistic view of 4Q and its textual relationships. To coun-
terbalance this, chapter VII will examine quantitatively a complete, continuous chapter of Samuel, 2 S 6.

Chapter VIII will treat the problem of the language of
Josephus' Vorlage. Insofar as it has been demonstrated in
chapters II-VII, and especially VI, that J used a bible close
to the 4Q tradition, we now ask: was that bible in the Hebrew
or Greek language? Part A will discuss the issues and possibilities. Parts B and C (Text and Commentary), building on the
detailed analysis of 2 S 6 from chapter VII, will examine
minutely J's Greek narrative to determine whether his Vorlage
for that chapter was in Hebrew or Greek. Part D, finally, will
consider the evidence of 4Q, Mez, Rahlfs, Thackeray, and Marcus
challenging the hypothesis that Josephus used a Greek Vorlage
for the narrative of 1-2 Samuel.

In summary, the method used will be an inductive line-up
of the 4Q readings insofar as they diverge from M or G. The
analyzed readings will be grouped primarily qualitatively according to the stated presuppositions of the hypothesis of recensional development, though 2 S 6 will be investigated continuously to put into focus the quantitative proportions of the
typical patterns. The narrative of Josephus' *Antiquities* will
have been kept under surveillance all the while and in the
final chapters the language of his Vorlage will be investigated
in an attempt to settle that question.

Texts and Editions

The texts and editions employed in this study are the following.[18]

The Qumran Samuel readings are taken from 4QSam[a]. They
are based primarily on the photographs of the scroll made
available to me through the kindness of Professor Frank Cross
and are for the most part checked against the leather scroll
itself in Jerusalem. Professor Cross has been consulted on
many readings and has given characteristically generous help,
for which I wish to express my gratitude. I wish also, however,

---

18. Full bibliographic data for the texts and editions
will be found grouped in the Bibliography.

to free him from liability for any misreadings in this volume,
for which I alone stand responsible.

For editions of 4QSam[a], see the forthcoming major publication of the scroll in *Discoveries in the Judaean Desert*, being
prepared by Cross with the collaboration of the present writer.
A preliminary publication of the first columns of the scroll
was published by Cross in *BASOR* 132 (1953), 15-26. Many of the
significant readings from the entire scroll, as well as from
4QSam[b,c], can be found in the "Textual Notes" of the *New American Bible*.

Palaeographically, 4QSam[a] dates from the first half of the
first century B.C.[19] and consists of fragments of a single,
continuous scroll containing 1-2 Samuel. A list of the passages for which fragments are extant can be found on page 271.
It is the hypothesis of this study that 4QSam[a] forms part of
the Palestinian text tradition which comprises the late sixth/
fifth century B.C. text of the Chronicler, the late third century B.C. text of 4QSam[b], the early first century B.C. texts of
4QSam[c,a] as well as the contemporaneous Vorlage of the proto-
Lucianic revisional activity.[20]

The Massoretic text of Samuel is cited from the fourteenth,
revised edition (1966) of *Biblia Hebraica*, edited by Rudolf
Kittel. For the other books the Massoretic text is from the
twelfth edition (1961). This Massoretic text tradition is
based on the Leningrad Codex B 19[A], dated 1008/9, which in turn
is a copy of a codex made by Aaron ben Moses ben Asher, who
stood at the pinnacle of Tiberian Massoretic achievement in the
middle of the tenth century.[21] The text tradition adopted by
the Massoretes can be traced back as far as the first century
of our era, thanks to the finds at Masada and Murabba'at, and

---

19. In BASOR, p. 16 and note 2, Cross dated the scroll to
the first century B.C. Since 1953 he has narrowed the possibility to the first half of that century.

20. Cf. HTR, p. 296.

21. Cf. *Biblia Hebraica*, Prolegomena, pp. XXIX-XXX, and
M. Greenberg, "The Stabilization of the Text of the Hebrew
Bible, Reviewed in the Light of the Biblical Materials from the
Judean Desert," *JAOS* 76 (1956) 158.

in the case of Samuel this tradition can be traced to the turn of the era, in the form of the Vorlage of the *kaige* recension.[22] Variant Hebrew readings, generally within the Massoretic tradition, are compiled in the volumes of Kennicott and de Rossi.

The Greek text of Samuel is cited from the edition of Brooke-McLean-Thackeray and, where not specified, represents primarily Vaticanus Codex B. Rahlfs' hand edition, however, has usually been consulted in addition, at the suggestion of Professor Dr. Dr. Robert Hanhart, director of the Septuaginta-Unternehmen in Göttingen.[23] For supplementary Greek evidence the volumes of Field, Holmes-Parsons, and Lagarde have been used as well as the conveniently-arranged Vannutelli synoptic edition. For books other than Samuel, the Cambridge or Göttingen critical editions have been used where possible, elsewhere the hand edition of Rahlfs.

It is axiomatic that LXX mss show different characteristics and different family groupings for the different books of the bible. The main groupings for 1-2 Samuel are the following:[24]

---

22. Cf. HTR, p. 289; and D. Barthélemy, "A Reexamination of the Textual Problems in 2 Sam 11:2 - 1 Kings 2:11 in the Light of Certain Criticisms of *Les Devanciers d'Aquila*," *1972 Proceedings*, pp. 60-61.

23. Professor Hanhart helpfully informed me that though Rahlfs professedly employed the uncials B S A for his edition, for the books of Samuel and Kings he also consulted many minuscules, especially the Lucianic mss, knowing their importance from his predecessor, Lagarde, and from his own *Lucians Rezension der Königsbücher*.

24. The writer acknowledges initial dependence on the groupings in Rahlfs, *Lucians*, pp. 9-80, Johnson, pp. 19-21, and Cross, Notes. The groupings presented above represent the writer's subsequent assessment, based on Rahlfs, Johnson, Cross, and his own observations. See also now Brock, "The Recensions," p. vi. All are in essential agreement.

Edition	Primary	Secondary	Versions
Old Greek (G) [25]	B y a_2	M N f m s w	ⱬ ⱷ (OL)
Lucianic (L)	b' b o c_2 e_2	g i z^{mg} M^{mg}	OL g^j Thdt Chr
Kaige (KR) [25]			
Hexaplaric (G^O)	A c x	d l p q t z	ⱷ Syh

Fragments of the Old Latin text are cited from Sabatier, *Bibliorum Sacrorum Latinae Versiones Antiquae, seu Vetus Italica*, and from the critical apparatus of Brooke-McLean, Vannutelli, and Vercellone. Critical sorting of the divers OL witnesses for 1-2 Samuel yet remains to be done (Cf. Wevers, *Genesis*, p. 35). The Old Latin, dating from approximately the second/third century A.D., is important for this study because it is translated from OG/pL, [26] often preserves Lucianic readings, and is thus an important witness to the Palestinian text type. The Vulgate, on the other hand, seldom enters our picture, due to its late date and its confessed correction to the *hebraica veritas*.

Targumic quotations are from Sperber's critical edition of the Aramaic Bible. The Targum of Jonathan for Samuel, dating from the early centuries of our era, is essentially a literal translation of M with expansions, and thus is not often valuable

---

25. The mss listed for the Old Greek are such up to 2 S 9:13. After 2 S 10:1 most G mss (except for boc_2e_2) display the *kaige* recension. All the texts have some mixing, but those listed under the family groupings exhibit sufficient stability to be dealt with as families.

26. Cf. the conclusion of B. Fischer, "Lukian-Lesarten in der Vetus Latina der vier Königsbücher," *Studia Anselmiana* 27-28 (Rome, 1951) p. 173: "Dieses *Ergebnis* beweist eindeutig den prälukianischen Charakter der Vorlage von VL. Oder genauer ausgedrückt: Die VL ist nach einem griechischen Texttyp geschaffen, der von Lukian stark zur Herstellung seiner Rezension benützt worden ist." But he goes on to say that certain "Lucianisms" (i.e., recensional characteristics usually associated with the later Lucianic recension) are already attested in OL and Cyprian, thus proto-Lucianic recensional characteristics. One of these characteristics attested by Cyprian is "Verbesserungen des *G*-Texts nach dem Hebräischen"!

as an independent witness.

The Peshitta is cited from Ceriani's photolithographic copy of the sixth-century Ambrosian Codex. The Syriac Version is generally considered to date from the second century A.D. and again is close to M for the books of Samuel, though its substratum preserves some Palestinian readings.

The Syro-hexaplar of Samuel, a Syriac translation of G^O, is no longer extant, except for some words and phrases attested by Masius and for a few extracts from Barhebraeus quoted by B-M. B-M also quote from the Syriac version of Jacob of Edessa "such readings as can reasonably be regarded as translations from a Greek Septuagint text."[27] This version is a revision of the Peshitta on the basis of Septuagintal mss, and consequently when it is quoted by B-M, it often agrees with G^{BL}, especially G^L. It was produced in 704-705, and the ms from which B-M quote is dated approximately 719.

For the text of Josephus' *Jewish Antiquities* V.338--VII, the critical edition of Niese is the primary edition used, supplemented by the Loeb edition of Thackeray and Marcus. The latter edition is also based on that of Niese, but "is the outcome of a careful and independent investigation of the MS. evidence in all cases."[28] Of the Greek mss of Josephus Niese considers R O "by far the best, freest from interpolation, and closest to the archetype."[29] They are fourteenth and fifteenth century mss, respectively. Next is M (thirteenth century) with not infrequent additions, followed by S P (each eleventh century) which both share interpolations common to M and add material of their own.[30]

---

27. B-M, p. viii.

28. H.St J. Thackeray in *Josephus*, Loeb edition, vol. I, p. xviii.

29. B. Niese,ed., *Flavii Iosephi Opera*, vol. I, Praefatio, p. XXXVII; cf. p. XXXII.

30. Niese, pp. XLI-XLVIII. Thackeray, however, criticizes Niese:

... Niese bases his text [of *Vita*] on the oldest MS., P....
  All textual critics of Josephus must gratefully

The Latin version of Josephus is of high importance.
Niese says that the text of Josephus was translated into Latin
"at the time when Christianity pervaded the Roman Empire,"[31]
and Cassiodorus refers to Josephus as "almost a second Livy"[32]
because the Latin version of the *Antiquities* was so widespread.
Franz Blatt, editor of *The Latin Josephus*,[33] agrees with Niese
that the oldest extant Latin ms of Josephus is "very close to
the Greek text."[34] This is the venerable sixth-century Ambrosian Codex from Milan, "of rare trustworthiness and quality...,
by far the best."[35] Although only a fragment, the fragment
covers *Ant.* V.334--X.204, fortunately spanning our section, its
gaps being supplied by an accurate seventeenth-century copy.[36]

---

acknowledge their indebtedness to Niese and their dependence upon the evidence collected in his edition. Yet one
may respectfully question whether he has established a definitive text. As Naber has remarked, he seems to have
somewhat overrated the value of a single ill-written MS.,
and the true text or the nearest approximation to it is
sometimes relegated to his *apparatus criticus*. The difficulties which confront the editor of Josephus arise from a
comparative paucity of ancient MSS., the inconstancy of
some MSS., which renders grouping uncertain, and the fact
that corruption has often affected the text of all. Each
variant has to be considered on its merits; and there is
considerable scope for conjectural emendation....
Loeb edition, vol. I, pp. xvii-xviii.
   31. Niese, p. XXVII.
   32. Quoted in Niese, p. XXVII.
   33. København, 1958.
   34. Blatt, p. 25.
   35. Niese, p. XXVIII.
   36. Blatt, pp. 26-27.

Chapter I
THE HISTORY OF THE PROBLEM

The problem with which we are dealing falls basically under
three headings: Qumran, proto-Lucian, and Josephus. We are
interested to know: (1) What new does the major Samuel scroll
from Qumran tell us about the ancient form of the text of
Samuel? What are its kindred text forms (e.g., OG, pL, OL, C,
J)? (2) What can we establish concerning the *early* stratum of
L? Since a 4Q texttype in Hebrew would have been unavailable
to Lucian, what can 4Q tell us about the proto-Lucianic text
which formed the basis of the Lucianic recension? (3) Can it
be known which type of Samuel text J used? In which language?
Where J is repeating actually attested S readings (from Hb,
Armc, Gk mss), which text family does he most regularly follow?

These general headings will be made more specific through
the development of this chapter. Anticipating conclusions, we
can sketch a synoptic preview of the history of the problem.
(A) There is a series of early references (*pace* Barthélemy),
especially by Jerome, sufficient to ground a triple variety of
ancient Greek text traditions, one of which was called and may
still legitimately be called Lucianic. (B) There is also a
line of 16th-19th century testimony and criticism about a certain variant text family, and this text family can be linked
with the Lucianic text. (C) From the turn of the 20th century
the text of Josephus is recognized as an important touchstone
for the proto-Lucianic text. (D) This line of study is generally on the right track, but since the Qumran discoveries all
must be rechecked and refined. This is where we are at present: A number of contemporary studies has helped lay the
groundwork for more controlled study of problems related to
ours.

A. Early References to the Lucianic Text

Since lists of excerpted notices concerning Lucian and his
training and industriousness in biblical scholarship are readily

found,[1] it will be necessary to present here only some salient features pertinent to the main line of our investigation.

Eusebius of Caesarea (c. 260-340) speaks twice in the *Church History* of his contemporary, Lucian (d. 311/12). Recording the presbyter's martyrdom in the time of Maximinus, he praises Lucian as "excellent in his whole life,"[2] and again as "excellent in all regards, both self-controlled in life and well trained in sacred learning."[3] Despite Lucian's Christological problems[4] and his (mistakenly) condemnatory inclusion in the *Decretum Gelasianum*,[5] Eusebius' contemporary witness to Lucian's illustriousness and sacred learning appears to withstand critical investigation.[6]

Jerome bequeathes four judgments on Lucian and his work, negative as well as positive. These testimonies are not confused or contradictory; they simply reflect different standpoints.

---

1. Especially helpful are H. B. Swete, *An Introduction to the Old Testament in Greek*, rev. ed. (New York, 1968), pp. 80-83; H. Dörrie, "Zur Geschichte der Septuaginta im Jahrhundert Konstantins," *ZNW* 39 (1940) 57-110; M. J. Routh, *Reliquiae Sacrae*, 2nd ed., vol. IV (Oxford, 1846), pp. 3-17; and B. Metzger, *Chapters in the History of New Testament Textual Criticism* (Leiden, 1963), pp. 1-7.

2. τον παντα βιον αριστος, MPG 20.773C.

3. τα παντα αριστος βιω τε εγκρατης και τοις ιεροις μαθημασι συγκεκροτημενος, MPG 20.808C-809A. τα ιερα μαθηματα, of course, refer preeminently to scriptural learning.

4. Cf. Metzger, pp. 1-2 and notes.

5. Cf. Ernst von Dobschütz, *Das Decretum Gelasianum de libris recipiendis et non recipiendis* [=TU 38/4] (Leipzig, 1912). Among the "subdenda" (p. 48) are "Evangelia quae falsavit Lucianus: apocrypha; Evangelia quae falsavit Hesychius: apocrypha" (p. 51). See also MPL 29.528D and Metzger, p. 5 and note 5.

6. Von Dobschütz (p. 292) concludes that the latter condemnation is the result of a misunderstanding of Jerome's statement (cf. note 7 below). For the former, cf. Metzger, pp. 1-2 and notes.

First, comparing Lucian's critical labors with his own,
Jerome denounces Lucian's emendational activity.[7]

Again, still somewhat negatively, after lamenting that the
old Septuagint "corrupta sit atque violata," he records the
localities in which the various Septuagintal texts, including
Lucian's, are honored.[8]

Thirdly, however, when Jerome doffs his critical and dons
his hagiographical biretta, his assessment parallels that of
Eusebius, praising Lucian as such a capable and industrious
Scripture scholar that one contemporary form of the Scriptures
still continues to bear his name.[9]

Finally, defending his Roman Psalter in the letter to Sun-
nius and Fretela, Jerome distinguishes the hexaplaric *Septuaginta* edition, which he had translated into Latin, from that
which had in Origen's day been called κοινη (common and widely
published) and was by Jerome's day also called Lucianic. About
15 lines later, he further defines that the κοινη is also

---

7. "Praetermitto eos codices, quos a Luciano et Hesychio
nuncupatos, paucorum hominum asserit perversa contentio: quibus
utique nec in veteri Instrumento post Septuaginta Interpretes
emendare quid licuit, nec in Novo profuit emendasse; cum mul-
tarum gentium linguis Scriptura ante translata, doceat falsa
esse quae addita sunt." *Praefatio Hieronymi in Quatuor Evangelia*, MPL 29.527B. Cf. also E. C. Ulrich, "4QSam[a] and Septuagintal Research," *Bulletin of the International Organization for
Septuagint and Cognate Studies* 8 (1975) 25-26.

8. "Alexandria et Aegyptus in Septuaginta suis Hesychium
laudat auctorem: Constantinopolis usque Antiochiam, Luciani
[*Al.* Juliani] martyris exemplaria probat. Mediae inter has pro-
vinciae Palaestinos [*Al.* Palaestinae] codices legunt; quos ab
Origene elaboratos Eusebius et Pamphilus vulgaverunt; totusque
orbis hac inter se trifaria varietate compugnat." *Praefatio
Hieronymi in Librum Paralipomenon*, MPL 28.1324B-1325A.

9. "Lucianus, vir disertissimus, Antiochenae ecclesiae
presbyter, tantum in Scripturarum studio laborat, ut usque nunc
quaedam exemplaria Scripturarum Lucianea nuncupentur." *De Viris
Inlustribus*, 77 [*TU* XIV, pp. 41f., ed. E. C. Richardson],
quoted in Metzger, p. 4, note 2.

Septuaginta, but that there is this difference: the κοινη is
the/an old edition which differing localities, ages, and scribal
interpretations have corrupted, whereas the hexaplaric text is
the translation of the Seventy preserved incorrupt and unblem-
ished in the books of the erudite.[10]

I would cautiously agree with Metzger[11] and Barthélemy[12]
that later testimonies of Suidas, Simeon Metaphrastes, Pseudo-
Athanasius, Epiphanius, and Josippus are possibly too late and
too open to suspicion to be included as indubitably credible
witnesses.

And so, the case can rest, relying basically on the testimony of Eusebius and Jerome. For we have one contemporary historian testifying to Lucian's good training in sacred learning
and one critical biblical scholar a century later who, while
praising Lucian's industrious labors in the scriptures, gives
valuable evidence through his criticism: that Lucian was

---

10.   "In quo illud breuiter admoneo, ut sciatis aliam esse
editionem, quam Origenes et Caesariensis Eusebius omnesque
Graeciae tractatores κοινα--i'd est communem--appellant atque
uulgatam et a plerisque nunc Λουκιανειος dicitur, aliam septuaginta interpretum, quae et in εξαπλοις codicibus repperitur et
a nobis in Latinum sermonem fideliter uersa est et Hierosolymae
atque in orientis ecclesiis decantatur....

"κοινη autem ista, hoc est communis, editio ipsa est, quae
et Septuaginta. sed hoc interest inter utramque, quod κοινη
pro locis et temporibus et pro uoluntate scriptorum uetus corrupta editio est, ea autem, quae habetur in εξαπλοις et quam
nos uertimus, ipsa est, quae in eruditorum libris incorrupta et
inmaculata septuaginta interpretum translatio reseruatur.
quicquid ergo ab hac discrepat, nulli dubium est, quin ita et
ab Hebraeorum auctoritate discordet." *Epistula* CVI, 2.2,
Sancti Eusebii Hieronymi Epistulae II (CSEL 55), ed. I. Hilberg
(Vienna, 1912), pp. 248-249.

11.   Pp. 5-6.

12.   "A Reexamination of the Textual Problems in 2 Sam
11:2 - 1 Kings 2:11 in the Light of Certain Criticisms of *Les
Devanciers d'Aquila*," *1972 Proceedings: IOSCS and Pseudepigrapha*, ed. R. Kraft (Missoula: Scholars Press, 1972), pp. 84-87.

responsible for a Greek text form at variance with Origen's,
that it was the emendational character of this text form that
he rejected, that this text form held sway over Syria and Asia
Minor, and that Lucian's text tradition was so common and
widely used that it was called (even by Origen, a century before Lucian!) κοινη.

B. 16th-19th Century History of Samuel Mss boc_2e_2

The great Complutensian Polyglot, a project begun in 1502
by the Spanish Cardinal Francisco Ximenes de Cisneros in honor
of the birth of Charles V and printed at Alcala *(Complutum)* in
the years 1514-1517, contained the first printed text of the
complete Greek Old Testament.[13] The Polyglot contains the OT
in Hebrew in the first column, the Greek in the third column,
and the Vulgate in the central column. Minutes still extant in
the Vatican library record that Leo X lent Vatican ms 330 (=H-P
108, =B-M *b*) to the editors in Spain,[14] and Delitzsch has shown
that this ms, supplemented by the Venetian ms Marc.5 (=H-P 68),
served as the basis for the Greek column,[15] though that column
was frequently corrected toward M.[16]

Vatican 330 (=H-P 108) is nearly identical with Chigi ms
R. vi.38 (=H-P 19), so that in the Brooke-McLean notation they
are *b* and b', respectively, and are cited together simply as b.

Monumental collections of variant readings from Greek OT
mss and quotations therefrom by the Fathers were amassed in the
seventeenth and eighteenth centuries, culminating in the praise-
worthy but not altogether trustworthy edition of Holmes and
Parsons at Oxford in 1798-1827. Through collections of variants

---

13. Swete, p. 171.

14. S. R. Driver, *Notes on the Hebrew Text and the Topography of the Books of Samuel* (Oxford, 1890), p. 1 [= Roman 50],
note 1.

15. *Fortgesetzte Studien zur Entstehungsgeschichte der
complutensischen Polyglotte* (Leipzig, 1886), pp. 2 and 19ff.;
cf. Swete, pp. 172-173.

16. Cf. Rahlfs' detailed textual analysis for 1 K 1 in
Lucians Rezension de Königsbücher, Septuaginta Studien III
(Göttingen, 1911), pp. 18-23.

such as these it was noticed that frequently H-P mss 19, 82,
93, 108 together preserved identical variants against all other
witnesses.[17]

In an 1853 dissertation from Münster, J. P. Nickes noted
that 108 "and other codices pertaining to that family" were
closer than the other Gk codices to the Old Latin version.[18]
Vercellone, to whom we owe the notice about Nickes, remarked in
1864 that 19, 82, 93, 108 tallied with the Old Latin marginal
notes of the Leon Vulgate, thus solidly establishing the link
of this Greek text with the Old Latin.[19]

But it was Ceriani in 1861 and 1863 who first recognized
that these mss, together with Chrysostom and the Complutensian
Polyglot, contain the "Lucianic recension."[20] The fundamental
connection was Chrysostom (d. 407), who as priest of Antioch
and patriarch of Constantinople would have been trained in and
would have made use of the Lucianic bible; for his contemporary,
Jerome, hád related that the area from Constantinople to Antioch used the Lucianic LXX.[21] Besides the readings from Chrysostom and the Complutensian Polyglot in common with 19, 82, 93,
108, Ceriani noticed that the Syriac version of Jacob of Edessa
(Brit. Mus. ms Add. 14,429) shared with the "recensione del
Patriarcato Antiocheno" both the same orthography of proper
names and the extension of Rgn β up to the death of David (1 Kg

---

17.   In 1904 Rahlfs was able to add ms 127 to this primary
group; cf. *Studien zu den Königsbüchern*, Septuaginta Studien I
(Göttingen, 1904), p. 18, note 1.

18.   Cf. Wellhausen, *Der Text der Bücher Samuelis* (Göttingen, 1871), p. 222, note *, who criticizes the work as "mehr
von gutem Willen, als von Gelehrsamkeit und Urtheil."

19.   *Variae Lectiones Vulgatae Latinae Bibliorum*, vol. II,
p. 436. Cf. also Wellhausen, pp. 221-222, and B. Fischer,
"Lukian-Lesarten in der Vetus Latina der vier Königsbücher,"
Studia Anselmiana 27-28 (1951) 169-177.

20.   Cf. Rahlfs, *Lucians*, p. 80, note 1.

21.   Cf. above, p. 17 and note 8. The text of Theodoret
(c. 393-466), bishop of Cyrrhus, is of similar importance; cf.
Rahlfs, *Studien*, pp. 16-54, *Lucians*, p. 81; and Ziegler, *Septuaginta* XIV: *Isaias*, pp. 79-80.

			Designations of the Primary Lucianic MSS of 1-4 Kgdms	
H-P	*B-M*	*Lagarde*	*Century*	*Library*
19	b'⎫	h	XI-XII	Rome, Chigi, R. vi. 38
108	b ⎬b	d	XIII-XIV	Rome, Vatican, Gr. 330
82	o	f	XII-XIII	Paris, Bibl.Nat. Coislin. 3
93	e₂	m	XIII-XIV	London, Br.Mus. Royal I D. ii
127	c₂		X	Moscow, Syn. Libr., Gr. 31.

2:11 in M).[22]

Similarly but independently in 1867, Lagarde, in compiling a register of biblical quotations from Chrysostom, concluded that the history of mss 19, 82, 93, 108 was to be traced to Lucian, the founder of the famous exegetical school at Antioch; the publication of this, however, did not appear until 1876.[23]

In 1871 Wellhausen's attention was drawn by Vercellone to this group of mss, and, though he was still unaware of their specifically Lucianic character, he did praise their quality in preserving superior readings where M and B were corrupt.[24]

To Field goes the credit for discovering in 1875 a second important connection between mss 19, 82, 93, 108 and the Lucianic text family. In a note introducing the Arabic translation of the Syrohexapla, Lucian's name is twice connected with the symbol ܠ (*lamad*) used to mark variant readings in the Syrohexapla. The same readings are found in the same places of the Gk mss 19, 82, 93, 108, marked with the siglum και λ, and again these texts display the same texttype used by Chrysostom and Theodoret.[25]

---

22. Cf. Rahlfs, *Lucians*, p. 49, note 1.

23. Cf. Rahlfs, *Lucians*, pp. 80-81, and note 1.

24. Cf. Wellhausen, pp. 221-224.

25. Cf. F. Field, *Origenis Hexaplorum quae supersunt sive veterum interpretum Graecum in totum Vetus Testamentum fragmenta* (Oxford, 1875), vol. I, pp. lxxxiv-lxxx; cf. also Swete, pp. 82-83; Driver, p. xlviii; and Rahlfs, *Lucians*, pp. 30-32, who shows that some of these readings are uniquely Lucianic, p. 31, note 2.

Barthélemy ("Reexamination," pp. 86-89) cross-examines

Lagarde then published in 1883 his edition of the Lucianic
text of Genesis-Esther.[26] A. Klostermann in his commentary
(1887) first perceived the importance of and consistently util-
ized the Lucianic recension for critical purposes,[27] and Driver
in 1890 followed his lead.

C. Josephus and the Proto-Lucianic Text

In 1895 the Lucian problem suffered a Copernican twist.
The fourth-century martyr was no longer the sole center around
which the L tradition revolved. Adam Mez demonstrated that
Josephus' *Jewish Antiquities* V.338-VII.394 (= 1-2 Rgn) exhibits
a text which agrees not with M or G^{BA} but with the Lucianic
text.[28] Since J completed the *Antiquities* around 93/94 A.D.,
this meant that "Lucianic" readings were numerous and influential two centuries before the man credited with producing them
lived. A list of other proto-Lucianic witnesses has subsequently been compiled.[29]

---

this evidence, concluding that "this siglum is therefore incap-
able of proving that a Lucianic recension existed." But his
touchstone is "the Lucianic recension" as a "recension comparable to that of Origen." He does agree that "while the old
readings of these 'loipoi' were still being recopied under this
siglum, others were added which were borrowed from the Antiochian text which circulated under the authority of Lucian."

26. *Librorum Veteris Testamenti Canonicorum Pars Prior
Graece* (Göttingen, 1883). Though basically successful for 1-4
Kgdms, this edition does not provide the (postulated) Lucianic
text of the Pentateuch, and it is without benefit of critical
apparatus. See the critique by Rahlfs (*Lucians*, pp. 23-30),
stressing (1) Lagarde's lack of time devoted to working thoroughly through the material, (2) his occasional departure from
all traditional ms readings, and (3) the lack of a critical
apparatus.

27. *Die Bücher Samuels und Könige* (Nördlingen, 1887). Cf.
Driver, pp. VIII and xliv-l.

28. *Die Bibel des Josephus untersucht für Buch V-VII der
Archäologie* (Basel, 1895), p. 80.

29. Cf. the conveniently arranged list in Tov, "Lucian

Mez' colorful *point de départ* is the controversy of the "whimsical" Whiston[30] in reaction to Hody[31] and Hyde.[32] He briskly and without further consideration moves over all names until he arrives at the critical edition of the J text prepared by Benedictus Niese,[33] which--he correctly points out--offers us not "verba Josephi" but the 2nd or 3rd century archetype of the extant J mss.[34]

Mez' methodology is clear and simple: his materials for comparison are J, M, A, B, L, T, P, OL, Jerome, and the *Onomastica Sacra*.[35] The compass of his study is Joshua--2 Samuel. His categories are two: proper names constitute his first series of readings, and positively reported facts his second series. The latter is "the more exact" series, since in the names J leaves himself some "Spielraum."[36] He confines his study to "the solid ground" of these two categories, eschewing the study of divergence or congruence between J and LXX in style, phraseology, and vocabulary, since J is slippery as an eel.[37]

The results obtained by Mez for 1-2 Samuel are similarly clear: B is not J's Vorlage, for in no single case does J = B alone against all other witnesses; rather, it is L which is J's bible, whose mistakes J follows, and whose words J misunderstands. In the more important second series "J goes against M, A, B with the so-called Lucianic text" in 10 readings; there are four explainable contrary readings. The first series yields the same conclusion, with 20 supporting readings and 6

---

and Proto-Lucian," *RB* 79 (1972) 103-104, with notes and bibliography; also Metzger, pp. 31-35.

30. William Whiston, *An Essay towards Restoring the True Text of the Old Testament* (London, 1722).

31. *De bibliorum textibus originalibus* (1704).

32. *Historia religionis veterum Persarum* (1700).

33. *Flavii Josephi Opera*, ed. B. Niese, 7 vols. (Berlin, 1885-1895). Cf. Mez, pp. 1-2.

34. Mez, p. 2.

35. For Mez' specific editions, cf. his pp. 2-4.

36. Mez, p. 79.

37. Cf. below, note 1 for Chapter VIII.

explainable exceptions.[38]

A proto-Lucianic text tradition is his obvious conclusion,
supporting and receiving support from a series of other findings already known in his day.[39]

In response to Mez I would say: (1) his work was a major
contribution for his day and remains of considerable value for
ours. (2) His text critical citations must be checked[40] against
more recent critical editions. (3) While it is legitimate to
confine himself to names and additions, there is confusion introduced due to the names, and there is considerable evidence
for the proto-Lucian-Josephus relationship that those categories exclude.

Rahlfs' prize-winning *Lucians Rezension der Königsbücher*[41]
is well enough known that we can proceed immediately to the
point that interests our discussion. In this study of L in the
books of Kings, Rahlfs devotes a chapter to the relationship of
J to L, in one section[42] of which he criticizes Mez' work on
the books of Samuel. Of Mez' second and "more exact" series,
Rahlfs accepts only two of the ten proofs, dismissing eight as

---

38. Mez, pp. 79-80.

39. He catalogs and summarily interrelates findings concerning the N.T., Peshitta, OL, and Justin texts as proto-
Lucianic witnesses. He concludes that 2 Greek bibles must have
predated Origen: an Egyptian (the B family) and a Syrian-
Italian (best preserved in the L mss). B formed the basis of
the fifth hexaplaric column; Origen must have known of pL; he
did distinguish θ' from α' and σ', treating θ' as a "brother"
to the old LXX; Harnack notes that the θ' tradition was contemporaneous with Jesus and Paul (thus proto-Theodotion); and so,
Mez concludes that θ' is based on proto-Lucian (pp. 81-84).
For qualified support of this last, cf. *DA*, p. 136, and Kevin
G. O'Connell, *The Theodotionic Revision of the Book of Exodus*
(Cambridge, Mass., 1972), p. 200.

40. Cf., e.g., Mez, p. 44: B Ιωναδαμ (Mez misses a very
important proof due to this); pp. 75-76, #LXIV: τεσσαρακοντα;
#LXV: וחפרש, αρωβωθωθ; #LXVII: עשרת.

41. Septuaginta Studien III (Göttingen, 1911).

42. Pp. 83-92.

inconclusive. Of Mez' first series he accepts only seven out
of twenty. Furthermore, while granting only those nine of Mez'
original thirty, Rahlfs finds ten where J and L conflict. His
conclusion is that the text which J used for 1-2 Samuel is *not*
"nearly identical" with L, but that J does prove in a considerable number of instances that readings peculiar to L are not
derived from the Lucian of the turn of the fourth century A.D.,
but were extant at least as early as the first century A.D.

Although Mez seems never to have replied, Rahlfs cannot
pass without rebuttal. Mez' study was short, limited, and
ground breaking, thus exposed to attacks on several flanks.
Rahlfs' analysis was comprehensive, detailed, and carefully re-
searched, thus advancing as a Goliath against a mere David.
But with regard to the theory behind this collection of readings, the decision must go once again to the little David.

For the first series one example will suffice: Mez' reading #120 (= J VII.121 = 2 S 10:6 // 1 C 19:6).[43]

VII.121   προς Συρον τον των Μεσοποταμιτων βασιλεα χιλια ταλαντα

2 S 10:6   M   וישכרו את ארם

            G   εμισθωσαντο την Συριαν

            L   μισθουνται τον Συρον

1 C 19:6   M   אלף ככר כסף לשכר להם מן ארם

            BL   χιλια ταλαντα αργυριου του μισθωσασθαι
                   εαυτοις εκ Συριας Μεσοποταμιας

Mez includes only the proper names from S, thus leaving
out of consideration the important "1000 talents" and "Mesopotamia" in both J and C but "not in S." Still he includes this
as proof that J = L on the modest basis of Συρον, which J has
mistaken for the name of the Mesopotamian king.

Rahlfs counters that J is following C here, for only C
names Mesopotamia and specifies the "1000 talents." Besides,
C[G] has Συρος in 19:10, 12. Accordingly, J is *not* reflecting L
of S; he is dependent upon C!

Thus far one must agree with Rahlfs over Mez. But a fragment of 4QSam[a] is extant for 2 S 10:6-9, most fortunately

---

43. Cf. Mez, p. 42; Rahlfs, pp. 87-88, and 86, note 2;
and below, pp. 152-156.

preserving three words (only) at the end of its first line:
אלף ככר כסף! This little lettered leather scrap disproves
Rahlfs and limelights Mez as correct (but for insufficient
proof), by showing that the "1000 talents" was in the text of
S, but only in the Palestinian tradition of S, from which C derived the detail.[44]

From Mez' second series Rahlfs accepts two of the ten
proofs. In all but one of the rejected cases Rahlfs' reason
for rejection is not that J ≠ L but that other mss besides L
display the given reading, therefore J could have derived the
reading from any of those disparate mss. Rahlfs' statement is
true that each of those seven rejected readings *taken individually* does not prove that J used exclusively a proto-Lucianic
Vorlage. But the seven *are* solid Lucianic readings, the only
common denominator is L, and it approaches the absurd to say
that each time J has a variant he is dependent upon a different
ms. For example:

in Mez #L $J = B \text{ bovza}_2 c_2 e_2$ ≠ M ANrell OL $\cancel{AE}$ σ';
in Mez #LXIV $J = \text{bgopuc}_2 e_2$ P   ≠ M BAMNrell α' σ' θ';
in Mez #LXXIV $J = \text{boc}_2 e_2$ OL C^{AN+} ≠ M BAMNrell C^M C^{BLS+}.

According to Mez this coaxes the conclusion that J = L, for L
is the solitary text tradition that could consistently ground
J's readings. Rahlfs apparently maintains that even though in
##LXXII and LXXIII (which are exclusively Lucianic!) J must
have used L, he could have used B in #L, could have used P in
#LXIV, and could have used C in #LXXIV. But while it is very
likely that over the years the biblical text of the historian
Josephus became dotted with marginal readings embodying diverse
corrections, variants, parallel references, etc., it baffles
the most elementary canons of elegance or concinnity to argue
that a historian would predominantly select his data through a
random[45] sampling of texts differing in text affiliation (B),

---

44. Cf. the NAB textual note for 10:6-9. Analysis shows
that C is dependent upon the text tradition displayed by 4Q,
and not vice-versa; see below, pp. 203-206 on the question.

45. The process would be random, for the only coherent
order posited is the proto-Lucianic Vorlage; no other pattern
has been proposed. Furthermore, even if Rahlfs were right, our

language (P), and even biblical book (C), when it can be shown
that all his data could derive from one single source. Should
assent be still hesitant, let אלף ככר כסף be remembered.

Alerted by the discovery of Mez, Henry St J. Thackeray
studied the text of Josephus as part of his preparatory research for the Samuel volume of the larger Cambridge *Old Testament in Greek*, and he found Josephus "a witness of first-rate
importance for the text of the Greek Bible."[46] One of the
major factors was the date of Josephus:

> A witness who takes us far back behind the three local re-
> censions of the Greek Bible known to Jerome in the 4th
> century, behind the Hexapla of Origen in the 3rd, and even
> behind or at least to the opening days of the great Rab-
> binical school of Jamnia at the end of the first, carries
> therefore considerable weight.[47]

In the Schweich Lectures[48] for 1920, he noted that there were
two major "translations" present in the four books of Reigns,
an early and a late translation:

	EARLY	The Reigns of Saul, David, and Solomon
α	1 S	(Reign of Saul; Preliminary Events)
ββ	2 S 1:1--11:1	(Reign of David in His Prime)
γγ	1 K 2:12--21:29	(Reign of Solomon; Monarchy Divided)

	LATE	The Decline and Fall of the Monarchy
βγ	2 S 11:2--1 K 2:11	(Uriah Story; Succession Narrative)
γδ	1 K 22:1--2 K 25:30	(Degeneration and Double Fall)

This distinction between translations was based on eight lexi-
cographic and two syntactic features[49] whose distributional

---

hypothesis considers B (in 1 S), C, and the substratum of P all
to be intimately bound with the Palestinian Samuel text tradition.

46. H. St J. Thackeray, "Note on the evidence of Josephus," B-M, p. ix.

47. Thackeray, *Josephus: The Man and the Historian* (New
York, 1929), p. 20.

48. Thackeray, *The Septuagint and Jewish Worship* (London,
1921), pp. 9-28.

49. Thackeray, *The Septuagint*, pp. 114-115.

28   CHAPTER I

patterns fairly clearly demarcated the sections above.

At the conclusion of his work on the text of Samuel and on
the Loeb edition of Josephus, Thackeray summed up his finds
concerning the biblical text used by Josephus:

> He employed at least two texts, one in a Semitic language,
> the other in Greek. Sometimes one was used almost to the
> exclusion of the other: sometimes both were consulted and
> amalgamated.... Throughout the Pentateuch his main author-
> ity is a Semitic text, and the use made of the so-called
> "Septuagint" is slight; here he is presumably justified in
> claiming that the translation is his own. From Samuel
> onwards to the end of the historical books the position is
> reversed: the basis of his text is a Greek Bible, and the
> Semitic text is only a subsidiary source. Here he found a
> large part of his work already done for him, his own share
> being confined to polishing the style and removing what he
> considered the vulgarisms of the existing translation.
> For the three intervening books (Joshua, Judges, Ruth) I
> find no certain evidence for the use of a Greek text; as
> between Hebrew and Aramaic, I suspect, in Judges at least,
> dependence on a Targum.[50]

Finally, singling out the Books of Samuel, Thackeray stated
that Josephus made use of a text "*uniformly* of this Lucianic
type."[51]

Building upon the lines of scholarship that had converged
in Thackeray, H. S. Gehman[52] and J. W. Wevers[53] advanced the
probe into the translational characteristics of sections of
Samuel-Kings dissected by Thackeray.

D. Light from Qumran

Suddenly, exploding the silence of nearly two thousand

---

50. Thackeray, *Josephus*, p. 81.

51. Thackeray, *Josephus*, p. 85, emphasis his.

52. "Exegetical Methods Employed by the Greek Translator
of I Samuel," *JAOS* 70 (1950) 292-296. Cf. below, p. 33 and
note 77.

53. "Exegetical Principles Underlying the Greek Text of 2
Sam. 11:2--1 Kings 2:11," *CBQ* 15 (1953) 30-45.

years, a missing link in the history of the Septuagint was re-
discovered in 1952 and published by D. Barthélemy.[54] That same
year the Samuel manuscripts were discovered in Cave IV Qumran,
and from that point the story is widely known and celebrated.
The progress of the ensuing scholarly discussion was synthe-
sized with clarity, adeptness, and fairness by Emanuel Tov in
the opening "State of the Question" address[55] at the 1972 Symposium of the International Organization for Septuagint and
Cognate Studies in Los Angeles.

At the same symposium Barthélemy and Cross presented re-
statements of their positions. With an assessment of these re-
statements we set the stage for the present study of 4QSam[a] and
Josephus.

On the basis of the Minor Prophets Scroll, Barthélemy
seems to have effectively laid to rest Kahle's "Targumic"
theory as the principal explanation of LXX origins[56] and at the
same time to have made an advance on the "later translation"
theory of Thackeray. These resulted from his discovery (the
converse of Thackeray's) that the Greek texts which differed
from each other showed a more fundamental common basis. Thus,
for example, βδ was not a separate Greek translation from a
Hebrew text, but a recension based on an already extant Greek
text. On this general point, Barthélemy, Cross, and others are
now in agreement.[57]

---

54. "Redécouverte d'un chaînon manquant de l'histoire de
la Septante," *RB* 60 (1953) 18-29.

55. "The State of the Question: Problems and Proposed
Solutions," *1972 Proceedings: IOSCS and Pseudepigrapha*, pp. 3-
15.

56. Kahle espoused this view even after the discoveries
of the scrolls from the Judaean Desert; cf. *The Cairo Geniza*,
2nd ed. (Oxford, 1959), pp. 209-239.

57. F. M. Cross, "The Evolution of a Theory of Local
Texts," *1972 Proceedings*, p. 108; J. W. Wevers, "Proto-Septua-
gint Studies," *The Seed of Wisdom: Essays in Honour of T. J.
Meek*, ed. W. S. McCullough (Toronto, 1964), p. 77; P. W. Skehan,
"The Biblical Scrolls from Qumran and the Text of the Old Testa-
ment," *Biblical Archaeologist* 28 (1965) 267-269; S. Jellicoe,

There are, in addition, some clarifications and qualifications of earlier views. Barthélemy now sees, as the result of Brock's[58] and Kraft's[59] critiques, that "one must expect to find a much more complex situation in the βγ section than I had envisioned in DA."[60] Incorporating the results of Johnson,[61] Barthélemy correctly holds that, even in the "OG" sections of Vaticanus, we meet an embedded hebraising revision:

> And if, as it seems, Johnson is correct in holding that MS B has not undergone contamination of Hexaplaric origin, it may very well be asked whether a certain number of these doublets of non-Hexaplaric origin are not juxtaposing the Old Septuagint and a *hebraising revision* which would be qualified as both "pre-Hexaplaric" and "non-καίγε."[62]

In addition to this text which was "substantially identical with the Greek form which served as a basis for the hebraising καίγε," Barthélemy posits that "at least two *non-καίγε* Greek forms are attested in the MSS of the α, ββ, and γγ sections of Reigns."[63] They are the Hexaplaric text (post-καίγε) and the Antiochian text.

> As regards the *Antiochian* Septuagint, if one accepts with Brock that it is the result of a "recensional activity... desiring to smooth over the roughness of the original translation and provide a more acceptable Greek," there is every motive for believing that this recensional activity

The Septuagint and Modern Study (Oxford, 1968), pp. 59-63; and O'Connell, pp. 3-4, 293. For a different view, see T. Muraoka, "The Greek Texts of Samuel-Kings: Incomplete Translations or Recensional Activity?" *1972 Proceedings*, pp. 90-107.

58. S. Brock, "Lucian *redivivus*: Some Reflections on Barthélemy's *Les Devanciers d'Aquila*," *Studia Evangelica* [=TU 103] (1968) 176-181.

59. R. A. Kraft, Review of Dominique Barthélemy, *Les Devanciers d'Aquila* in *Gnomon* 37 (1965) 474-483.

60. "Reexamination," p. 29.

61. Bo Johnson, *Die hexaplarische Rezension des 1. Samuelbuches der Septuaginta* (Lund, 1963).

62. "Reexamination," p. 23; see also below, pp. 197-202.

63. "Reexamination," p. 19.

must have extended over a definite period and must have taken place especially after the period of the hebraising καίγε recension.[64]

Barthélemy, in fact, offers no motive for believing this last statement. Obviously, the post-hexaplaric stratum of L is post-*kaige*, but that entirely begs the question of the early stratum of L.

In *DA*, Barthélemy had denied both early revision in the L text and the "pretended 'Lucianic recension.'" Jellicoe may perhaps have been too lenient[65] concerning the cavalier treatment by Barthélemy of the evidence for a Lucianic tradition. For Barthélemy still maintains in his "Reexamination" this distorted manner of handling the evidence concerning the L recension.[66]

He also insists on discussing "the Lucianic recension" (a) only in connection with *Lucianus ipse*, (b) only as a revision "de faire du grec un meilleur témoin de l'hébreu,"[67] and (c) only "comme une recension comparable à la recension origénienne."[68]

But (a) concentration on Lucian begs the question of the acknowledged early stratum of L; (b) Barthélemy himself has just defined a recension as including an effort "pour améliorer cette traduction ou bien en en corrigeant la langue...";[69] and (c) neither must a recension be of the exact nature of

---

64. "Reexamination," p. 21.

65. Review of D. Barthélemy, *Les Devanciers d'Aquila* in *JAOS* 84 (1964) 179: "While it is true that some obscurity attaches to this recension, including its attribution to the martyr of Antioch, the evidence is much stronger than the author [Barthélemy] allows."

66. Check the misrepresentation of the Ziegler evidence (p. 66), the emotional judgments ("ambitions littéraires relevant du snobisme atticist," and "un complexe d'infériorité," p. 74), and the biased translation (e.g., "les évêques, dit il, *prétendirent*" for the historian Sozomen's ελεγον).

67. "Reexamination," p. 74.

68. "Reexamination," p. 88.

69. "Reexamination," p. 72.

Origen's,[70] nor must it be of the "titanesque" scope of Origen's[71] to be a recension.

In brief, Barthélemy has made a major contribution to LXX
studies in his analysis of the Greek Minor Prophets scroll,
but, with regard to the specific question of the early Lucianic
tradition, his conclusions may be of value but only when used
with constantly critical caution.

At the Los Angeles Symposium Cross restated his theory of
three local Hebrew texts and their reflection in the Old Greek
translation plus the three recensions based on it (see above,
pages 4-5). For the books of Samuel, specifically, he posits
(1) an Egyptian Hebrew Vorlage behind the OG translation; (2) a
proto-Lucianic recension, which "consists apparently of a light
sprinkling of readings derived from the Palestinian textual
family of the type found in the three Samuel manuscripts from
Qumran, to which the Old Greek was sporadically corrected"; (3)
a *kaige* or proto-Theodotionic recension, as in βδ, based on the
proto-Massoretic text; and finally (4) the recensions of Aquila
and Origen, based on the authoritative Massoretic Hebrew.[72]

With regard to the Lucianic recension, Emanuel Tov pro-
poses a two-strata hypothesis: the "substratum contained
either *the* Old Greek translation or any Old Greek translation,"
and the "second layer is the historical Lucian."[73] Three
strata can be perceived in Rahlfs' work: (1) the Old Greek
text of B 𝔅, from which the proto-Lucianic text differed; (2)
the proto-Lucianic substratum ("Lucians Vorlage"), influencing
Josephus; and finally (3) the Lucianic revision.[74]

Cross, adopting the Lagarde-Rahlfs position generally on
the basis of his analysis of the Qumran scrolls, agrees with
Tov concerning the late stratum; he agrees concerning the early
stratum

to the degree that [Tov] reckons with the Old Greek as the

---

70.   Brock, "The Recensions," does successfully demonstrate that L is a genuine recension.

71.   "Reexamination," p. 74.

72.   "The Evolution," pp. 115-118.

73.   "Lucian and Proto-Lucian," *RB* 79 (1972) 103.

74.   *Lucians*, pp. 283-284 and 290-291.

substratum of [the] Lucianic text. There are in my view,
however, three strata, not two, in the Lucianic text of the
Pentateuch and the Former Prophets..., where the *textus*
receptus is *non-Palestinian*. The strata of the Lucianic
recension are thus symmetrical with the three text types:
Old Greek (Egyptian), proto-Lucian (Palestinian), Lucianic proper (Babylonian).[75]

Brock also finds three stratigraphic elements: "very considerable" hexaplaric influence in the Antiochene text, and
apart from the hexaplaric "there still remains a considerable
recensional element in Ant.," although Ant. "often *alone* retains the original LXX translation of this book" (= 2 Sam).[76]
Brock, however, does not affirm or even necessarily imply that
the secondary and tertiary elements of his strata are chronologically distinct; that is, Lucian himself could have been responsible for both the atticising and the hexaplaric elements.[77]

A series of attempts has been made to test critically the
theories of Barthélemy and Cross by students of the latter.
Werner Lemke, in his 1963 dissertation, was able better to
assess the tendential nature of the Chronicler by demonstrat-
ing--partially on the basis of the Qumran Samuel mss--that some
of the Chronicler's differences from the Samuel-Kings narrative
are due to differences in the text tradition of his Vorlage,
not to alleged theological *Tendenz*.[78]

Ralph W. Klein outlined a theory of the early history of

---

75. "The Evolution," pp. 118-119. For critique of Cross's
theory of local texts, see Barthélemy, "Reexamination," pp. 55-
65.

76. Brock, "Lucian *redivivus*," p. 177. The last clause
is quoted by Brock from Barthélemy, but with approval as "entirely convincing," p. 177.

77. In this connection, see Fischer's view cited above in
note 26 to the Introduction; cf. also Tov, "Lucian and Proto-
Lucian," *RB* 79 (1972) 107.

78. "Synoptic Studies in the Chronicler's History" (Th.D.
dissertation, Harvard University, 1963). See also his article,
"The Synoptic Problem in the Chronicler's History," *HTR* 58
(1965) 349-363.

the Hebrew and Greek text of the Chronicler's history. He
found that "1 Esdras often preserves a form of the text older
than Ezra MT-G," and that "Chronicles-Nehemiah G are not directly connected with the *kaige* recension."[79]

James D. Shenkel unraveled the chronological problems of
the divided monarchy through his application of the hypothesis
of recensional development.[80]

Daniel J. Harrington analyzed the *Liber Antiquitatum Biblicarum* of Pseudo-Philo. After showing that that work was originally written in Hebrew (or possibly Aramaic), he demonstrated
that "the biblical citations in *LAB* cannot be explained as insertions of the Old Latin, the LXX, the Greek Lucian or any
other known Greek or Latin biblical text. Therefore, we have
in *LAB* witnesses to a Hebrew biblical text. There is consistent agreement of the biblical text in *LAB* with representatives
of the Palestinian biblical text, especially as glimpsed in the
Greek Lucian and in Josephus."[81]

Kevin G. O'Connell investigated the Theodotionic material
in Exodus and established (1) that it "comes from a systematic
revision of the OG to reflect the present MT"; (2) that "Aquila
knew and used Theodotion's recension as the basis for his own
further revision to the MT"; (3) that the Theodotionic recension "existed in substantially its final form at least by the
late first century A.D."; and (4) that "Theodotion's version
in Exodus is an integral part of the general KAIΓE recension
identified by Barthélemy."[82]

J. Gerald Janzen demonstrated for the book of Jeremiah the
essential integrity and superiority of the short Septuagintal

79. "Studies in the Greek Text of the Chronicler" (Th.D.
dissertation, Harvard University, 1966), p. 323. See also "New
Evidence for an Old Recension of Reigns," *HTR* 60 (1967) 93-105.

80. *Chronology*. See also "A Comparative Study of the
Synoptic Parallels in I Paraleipomena and I-II Reigns," *HTR* 62
(1969) 63-85.

81. "Text and Biblical Text in Pseudo-Philo's 'Liber
Antiquitatum Biblicarum'" (Ph.D. dissertation, Harvard University, 1969), p. 183.

82. *The Theodotionic Revision*, pp. 292-293.

text over the Massoretic text, with partial but strong confirmation from 4QJer[b].[83]

Walter R. Bodine, applying the theory of recensional development, isolated the different strata of the Greek text of
Judges.[84]

In addition to this series of dissertations, several further contributions should be mentioned. Patrick W. Skehan published "A Fragment of the 'Song of Moses' (Deut. 32) from Qumran,"[85] and concluded:

> Thus for this very limited portion of the Old Testament,
> the new Qumran materials serve to confirm the existence of
> a divergent ancient text which the LXX translators had be-
> fore them, and followed far more closely than has gener-
> ally been supposed. They also give us, in Hebrew, a num-
> ber of specific divergent readings whose usefulness for
> the criticism of the text has long been recognized on the
> basis of the unsupported Greek.

We have already referred to the excellent Oxford dissertation of Sebastian Brock, "The Recensions of the Septuagint Version of I Samuel." He argues that "the Greek Version of I
Kingdoms is the work of a single hand,"[86] in line with the
Lagarde hypothesis built upon by Barthélemy and Cross. Against
Barthélemy, he demonstrates and carefully characterizes the
nature of the Lucianic recension. Against the present writer's
view, Brock's "independent investigation of the Josephan material for I Kms in general confirms Rahlfs' criticism of Mez,"
and maintains that "Josephus quite definitely made use of both
LXX and the Hebrew, although much of the time it is impossible

---

83. *Studies in the Text of Jeremiah* (Cambridge, Mass.,
1973).

84. "KAIΓE and Other Recensional Developments in the Greek
Text of Judges" (Ph.D. dissertation, Harvard University, 1973).

85. *BASOR* 136 (1954) 12-16. Cf. also his "The Qumran
Manuscripts and Textual Criticism," *VTS* 4 (1957) 148-160, and
"The Biblical Scrolls from Qumran and the Text of the Old Tes-
tament," *Biblical Archaeologist* 28 (1965) 87-100.

86. Abstract, p. 1.

to say which of the two he is currently using."[87] With regard
to Cross and the proto-Lucianic recension:

> In the main Cross' analysis is probably correct....
> Where Cross goes against, or perhaps one should say, be-
> yond, Barthélemy, is in his postulate of a 1st century BC
> "'proto-Lucianic' recension." This indeed neatly explains
> the agreements between L and 4QSam, but according to Cross
> himself (p. 292) these are very few, and might rather be
> explained as original readings preserved only in L, but
> corrected to the (proto-)masoretic norm in the rest of the
> LXX tradition (pre-hexaplaric).[88]

A. Schmitt's work on Theodotion in Daniel demonstrates
that the strict identification of KR with ϑ' is untenable,
since the text of Daniel-Theodotion is not identical with the
text of the sixth column of the Hexapla.[89]

Finally, George Howard seeks to find KR readings in the
text of Josephus.[90] The nine readings he offers from Samuel,
however, do not link Josephus with the specifically *kaige* revisional element of the *kaige* text, which must be carefully
distinguished from the OG/pL substratum of the *kaige* text.
Howard does, nonetheless, point us toward Josephus' use of a
slightly revised (pL) Greek text.[91]

In conclusion, the Lucianic text can be identified in 1-2
Samuel. Brock has established that it is a recensional text
focused around fourth-century Antioch and based ultimately on
the single original OG translation. Jerome criticized this
"Lucianic" text and testified that it had been noticeably cor-
rected/corrupted and widely known as the κοινη Septuagint already in Origen's day, several generations prior to Lucian.

---

87. Brock, "The Recensions," pp. 215-216; in response,
see above, pp. 24-27, and chapter VIII.

88. P. 171; in response, see chapter III below, and the
Conclusion to this volume, and my "4QSam[a] and Septuagintal Research," p. 30.

89. *Stammt der sogenannte "Θ'"-Text bei Daniel wirklich
von Theodotion?* MSU 9 (Göttingen, 1966).

90. "*Kaige* Readings in Josephus," *Textus* 8 (1973) 45-54.

91. See below, p. 191.

And Mez has demonstrated that this earlier, κοινη form of the Lucianic text was the textform used by Josephus, thus proto-Lucianic. Whether and how the pL text differs from OG remains to be seen.

With this survey of past scholarship, the stage is now prepared, set more than a century before Josephus, for our analysis of the fragments of 4QSam[a].

Chapter II

THE AGREEMENT OF 4QSAM[a] WITH THE GREEK VERSION

In this chapter we will examine the readings in 4QSam[a]
which vary from the Massoretic Text yet display agreement with
the Greek Version. Rather than being presented simply seriatim,
the analyses of the variant readings will be grouped qualitatively in accord with the theories and presuppositions discussed in the Introduction (pp. 4-9 above).

A. The Pattern 4Q = G ≠ M in Section α ββ

1. Plus

We may begin with several striking pluses shared by 4Q and
G. The very first words of the first fragment extant for 4Q
offer this evidence:

1 S 1:11   *V.344*

4Q

אנשי]ׄם ונתחיהו ל[פֿניך נזיר]   ]

]עד יום מותו ויין ושכר לא ישתה ו[מׄורה לא יעבור עׄ]ל ראשׄו   [

M P

אנשׁים ונתתיו ליהוה

כל ימי חייו   ומורה לא יעלה על ראשו

T

אנשא ואמסרניה דיהי משמיש קדם יוי

כל יומי חיוהי   ומרות אנש לא תהי עלוהי

G[V]

אנשים ונתחיהו לפניך נזיר

עד יום מותו ויין ושכר לא ישתה ומורה לא יעלה על ראשו

G OL[SV]

ανδρων, και δωσω αυτον ενωπιον σου δοτον (om OL) εως ημερας
θανατου αυτου˙ και οινον και μεθυσμα ου πιεται, και σιδηρος
ουκ αναβησεται επι την κεφαλην αυτου.

J

καθιερωσειν επι διακονια του θεου, διαιταν ουχ ομοιαν τοις
ιδιωταις

39

Cf. Driver, Notes, BASOR 18, NAB. The issue here is not
the exact wording of the 4Q reconstruction (לפניך vs. ליהוה;
נזיר?; עד יום מותו vs. כל ימי חייו) but the fact of a considerable 4Q plus, lacking in M T P, present in G OL J. It is
necessary, moreover, in conjunction with this reading to study
1 S 1:22, where the נזיר wording will be discussed (cf. below,
pp. 165-166).

4Q must be reconstructed with a plus of approximately 5
words or 20 letters. The only other pair of lines extant for
this column shows a length of 54 spaces per line. If 4Q were
reconstructed according to M, this line would exhibit 33 spaces
--implausibly short; the reconstruction according to G exhibits
53 spaces, helps explain the G OL J reading, and receives cogent confirmation from the 4Q reading at 1:22 (see next paragraph).

J relates this feature in its proper sequence. Though
here he summarizes, below in V.347 he gives the details as the
vow is carried out: προφητην . . . κομη . . . υδωρ. This
corresponds to 1:22, where neither M nor G gives any details of
Samuel, but where 4Q has an addition of an entire line, including [חייו] /ונת[ת]יהו נזיר עד עולם כול ימי.

When the two readings are studied together, one is forced
to conclude that J followed a text of the 4Q type both at 1:11
and at 1:22, and that for the plus under discussion 4Q = G OL J
≠ M.

1 S 1:24   V.347~
4Q

```
                     בי]ת יהוֹה שילה והנער                      ]
            [עמם ויבאו לפני יהוה וישחט אביו את ] הזב[ח כ]אֹשֵׁר
            [ויעשה מימים ימימה ליהוה ותבא את הנער     25 רי]שחט
```

M T P

```
            בית יהוה שלו   והנער

            נער 25 וישחטו
```

G OL

εις οικον Κυριου εν Σηλωμ, και το παιδαριον μετ αυτων· και
προσηγαγον ενωπιον Κυριου, και εσφαξεν ο πατηρ αυτου την θυσιαν
ην εποιει εξ ημερων εις ημερας τω Κυριω. και προσηγαγεν το

παιδαριον, [25]και εσφαξεν

For the reconstruction based on G, cf. BASOR 26, plus JBL
165, n. 40; NAB. This reading has already been discussed in
BASOR 19-20:

> MT *whn‘r n‘r* is the tell-tale remnant of a lengthy
> haplography due to *homoioteleuton*, supplied by LXX and 4Q.
> Both requirements of space, and the clear traces of *hzbḥ*
> *k'šr* (LXX θυσίαν ἦν), as well as [*wy]šḥṭ* in v. 25 (1. 10),
> make the full reading certain. The obvious character of
> the haplography in MT between *hn‘r* (=1. 8 in 4Q) and
> [*(h)n‘r*] (=1. 10) indicates that the Hebrew tradition be-
> hind both MT and LXX once read the full text, and described
> Elkanah's part in the proceedings.

Thus, we have here another plus in which 4Q = G OL ≠ M.

1 S 2:23-24   V.340 om

4Q

[   ]דבר[עׄ]מׄ[שׁו] אני [שׁ]ר[שׁ]א הׄ[ל]א[ל]ה כדברים [ן]שׁׄעת
[לע אל]מׄ[ולׁש יכׁל]א רשא העו[ר]מׄ[שׁה טובה לוא יכ בני ל]א ²⁴
[   ]בׄמע שומע ני[א רשׁ]א [שׁמועות]ה תׁ[ולׁ]בוט[א לו יכ ן]שׁעת[

M T P

כל מאת רעים דבריכם את שמע אנכי   אשר האלה כדברים ן[שׁ]עת
אנכי אשר השמעה טובה לוא כי בני ל]א ²⁴אלה העם
מעברים שמע

G^V

כל פׄי מׄ[L בכם מדברים+]< שומע אני אשר האלה כדברים ן[שׁ]עת
אל שומע אני השמועה טובה לוא כי בני ל]א ²⁴יהוה עם
)   (שומע אני אשר השמועות טובות כי ן[שׁ]עת

G

ποιειτε κατα το ρημα τουτο ο εγω ακουω
εκ στοματος παντος του λαου Κυριου; ²⁴μη τεκνα
οτι ουκ αγαθη η ακοη ην εγω ακουω   μη ποιειτε ουτως
οτι ουκ αγαθαι αι ακοαι ας εγω ακουω
του μη δουλευειν λαον

L

ποιειτε κατα τα ρηματα ταυτα α εγω ακουω καταλαλουμενα καθ υμων
εκ στοματος   του λαου Κυριου; ²⁴μη τεκνα μη ποιειτε ουτως
οτι ουκ αγαθη η ακοη ην εγω

ακουω περι υμων

του ποιειν τον λαον μη λατρευειν

OL^S

facitis verba haec, quae ego audio de vobis mala
ab omni populo? ²⁴Nolite filii mei
quoniam non est bona fama quam ego

audio de vobis [. . .]

Cf. Well, Driver, Notes, NAB, and esp. BASOR. There is
multifarious disagreement among mss concerning details within
this reading, but in general M preserves the preferable short
text, followed by T P L OL^S. 4Q presents a double rendering,
followed by most G mss (and probably by OL^V, but the latter is
too fragmentary for certain judgment). Our aim is not necessarily to reach the original reading, but to decide 4Q's text
affiliation, and clearly in this inferior plus, 4Q = G ≠ M (L
OL^S).

The next "striking plus" shared by 4Q and G against M
could be presented briefly:

2 S 4:1   VII.46   4Q   [וי]שמע מפיב[שת]

M   וישמע

G   και ηκουσεν Μεμφιβοσθε (Ιεβοσθε MN++).

But it is only one star in a constellation of widespread and
varied readings all of which should be studied together:

2 S 2:15   VII.9, 12

4Q   [שנים/[ל]עשר לבני בנימין איש]

M T   שנים עשר לבנימין ולאיש בשת

P   דאשבשול

BAM   των παιδων Βενιαμειν δωδεκα των Ιεβοσθε (-θαι A)

LN   δωδεκα των υιων Βενιαμειν του Μεμφειβοσθε
                                    (-βος N; Εισβααλ e₂)

cx   των παιδων Βενιαμην των Ιεβουσθε...δωδεκα

J   om VII.12, but in VII.9: Ιεβοσθος

2 S 4:1   VII.46

4Q   [וי]שמע מפיב[את בן שאול]

M T   וישמע   בן שאול

P   ושמע   אשבשול בר שאול

G L   και ηκουσεν Μεμφιβοσθε (Ιεβοσθε MN++) υιος Σαουλ

J   Ακουσας δε...ο Σαουλου παις Ιεβοσθος (Ιεβωσ- RO)

2 S 4:2   VII.47

4Q	[ם למפיבשת בן שאול]
M	שרי גדודים היו בן שאול
T P	משרין הור עם בר שאול
G L	ηγουμενοι συστρειμματων τω Μεμφιβοσθε (Ιεβ- MN++) υιω Σαουλ
J	Ιεβοσθου

2 S 4:12   VII.52

4Q	מפיבשת לקח ו[ויקבר]
M T P	אישבשת לקחו ויקברו
G L OL^b	Μεμφιβοσθε (Ιεβ- MN++ OL^b) εθαψαν (-ψεν N)
J	Ιεβοσθου ... εκηδευσε

Cf. Well., Driver, Notes, NAB, *DA* pp. 37-38. There are two people under consideration: Ishbaal (Ishbosheth in scribal tradition), son of Saul, king of Israel briefly at the beginning of David's reign over Judah; and the lame Meribbaal (Mephibosheth), son of Jonathan and grandson of Saul. The chart displays the selected witness of the mss--selected because (1) 4Q is extant, (2) hexaplaric witness is avilable, or (3) a parenthesis concerning Meribbaal is inserted in an Ishbaal passage, confusing certain text traditions.

4Q has Ishbosheth correctly in 2:15, but in 4:1, 2, 12 it has Mephibosheth, displaying a Hb basis for the confusion in the Gk mss.

M, when it does present a name, names the correct individual. It fails, however, to name Ishbosheth in the opening verses of chapter 4, leaving Mephibosheth in the parenthetical insert 4:3-4 as the first encounter of either person for 28 verses. Barthélemy (*DA*, p. 28 n.) correctly considers Μεμφι-βοσθε to be the OG reading here, and thus OG has followed 4Q in a clear error, which is corrected in some later G mss. Skehan and Cross (*ALQ*, p. 191 n.) attribute the error to an earlier stage of M as well, excised but not corrected by the reviser of M.

T follows M throughout, while P follows M with these exceptions: Ishbosheth becomes Ishbashul, and Ishbashul is supplied in 4:1 (but not 4:2) when M omits.

BAcx always group together and always agree with 4Q where the latter is extant. MN also group together (after 2:15--cf. B-M for N's textual trouble here), but they level Ishbosheth

locus in 2 S	2:15	4:1	4:2	4:4	4:12	9:6	19:25(24)
correct name	I	I	I	M	I	M	M
4Q	I	M	M	de	M	de	de
M T	I	om!	om!	M	I	M	M
P	I**	I**	om	M	I**	M	M
B	I	M	M	M	M	M	M
A	I	M	M	M	M	M	M
M	I	I	I	I	I	M	M
N	M**	I	I	I	I	M	M
L	M**	M	M	M*	M	M*	M*
OL					I**	M*	
𝔤ʲ				M*		M*	
cx	I	M	M	M	M	M	M
α'						M	
σ'						M	
ϑ'						M	
o'						M	
αλλος						M*	
sin nom							M*
J	I	I	I	om	I	M	M

(An asterisk [*] indicates a "-baal" name; a double asterisk advises the reader to note a special form in the readings.)

---

throughout chapter 4.

L has leveled Memphibosthe throughout where Ishbaal should be, and Memphibaal where Meribbaal should be. But note that at 2:15 e₂ alone reads Eisbaal. 𝔤ʲ, where quoted by B-M, agrees with L; and OLᵛ similarly agrees with L's Memphibaal, while OLᵇ agrees with M T P MN (J).

According to a marginal note in ms j, α'σ'ϑ'o' have Memphibosthe, while "αλλος" has Memphibaal--the L (𝔤ʲ OLᵛ) reading! Does "αλλος" sometimes mark L readings the same way λ does? jᵐᵍ also offers Memphibaal, without attribution, at 19:24.

Finally, J, as a historian, always names his characters correctly, while omitting the confusing insertion about Mephibosheth (4:4) in the Ishbosheth section. The claim might be

made, therefore, that J = M ≠ G; but the claim would not be
sound. J has the correct names precisely because his attention
is on his story, not primarily on his Vorlage (thus he has the
name where the narrative demands it at 4:1, 2, and he chooses
not to break his narrative with the 4:4 insertion--in all three
cases J ≠ M!). Thus, J should not be considered a witness to
any of the Vorlagen as such, but his general choice of the
forms Ιεβοσθος and Μεμφιβοσθος shows dependence on a Gk not a
Hb Vorlage; they also show dependence on S not on C, for the
names appear as אשבעל/Ασαβαλ, Ισβααλ, Ιεβααλ in 1 C 8:33, 9:39,
and מריב בעל/Μεριβααλ, Μεμφιβααλ in 1 C 8:34, 9:40.

Returning to the individual readings, we can note in 2:15
that M lacks בני 4Q, παιδων/υιων G. The possibility of haplography in M or of dittography in 4Q OG^V somewhat weakens the
force, but nonetheless for this plus, 4Q = G ≠ M.

In 4:1 M omits the name and 4Q G (J) include it (B and L
specifically agreeing with 4Q): 4Q = G ≠ M. The same phenomenon recurs in 4:2: 4Q = G ≠ M.

In 4:12 (B and L once again agreeing specifically with 4Q
on the name), 4Q ≠ M ≠ G on לקח.

The strongest, most consistent trend throughout these
readings is: 4Q = G ≠ M, and specifically in the pluses of 4:1
and 4:2 OG follows 4Q in clear errors.

2 S 8:7-8	*1 C 18:7-8* *VII.104-106*	

4Q

 וי[קח דויד א]ת שלטי הזהב אשר היו על עבדי [   ]^7

הדדעזר ויביאם ירוש[ל]ים [וי]גם [ל]אותם [לקח אחר ששק מלך מצרים]

ב]על]ותו אל יר[ושלים] בימי רחבעם בן שלו[מה]רמ-^{8} רמ-   עד-[י]

הדדעזר לקח המלך דויד נחושת רבה מא[ד בה עשה שלומה את ים... [

M T P   ויקח דוד את שלטי הזהב אשר היו אל עבדי^7

הדדעזר ויביאם ירושלם:

ומבטח ומברתי עד-י^8

הדדעזר לקח המלך דוד נחשת הרבה מאד:

G^V(OL^{SV})   ויקח דויד את שלטי הזהב אשר היו על עבדי^7

הדדעזר   ויביאם ירושלים (גם אותם לקח אחר ששק) מלך מצרים

בעלותו אל ירושלים בימי רחבעם בן שלומה^8 רמ- ?   רמ- ?   עד-י

הדדעזר לקח המלך דויד נחושת רבה מאד בה עשה שלומה את ים...

G OL^S ⁷και ελαβεν Δαυειδ τους χλιδωνας τους χρυσους

οι ησαν (ους εποιησεν B+) επι των παιδων των

Αδρααζαρ βασιλεως Σουβα (om β'Σ' C^{M,G}; de OL)

και ηνεγκεν αυτα εις Ιερουσαλημ

και ελαβεν αυτα Σουσακειμ (et haec accepit postea Susac)

βασιλευς Αιγυπτου

εν τω αναβηναι αυτον εις Ιερουσαλημ εν ημεραις

Ροβοαμ (Ιεροβ- B+) υιου Σολομωντος (in diebus

Roboam filii Salomonis cum ascendisset in Ierusalem)

⁸και εκ της Μασβαα (Machinas) ελαβεν (AMN++ε^j = L; om OL)

ο βασιλευς Δαυειδ εκ των εκλεκτων πολεων του

Αδρααζαρ χαλκον πολυν σφοδρα

εν αυτω εποιησεν Σαλωμων την θαλασσαν...

L   ⁷και ελαβε Δαυειδ τους χλιδωνας τους χρυσους

οι ησαν επι των παιδων

Αδρααζαρ του βασ. Σουβα και παντα τα οπλα τα χρυσα και τα δορατα

και ηνεγκεν αυτα εις Ιερουσαλημ

και ελαβεν αυτα Σουσακειμ βασιλευς Αιγυπτου

εν τω αναβηναι αυτον εις Ιερουσαλημ εν ημεραις

Ροβοαμ υιου Σολομωντος

⁸και εκ της Ματεβακ εκ των εκλεκτων πολεων του

Αδρααζαρ ελαβεν ο βασιλευς Δαυειδ χαλκον πολυν σφοδρα

εν αυτω εποιησεν Σολομων την θαλασσαν...

C^{MG}

⁷ויקח דויד את שלטי הזהב אשר היו על עבדי

הדדעזר ויביאם ירושלם:

⁸ומטבחת ומכון ערי

דויד נחשת רבה מאד בה עשה שלמה את ים...   הדדעזר לקח

J   και τας τε χρυσας φαρετρας και τας πανοπλιας, ας οι του Αδαδου
σωματοφυλακες εφορουν, ανεθηκε τω θεω εις Ιεροσολυμα· ας υστερον
ο των Αιγυπτιων βασιλευς Σουσακος στρατευσας επι τον υιωνον αυτου
Ροβοαμον ελαβε και πολυν αλλον εκ των Ιεροσολυμων εξεφορησε πλουτον·
... ο δε των Εβραιων βασιλευς ... και ταις καλλισταις των Αδραζαρου
πολεων επεστρατευσε Βατταια και Μαχωνι, και λαβων αυτας κατα κρατος
διηρπασε. χρυσος δ' εν αυταις ευρεθη παμπολυς ... και χαλκος...,
εξ ου και Σολομων το μεγα σκευος θαλασσαν δε καλουμενον εποιησε...

Cf. Well., Driver, Notes, NAB.

G^{LBAN} OL^S J all exhibit two long pluses not found in M T P.
The G uncial M and C^{MG} lack the first plus but have the second.

4Q contains the first plus, but breaks off in the final line of
this column one word before we could tell whether it contains
the second plus, while nothing remains of the entire next
column. It is plausible, however, that 4Q has the second plus,
for no ms which has the first plus lacks the second. At any
rate, Wellhausen's suggestion that the plus in 8:7b derives
from 1 Kg 14:25ff. is now correctly set aside by Cross (Notes),
for the text there is quite different.

4Q here consists of two fragments: one small fragment containing the first line and גם ס̇[ו]ל̇[   ] of the second line,
and another larger fragment beginning with א̇ותם and continuing
to מא̇[ד], on the bottom line of this column in 4Q. It is almost
certain that these two fragments join together precisely here:
(a) the spacing not only fits beautifully, it cannot be altered
by more than 4 or 5 letters. (b) גם is clear and follows
[ירוש]ל̇[ו]ם̇ precisely where M breaks off with ירושלים, and
there is no other word ending with ־לים in the vicinity either
actually present or reconstructed from any ms. (c) In the line
above the ם in בימי there is the trace of final *mem*, again fitting the final *mem* in ירושלים perfectly when constructed exactly
after M, and again, otherwise unexplained. (d) 4Q OL^S J show
astounding resemblances through this whole passage, and OL has
"et haec accepit postea Susac" (ας υστερον ... Σουσακος J)
which would derive ultimately from the Hb Vorlage: גם אותם לקח
אחר שושק (or ואותם, or ויקחם as NAB). But the Latin has an un-
usual word order, emphasizing "haec." Were it translating
ויקחם/και ελαβεν αυτα, it would read "et accepit ea." Though
the emphasis may come from the OL translator, it must be judged
to come from the Vorlage if such a Vorlage can be produced.
And 4Q definitely does have גם in this locus, and it definitely
has [א̇ותם   ] in the very near vicinity otherwise unexplained;
finally, note גם אתם introducing a clause three verses later in
8:11. 4Q is to be reconstructed as above.

Further, the combination of witnesses indicates that the
following formed part of the Palestinian text of Samuel: the
first plus (4Q G L OL J), the second plus ([4Q] G L OL C J),
היו על (T P C^MG G; εποιησεν, -ησαν BA+ is a corruption of οι
ησαν), גם אותם (4Q OL [J]), אחר (OL J), and רבה (4Q C^M).

In addition to several details, for the first plus 4Q = G

L OL^S J ≠ M C; for the second plus J = (4Q) G L OL^S C^{MG} ≠ M.

Having presented the more striking examples from among the pluses shared by 4Q and G against M in the section α ββ, we may now consider the remainder of those pluses in order.

1 S 1:24   V.346

4Q   ותעל אותו שילה כאשר
         שילה בפר בן[בקר משלש ולחם ////]
                     בי]ת יהוֺה שילה]

M   כאשר   ותעלהו עמה
         שלשה ואיפה   בפרים   גמלתו
     אחת קמח ונבל יין ותבאהו בית יהוה שלו

G   και ανεβη μετ αυτου εις [Σηλωμ ...]
     Σηλωμ εν μοσχω τριετιζοντι και αρτοις και οιφι
     σεμιδαλεως και νεβελ οινου. και εισηλθεν εις οικον Κῡ εν Σηλωμ

J   παρησαν ουν υπερ της του παιδος θυσοντες γενεσεως
     δεκατας τ΄ εφερον.

For consideration of the reconstruction of 4Q, cf. BASOR 19. These lines immediately precede the lines discussed above (p. 40), in which 4Q G agree in preserving a long reading lost by haplography in M. Though here each of the texts shows independent development, it can be seen that G was dependent on a 4Q texttype as opposed to an M texttype.

          1)   4Q   שילה   אותו   ותעל
                 M   עמה   ותעלהו
                 G^V שילה   אתו   ותעל
                 G   Και ανεβη μετ αυτου εις Σηλωμ
                 J   παρησαν

G's translation, pre-dating by a century the orthography of 4QSam^a, is clearly following here a 4Q texttype. The ambiguity of the early *ותעל אתו was interpreted one way by the original G translator, another way by the orthographic interpretation of the subsequent scribe of 4QSam^a (or by a near ancestor of this ms). This phenomenon recurs at 2 S 12:17 (cf. p. 129).

J has παρησαν ("they came"), demonstrating his dependence on the intransitive G reading (not on M or 4Q). His addition of δεκατας (= G 1:21) a few words later clinches that dependence, since M lacks that detail (de 4Q).

For this variant, then, 4Q = G ≠ M in textual affiliation.

2) 4Q and G add Shiloh, against M. G has subsequently lost a line through haplography, but the haplography is
based precisely on this expansion shared with 4Q. For the plus
εις Σηλωμ, 4Q = G ≠ M.

3)	4Q	בקר משלש [ובפר בן]	
	M	בפרים שלשה	
	G^V	בפר משלש	
	G	εν μοσχω τριετιζοντι	

τριετιζειν is used only here and in a triple occurrence at Gen
15:9, which similarly deals with cultic animals. The triple
use there to translate the Pual participle indicates that for
the variant here, 4Q = G ≠ M.

To judge from Lev 16:3 (cf. 2 C 13:9 similarly) where בפר
בן בקר in M is rendered by εκ μοσχω εκ βοων, בקר [בן] may be a
gloss in the 4Q tradition subsequent to the translation of G.
At any rate for this variant as well 4Q = G ≠ M.

4)	4Q	ולחם
	M	om
	G	και αρτοις

Finally, for this plus 4Q = G ≠ M.

In sum, we can see that (1) M goes its separate way in
each reading, including the developments בפרים ותעלהו עמה and
שלשה; (2) 4Q has developed: [בן] בקר, שילה, אותו; and (3) G
has developed: the Σηλωμ haplography. But 4Q and G stand out
as two closely allied members of a single texttype, agreeing in
2 pluses and 3 variants against M, before their separate developments.

1 S 2:2	4Q	כ[יא אין קדוש	]
	M	אין קדוש	
	G	οτι ουκ εστιν αγιος	

1 S 2:10   Between מריבו and ירעם M has two words, 4Q has
four lines and G has approximately three verses which bear
strong relation to G of Jer 9:22-23. 4Q is too fragmentary for
reconstruction, but its traces indicate that 4Q ≠ G. Even
though 4Q and G probably do not read the same plus, they nonetheless agree in having some similarly long plus at this point.
Compare the similar phenomenon at 1 S 1:24 just discussed on p.

48.

1 S 2:20	4Q	וילך האיש
	M	והלכו
	G	και απηλθεν ο ανθρωπος

1 S 2:21	4Q	ותלד עוד
	M	ותהר ותלד
	BM++	και ετεκεν ετι
	ANcx+	και συνελαβεν και ετεκεν ετι
	L	και συνελαβεν ετι και ετεκεν

4Q and M preserve two variants. OG (BM++) follows the 4Q
texttype; ANcx conflate by inserting the approximation toward
M; L follows the revision, further shifting ετι in needless precision. 4Q = OG ≠ M G^h.

1 S 2:25	4Q	[אם] חטא [יחטא]
	M	אם יחטא
	G	εαν αμαρτανων αμαρτη

1 S 2:27	4Q	[במצ]ר̊ים עבדים
	M	במצרים (haplography)
	G	Αιγυπτω δουλων

1 S 2:29	4Q	ולמה
	M	למה
	G	και ινα τι

1 S 2:32	4Q	[ולוא] יהיה לך
	M	ולא יהיה
	G	και ουκ εσται σου

See the fuller discussion on pp. 58-59.

1 S 5:8^{fin}	4Q	[אלוהי]/[ ]ישראל ג[תה]
	M	אלהי ישראל
	G	του θεου εις Γεθ(θα)

Confirming this reading is גתה in the following line of 4Q,
where M has the corrupt אתו, G omits, and L has προς τους Γεθθαιους. Though G does not share the ישראל expansion of 4Q and
M (cf. p. 123), for [גתה] 4Q = G ≠ M.

1 S 5:10   4Q   לא[מור] למה

                  M   לאמר

                  G   λεγοντες τι

λεγων, -οντες is the usual G equivalent for לאמר; cf. 2 S 1:16,
2:4, 5:6, 13:30, etc., and immediately below.

1 S 6:2

4Q   [לכהנים ולקסמים] ולמעונ[ני]ם לאמור

M   לאמר   לכהנים ולקסמים

G   τους ιερεις και τους μαντεις και τους επαοιδους αυτων λεγοντες

επαοιδος usually reflects (חרטמ(ים or ידעני and does not
reflect מעונן elsewhere. But מעונן occurs in Dt 18:10, 14
(where G = κληδον-), and it is strikingly coincidental that
επαοιδος occurs only five words later in the same list, rendering חבר--also the only instance of this correspondence. The
old Palestinian text probably expanded here with a third group
from its thesaurus of "diviner" terms, and G similarly rendered
it by one of its stock "diviner" terms; or M is haplographic.

1 S 6:3

4Q   אם/ [משלחים אתם את ארון] ברית יהוה אלוהי ישראל

M   אלהי ישראל   את ארון   משלחים   אם

G   Ει εξαποστελλετε υμεις την κιβωτον διαθηκης
         Κυριου θεου Ισραηλ

        In addition to the visible plus ברית יהוה in common with
G, 4Q most probably preserves with G the אתם glaringly absent
(by haplography) from M. 4Q's spacing requires it, for the
line is two letters short of the average even when it is included. And the presence of υμεις in G presupposes אתם in its
Vorlage, for--although אתם is necessary for the Hebrew--G's
customary translation of a Hb participle by a finite verb renders υμεις not entirely necessary (cf. 1 S 24:15, p. 54).

1 S 7:1 VI.18   4Q   [בית אבינ[דב אש̊ר/בגבעה]

                   M   בגבעה   בית אבינדב   (M note 7:1α)

                   G   οικον Αμειναδαβ τον εν τω βουνω

                   J   Αμιναδαβου...εις οικιαν

1 S 8:17   4Q   וצא̊נ̊כם

                  M   צאנכב

                  G   και τα ποιμνια υμων

1 S 10:4   *VI.55*

4Q   ‏ונתנו לך שתי ת[נ̇ופות לחם ולקחת‏

M   ‏לחם ולקחת   ונתנו לך שתי‏

G   και δωσουσιν σοι δυο απαρχας αρτων και λημψη

L OL^v   και δωσουσιν σοι   απαρχας αρτων και λημψη

dpqtz   και δωσουσιν σοι δυο αρτους απαρχων (αρτων απαρχας z)...

α'   δυο αρτους

OL^b   duo trium   panum   +ea

J   και δωσουσι σοι αρτους δυο, συ δε λημψη

    4Q can be confidently reconstructed with ‏חנופות‏ (= G);
απαρχη = ‏חנופה‏ in Ex 38:24 (39:1 G). Furthermore, Lev 23:17
mentions as a wave offering: ‏לחם חנופה שתים‏ (though there G
uses επιθεμα).

    L OL^v anomalously lack δυο, though OL^b (despite "trium")
has it.

    M, as in the preceding verse, shows non-agreement in the
gender of the numeral (cf. pp. 125 and 53 below: probably a
convention to indicate an acceptable but non-incorporated variant).

    J speciously agrees with M α' in omitting απαρχας. But
(1) he uses απαρχη infrequently (only 10x in *Ant.*, compared
with 44 occurrences in G of the historical books). The only
occasions on which he does use it are when specifically quoting
legal sections (III.235, 250; IV.70f, 226; V.26), when specifically describing the Temple and its cult (VII.378, IX.273),
or when quoting letters (XII.50, XVI.172). J never uses απαρχη
in simple narrative as here. (2) J is obviously echoing G
almost *literatim* here, as in the preceding verse.

    Thus 4Q = G ≠ M in this plus, while J is quoting G almost
literatim: 4Q = G (J) ≠ M.

1 S 10:25   4Q   ‏וילכו איש‏

               M   ‏איש‏

               G   και απηλθεν εκαστος

Cf. the variant on p. 77, where 4Q = G ≠ M in the following
word, as well as in this plus.

1 S 10:26   4Q   בני החיל

M   החיל

G   υιοι δυναμεων

α'   η ευπορια

σ'   η δυναμις

1 S 12:7-8   VI.89

4Q   [אׄ]בותיכם כאׄשׄ]ר בא יעקב ובניו מצרים ויענום מצרים ויזעקו[

[אבו]תׄיכם אל יה]וה [

M   ויעזקו   מצרים   כאשר בא יעקב [8] : אבותיכם

אבותיכם אל יהוה

G   πατρασιν υμων· ως εισηλθεν Ιακωβ και οι υιοι αυτου

εις Αιγυπτον, και εταπεινωσεν αυτους Αιγυπτος·

και εβοησαν οι πατερες ημων προς Κυριον

J   οτι συν εβδομηκοντα μονοις εκ του γενους ημων ο παππος

Ιακωβος δια λιμον εις Αιγυπτον ηλθε,...

ας εις δουλειας και χαλεπας υβρεις ηγαγον οι Αιγυπτιοι

4Q is reconstructed according to M, with the two pluses
filled in from G (cf. Kittel's apparatus). 4Q's spacing requires the two pluses: without them the line (counting from
בַאשר to אֶל) has 35 spaces, and with them it has 55. On the
other three fragments of this column there are five other lines,
whose counts are 52, 54, 54, 53, 54, as reconstructed from M.
In confirmation, see the 1 S 2:27 reading on p. 50 above, where
a very similar M haplography has occurred with מצרים עבדים.   J
also read both pluses.   4Q = G J ≠ M.

1 S 14:29   4Q   הדבש הזה

M   דבש הזה

G   του μελιτος τουτου

M may be attempting, through syntactic tension, to preserve two
variants, מעט דבש (cf. 14:43) and הדבש הזה (מעט), or it may
simply err. Whichever, 4Q = G ≠ M.

1 S 14:30   4Q   רׄבה המכׄה

M   רבתה מכה

G   μειζων ην (εγεγονει L) η πληγη

4Q and G preserve the expected definite article. The form of

4Q's verb is from רבב, that of M's verb from רבה. This could
conceal an earlier reading in the M tradition of רבה המכה,
where רבתה > רבחה after a misdivision of the words.

1 S 15:27	*VI.152*	4Q	[ו]יחזק שאול
		M	ויחזק
		G	και εκρατησεν Σαουλ
		L	και επελαβετο Σαουλ
		OL^V	et retinuit Saul
		J	Σαουλος δε ... ελλαμβανεται
			(επιλ- S^2 Zon)

1 S 24:15	4Q	מי אתה [ויצא מ]לך
	M	מי יצא מלך
	G	τινος συ εκπορευη (καταδιωκεις L) βασιλευ

1 S 25:4	4Q	כי ג[ורז נבל הכרמלי]
	M	כי גזז נבל
	G	οτι κειρει Ναβαλ ο Καρμηλιος

4Q spacing requires the inclusion of הכרמלי. In further support of its inclusion, cf. the reading of 2 S 3:3 on p. 64 below, where 4Q G C describe Abigail as הכרמלית, omitting M's אשת
נבל, while M reads הכרמלי instead, after inserting the gloss
אשת נבל.

2 S 2:13	4Q	[ויצאו מחברו]ן
	M	ויצאו (cf. M note)
	G	εξηλθοσαν / εκ Χεβρων (trp LN)

4Q spacing requires the inclusion of the expected מחברון, indicated in Kittel's apparatus.

2 S 2:15	4Q	לבנֿי בנימין
	M	לבנימן
	G	των παιδων Βενιαμειν

2 S 2:31	4Q	[מבני]/[בנימין מאנשי [אבנר
	M P	מבנימן ובאנשי אבנר
	T	מדבית בנימין ובגברי אבנר (om דבית af)
	G	των υιων Βενιαμειν (+εκ z) των ανδρων Αβεννηρ

Syntax (-מ) and spacing require the plus מבני in 4Q (= G T ≠ M
P). G's partitive genitive των ανδρων reflects the 4Q variant

מַאֲנָשִׁי, as in מַבְּנֵי immediately before and as מַעֲבָדֵי in the preceding verse. 4Q = G ≠ M T P.

2 S 3:7   VII.23~

4Q 11. 14/13	[וַיֹּאמֶר מְפִיבֹשֶׁת בֶּן] / שָׁאוּל אֶ֥ל אַבְנֵ֗ר	
M T	אֶל אבנר	ויאמר
P	לאבנר	ואמר אשבשול
Bya₂L 𝔤ʲ	και ειπεν Μεμφιβοσθε υιος Σαουλ προς Αβεννηρ	
AMN++ ¢	και ειπεν Ιεβοσθε υιος Σαουλ προς Αβεννηρ	
οι λ	Ιεσβααλ	
OL de; Vulg:	dixitque Isboseth ad Abner	
J	Ιεβοσθου	

    Cf. M note 3:7a, Well., Driver, Notes, NAB. If 4Q's line
13 were to follow M, it would contain only 34 characters, which
would be too short. If it follow G, the count becomes 50 (this
column's variation is 48-55). Line 14 shows that 4Q does contain more material than M and in fact coincides with G. מפיבשת
is reconstructed after G because the name occurs further in 4Q
at 4:1 (cf. pp. 42-45 above), where again M omits and G has
Μεμφιβοσθε (var.: Ιεβοσθε). Thus, again in having this plus,
4Q = G (J) ≠ M.

2 S 3:8	4Q	[בנר הראש] לו אָ֣ ויאמר
		[ראש] הֹ֗
	M	הראש ויאמר
	G rell	και ειπεν Αβεννηρ προς αυτον Μη κεφαλη
	L	και ειπεν αυτω Αβεννηρ Κεφαλη

The letter after לו is the last on this 4Q fragment, and it is
difficult to determine whether it is א (of אבנר) or ה (of הראש).
But the plus לו is clear and is reflected in (G) L.

2 S 3:27   VII.35

4Q	[ש]ם עד החמש
M	החמש שם
T	תמן בסטר ירכיה
P	תמן בחומשה
G	εκει επι (εις B) την ψυαν (ψοαν B, ψοα e₂, etc.)
σ'	κατα της λαγονος
J	υπο την λαγονα

    Cf. M note 3:27b, Well., Driver, Notes, NAB. Though M may

be using החמש adverbially (as חברון earlier in the verse), it
is better to conclude with Well., Driver, and M note that the
preposition has been lost, for 2:23, 4:6, and 20:10 all have
אל החמש.

   But which preposition has been lost? עד is used after נכה
for "time until which" (Josh 8:22, 1 S 11:11), but על should be
used after נכה for parts of the body (as is the case here; cf.
1 K 22:34 // 2 C 18:23, Jon 4:8), and על is indeed the Vorlage
for G here (B alone has εις, reflecting עד 4Q or אל). על is
probably the original expression: cf. [ש]החמל על בה ויכהו יואב in
4Q at 2 S 20:10 (de at 2:23, 4:6) in a nearly identical context,
where (as here) Acx boc₂e₂ have επι for B's εις (M has אל).
And על best explains the assortment of variants אל, עד, επι.

   In this plus then 4Q = B (G) ≠ M.

2 S 6:6   1 C 13:9   VII.81
4Q   וישלח עזא [את] ידוֹ
M   וישלח עזה
G   και εξετεινεν Οζα την χειρα αυτου
c^M   וישלח עזא את ידו
c^G   και εξετεινεν Οζα την χειρα αυτου (om την χ. α. Se₂)
J   Οζας . . . εκτειναντα την χειρα

   For fuller discussion, see pp. 195-197. After misspelling
the name of עזא, M omits את ידו by haplography through homoioarchton: וישלח עזא את ידו אל ארון. 4Q = G C J ≠ M.

2 S 8:4   1 C 18:4   VII.99
4Q   [   ] ד̊ויד אלף ר[כב ושבע]
M T P   דוד ממנו אלף   ושבע
G   Δαυειδ των αυτου χιλια αρματα και επτα
p   Δαυειδ   χιλια αρματα και επτα
OL^V   David mille vehicula eius et septem
c^M   דויד ממנו אלף רכב ושבעת
c^G   Δαυειδ / αυτων (trp bdjpqtze₂) χιλια αρματα και επτα
J   αυτου αρματα χιλια

   Cf. Well., Driver. 4Q's leather is marred just as the
fragment breaks off, but the last letter has a wide, broad head,
the size and shape of *resh*. If it is all ink--and it seems to
be--then 4Q inserts רכב before ושבע with G OL^V C J.

   4Q does not display the ממנו present in all other mss--

perhaps it has the transposed ממנו דויד of c^G mss bdjpqtze$_2$ and
of 𝔄 in Samuel. Or perhaps it omits altogether, as p. (OL^V,
undoubtedly from a Gk Vorlage in general, patently derives from
G here specifically; were it to translate ממנו directly, it
would employ *ab eo*.)

For the plus רכב, 4Q = G OL^V C J ≠ M; for the minus ממנו,
4Q ≠ M G C.

2. Minus

We may introduce this section with three M readings strikingly absent from 4Q in common with G:

1 S 2:22^{fin} V.339

4Q   לפני י]הוה[^{22}ועלי זקן מאד בן תשעים שנה [ושמונה שנים]
            וישמע [את] אשר [עו]ש[ים בניו לבני ישראל]^{23}ויאמר להם למה[
            תעשׂו̊]ן   [

M   עם יהוה ^{22}ועלי זקן מאד
            ואת אשר ישכבון   ושמע את כל אשר יעשון בניו לכל ישראל
            ויאמר להם למה^{23} את נשים הצבאות פתח אהל מועד
                                                         תעשון

G^V לפני יהוה ^{22}ועלי זקן מאד
            וישמע את   אשר עושיט בניו לבני ישראל
            ויאמר^{23} . . .

G   ενωπιον Κυριου. ^{22}Και Ηλει πρεσβυτης σφοδρα,
           και ηκουσεν α εποιουν οι υιοι αυτου τοις υιοις Ισραηλ

Acdpqt(sub ※)xz(txt) 𝔄   +και ως εκοιμιζον τας γυναικας
           τας παρεστωσας παρα την θυραν της σκηνης του μαρτυριου

N   +και ως εκοιμωντο μετα των γυναικων
           των παρεστηκυιων παρα την θυραν της σκηνης του μαρτυριου

bghoz(mg)c$_2$(sub ※)e$_2$ ₵(vid) +παντα και οτι συνεκοιμωντο
           οι υιοι αυτου μετα των γυναικων
           των παρεστηκυιων παρα τας θυρας της σκηνης του μαρτυριου

J   γυναικας τε τας επι θρησκεια παραγινομενας υβριζον φθοραις
           ταις μεν βιαν προσφεροντες τας δε δωροις υπαγομενοι

Cf. Well., Driver, BASOR, NAB. The expansion giving Eli's
age will be discussed on p. 133; our present interest concerns
the notice about the women, which 4Q definitely lacks.

Bya$_2$ 𝔏 lack it (though 𝔏^a has it in the margin), indicating that it was not part of the OG translation. In support of
4Q = OG, note the clear agreement for לפני, לבני, and the omission of כל; and the probable agreement for וישמע and עושים.
Note also the three texttypes: 4Q and OG are close (the only
difference being 4Q's characteristic expansion of Eli's age),
while M is distinctive.

Acx dpqtz(txt) 𝔄 preserve a translation of the gloss in M,
probably the earliest Gk form of it. Two possible clues for
the priority of this translation are:

    1) εκοιμιζον: καθευδειν, κοιμαν, and κοιμιζειν are
all used for שכב in α ββ, whereas (a) only κοιμαν is used in
βγ, and (b) α'θ' use κοιμαν for שכב, suggesting that κοιμαν is
the revisional word.

    2) παρεστωσας: παριστανaι = צבא only here, and α'θ'
use παριστανaι for יצב, both suggesting that Acx+ preserve a
freer (and therefore probably earlier) translation.

N has a revised form of the plus, which L+ have amplified
and "improved."

The gloss was made at the Hb stage and was translated directly from the Hb of this verse of Samuel. Note the exact
borrowing of the last four Hb words from Ex 38:8 (the only
other occurrence of the הצבאות). While the Gk of S accurately
translates the S gloss, it is obviously not borrowed from the
Gk of Ex 38:8 which reads των νηστευουσων (= הצמות*)...παρα τας
θυρας της σκηνης του μαρτυριου.

J uses the plus in his opening paragraph of the whole
Samuel narrative (!), attesting the early date of the plus,
though his recasting of the details (leaving only γυναικας from
LXX) throws off any possible clues as to precise Vorlage.

For this minus, 4Q = OG ≠ M G$_2$ J.

1 S 2:31-32   V.340, 351 om
4Q

    [את‬ ‬וראעך את ‬ וגדעת[י ‬ באֹ֗ים ‬ י[מֹ֗ים ‬ הנה   ]
    [‬ הימים] כול ‬ בביתי ‬ זקן ‬ לך ‬ יהיה [ולוא ‬ אביך ‬ בית ‬ זרע   [

M (T P)

31הנה ימים באים וגדעתי את זרעך ואת

זרע בית אביך   מהיות   זקן בביתך 32והבטת צר מעון בכל אשר

ייטיב את ישראל ולא יהיה   זקן בביתך כל   הימים:

G^V

31הנה ימים באים וגדעתי את זרעך ואת

זרע בית אביך 32ולא יהיה לך זקן בביתי כל   הימים

G OL^S

31ιδου ημεραι ερχονται και εξολεθρευσω το σπερμα σου και το
σπερμα οικου πατρος σου 32και ουκ εσται σου πρεσβυτης
         εν οικω μου πασας τας ημερας.

Acx

31ιδου ημεραι ερχονται και εξολεθρευσω το σπερμα σου και το
σπερμα οικου πατρος σου και ουκ εσται σου πρεσβυτης
         εν οικω μου 32και επιβλεψει κραταιωμα
(+μουων A) εν πασιν οις
αγαθυνει τον ισραηλ   και ουκ εσται   πρεσβυτης
         εν (+τω A) οικω σου πασας τας ημερας.

L OL^V

31και ιδου ημεραι ερχονται και εξολεθρευσω το σπερμα σου και το
σπερμα του οικου του πατρος σου 32και επιβλεψει κραταιωμα
         μαων (e₂; ναων b'; νωων b; λαων c₂; ων o) εν πασιν οις
αγαθυνει τον ισραηλ   και ουκ εσται   πρεσβυτης
         εν τω οικω σου   και ουκ εσται σοι πρεσβυτης
         εν τω οικω μου πασας τας ημερας.

Cf. Well.; Notes; NAB (at 2:33). With Well. and Cross it
is likely that the short text of 4Q G OL^S is original and that
M is expanded and corrupt (29a and 32a are corrupt variants;
31b is a variant of 32b; and pages 67-69 below exhibit two two-
part readings in 29 for which 4Q = G ≠ M).

Even if 4Q G were haplographic, no matter. The point at
present is that 4Q = G ≠ M in a noticeably shorter text. In
minor confirmation, 4Q G OL^S add לך and read בביתי against M
for the only two visible variants.

Acx and L OL^V are closely related variants of the expanded
text, OL^V following L as best it could: και επιβλεψει κραταιωμα μαων (?) becoming *et attendit fideliter manens*.

For this one-line minus, 4Q = G OL^S ≠ M G^h L₂ OL^V.

2 S 5:4-5   *1 C 11:4*   *VII.54, 61, 65*

4Q	om
M T P G	hab
OL^b	om
C^MG	om
J	om

Cf. Notes: "An apparently proto-Lucianic omission."

Fortunately, large fragments of 4Q are preserved for the preceding column and for this column, including the top and right margins. The present fragment (5:3-16) is attached to the preceding column which has continuous lines up to its top margin, and the scribe's lineation of the leather is trans-columnal. Calculations of lines and space therefore become certain. The preceding fragment in our column continues up to the *athnaḥ* in 5:2; the present fragment has בחברוֹן of 5:3a at the right margin of line 14, and ואנשׁיו of 5:6a occurs at the right margin of the next line. There is no uncertainty: 4Q lacks 5:4-5.

In VII.53-54 J narrates the bulk of the details in 2 S 5:1-3 // 1 C 11:1-3. He then inserts a list of the tribal army (VII.55-60 = 1 C 12:24-37) and resumes at VII.61 with 2 S 5:6 // 1 C 11:4. He lacks entirely (and only) the data of 5:4-5, thus falling in step with the Palestinian family 4Q OL C.

Later, at VII.65 J does relate the length of David's rule in Hebron, but does this mean that his Vorlage contained 5:4-5? That J's Vorlage lacked 5:4-5 can be recognized from a comprehensive and detailed look at the chronological data for David's reign.

The length of David's reign in Hebron is noted in 2 S 2:11 (no parallel in C), 2 S 5:5 (cf. 1 C 3:4), and 1 K 2:11 (final verse of 2 Rgn // 1 C 29:27, the end of 1 C). In each of the S K and C chronological notices--except 2 S 2:11--the length of the reign in Hebron is accompanied by the length of the reign in Jerusalem. At the end of David's life J does repeat the length of the Hebron reign, accompanying it there with the record of the Jerusalem reign (1 K 2:11 // 1 C 29:27 = VII.389). But here at VII.65 J notes only the length of the reign in Hebron, suggesting that he took his datum from 2 S 2:11. A detailed comparison confirms the suggestion:

G^{LAMN} (de B)   2 S 2:11   J VII.65

και <u>εγενοντο</u>	ο δε <u>χρονος ον</u>
αι <u>ημεραι ας</u>	της Ιουδα <u>φυλης</u>
Δαυειδ εβασιλευσεν	ηρξε μονης
εν Χεβρων	εν Χεβρωνι
επι τον <u>οικον</u> Ιουδα	<u>εγενετο</u>
επτα ετη	ετη επτα
και εξ μηνας.	και μηνες εξ.

At 2 S 5:5a G^{BMN} reads: (G^A is revised toward M); G^L reads:

επτα ετη	και εβασιλευσεν
και εξ μηνας	εν Χεβρων
εβασιλευσεν	επι Ιουδαν
εν Χεβρων	ετη επτα
επι τον Ιουδα....	και μηνας εξ....

J includes every detail from 2:11 and adds no other; even his
order and syntax are unusually faithful to his Vorlage. On the
other hand, 5:5a displays considerably less agreement with J,
and both 5:4 (David's age and the total length of his combined
reign) and 5:5b (the length of the Jerusalem reign) are absent
from J. Finally, J has omitted the chronological detail of
2:11 from his narration of that pericope (VII.9) to place it
here logically at the end of the (Hebron) reign which it is
tallying, the end being signalled by David's capture of Jerusalem.

Thus, J, following 4Q (as do C and, indirectly, OL), lacks
5:4-5 entirely. Though it may at first seem that J echoes 5:5a
(out of place) at VII.65, this turns out to be specious; VII.65
is taken (in its completeness, word order, and syntax) from
2:11 and placed here where a historian would logically place it
(cf. similarly, VI.18 occurring at 1 S 7:1 instead of 6:1).

Our primary question, once all this evidence is in and has
been evaluated, is: did OG echo the addition (with M) or lack
it (with 4Q)? Since all G mss contain the reading, the spon-
taneous answer would be that OG contained it. But two larger
issues should be considered to place the evidence in focus.

First, the material is found in all traditions at the end
of David's reign, suggesting that it may be secondary here
where half the traditions lack it.

Secondly, though we are dealing with 2 S 5 here, in Chapter VII below a detailed analysis of 2 S 6 finds that 4Q preserves the best Hb witness to that material, with C a close second, and M inferior to both. Analysis of what is commonly considered the OG text there isolates six examples of hebraizing revision of the OG, including examples of the OG being revised toward both errors and pluses in M. And these revisions toward M, though not in OG, have penetrated the universal G ms tradition.

The hypothesis is consequently proposed that, even though the universal G ms tradition attests the reading, the original Septuagint did not contain it. Everything then falls neatly into place. The old Hb tradition lacked the gloss, and 4Q and C^M accordingly lack it. OG, translated from a similar Vorlage, lacked it, and J OL (C^G) accordingly lack it. The gloss was inserted into the M tradition and was subsequently reflected by T P and an early reviser of G. All subsequent G mss included this gloss the same way they included the early doublets and other revisions which are universally attested.

The alternative is to argue, as Cross suggests, that the OG contained the plus, that a proto-Lucianic reviser excised the gloss on the basis of 4Q, that J and OL are dependent upon the proto-Lucianic shorter text, and finally that the plus was subsequently restored to the Lucianic mss.

The possibly secondary nature of the material plus concinnity of argument suggests the former solution, and thus in this minus, $4Q = OG\ OL\ C\ J \neq M\ T\ P\ G_2$.

Having seen three striking examples from among the minuses shared by 4Q and G against M in the section α ββ, we may now consider the remainder of those minuses.

1 S 1:13	4Q	והיא
	M	וחנה היא
	G	και αυτη (pr Αννα cxc$_2$; Αννα A)

1 S 2:17	4Q	נאצו את
	M	נאצו האנשים את
	G	ηθετουν την

1 S 2:22   4Q   רישמَע [ואת] אשר

             M   ושמע את כל אשר

             G rell   και ηκουσεν α

             c   και ηκουσεν συν παντα α

             Adpqtxz 𝔤ʲ 𝔄   και ηκουσεν συμπαντα α

See the fuller exposition of this verse presented above (p.
57) where 4Q = OG ≠ M G₂ in a striking minus. 4Q's spacing is
tightly controlled here, and there is no room for כ(ו)ל with
the subsequent space required for word-division. Note in c(Ax+)
the characteristically Aquilan συν for את.

1 S 2:27   4Q   [ו]יֹאמר כה

             M   ויאמר אליו כה

             G   και ειπεν Ταδε

             LN 𝔼   και ειπεν αυτω (προς αυτον N) Ταδε

1 S 2:28   4Q   אפוֹד

             M   אפוד לפני

             G   εφουδ

             LAcx+   εφουδ ενωπιον μου (εμου A)

1 S 2:30   4Q   יֹ[שרא]לֹ אמרתי

             M   ישראל אמור אמרתי

             G   Ισραηλ Ειπα

             LAN   Ισραηλ Ειπον (Ειπας AN; om cx)

1 S 3:4   4Q   [ויקרא יהו[ה שמֹ[ואל

             M   ויקרא יהוה אל שמואל

             G OL   και εκαλεσεν Κυριος Σαμουηλ Σαμουηλ

One cannot say definitely whether 4Q had a second שמואל,   for
this is the last phrase of the fragment containing the last
line of this column. But there is room for it, and with its
inclusion the line is well finished, totalling 48 spaces in
comparison with 51 and 49 in the immediately preceding lines.
But clearly, 4Q G omit אל.

1 S 6:4
4Q   עֹפֹלי זהב כי

M   עפלי זהב וחמשה עכברי זהב כי

Bya₂++ OLᵇ   εδρας χρυσας οτι

L OL^V εδρας χρυσας ομοιωμα των εδρων υμων οτι
ANcx+ εδρας χρυσας και πεντα μυας χρυσους οτι

Whether 4Q is haplographic or M is glossed, 4Q and OG agree in their shorter text.

1 S 6:20   4Q   [לפני] יהוה הקדוש

M   לפני יהוה האלהים הקדוש

By Ʞᄃ   ενωπιον   του αγιου

LN++   ενωπιον κ̅υ̅ του αγιου

Acx+   ενωπιον κ̅υ̅ του (om cx) θ̅υ̅ του αγιου

4Q = G ≠ M G^h in lacking האלהים. If By Ʞᄃ really do represent OG, as they characteristically should, L is here a proto-Lucianic revision toward 4Q which nearly thoroughly penetrated the tradition. Acx+ have revised toward M.

1 S 15:31   VI.154

4Q Kenn-151   [ ]וי[שוב שמוͦ]אͦ[ל]אח[ ]רͦ̊י [שאול וישת]חͦ[ו ליהוה

M P   וישב   שמואל אחרי שאול וישתחו שאול ליהוה

T   ותב שמואל בתר שאול וסגיד שאול (om F r) קדם יוי

G   και ανεστρεψεν Σαμουηλ οπισω (μετα cx+) Σαουλ
                και προσεκυνησεν (+Σαουλ A) τω κυριω.

J   συν αυτω ... προσκυνησαι. διδωσι δε τουτο
                Σαμουηλος αυτω και συνελθων προσκυνει τω θεω.

    A syntactic and scribal problem. The original Hb (= 4Q) lacked שאול 2°. The resulting sense is that, upon Saul's request that Samuel worship with him, Samuel turns back after Saul and worships (singular verb though both men worship). J clearly follows this syntax and sense of 4Q G. A nodding scribe inserted the erroneous שאול in M, and A "corrects" accordingly. T P also follow the M error.
    4Q = G J ≠ M (T) P G₂.

2 S 3:3   4Q   [לאביגיל ה]כרמלית

M T P   לאביגל אשת נבל הכרמלי

G   της Αβειγαιας της Καρμηλιας

c^M   לאביגיל הכרמלית

c^G   τη Αβειγαια τη Καρμηλια

For fuller exposition, see pp. 81f. below, where in a single phrase 4Q = G C ≠ M for two variants in addition to this omission of אשת נבל.

2 S 3:7	VII.23	4Q	פילגש ̇רצפֹה
		M	פלגש ושמה רצפה
		G	παλλακη Ρεσφα
		Niv Ӿ	παλλακη η ονομα Ρεσφα
		L ɤ̶ˢᵃ	παλλακη και ονομα αυτη Ρεσφα
		j(mg)	❈ α' λ̸ και ονομα αυτη
		J	παλλακη Ραισφα μεν τουνομα

For the omission of ושמה 4Q = G ≠ M L α' J. The fact that N,
J, and the early Ethiopic mss already have ονομα suggests that
the plus was already in the early stratum of L.

2 S 3:36	4Q	̊
		והע[ם
	M	העם טוב
	G	του λαου
	Gʰ	του λαου αγαθον

For fuller presentation, see below, pp. 97 and 116.

2 S 5:1	1 C 11:1	4Q	לאמר
		M	ויאמרו לאמר (8 mss ויאמרו לו)
		T	ואמרו למימר (c, f ואמרו ליה)
		MN++ OL	λεγοντες
		L	και λεγουσιν
		BAnvy Cyr	και ειπαν αυτω
		acx	και ειπον αυτω
		Cᴹ	לאמר
		Cᴳ	λεγοντες

The old Palestinian reading here is לאמר, preserved faithfully by 4Q, MN++, OL, Cᴹᴳ.

The OG here is either και λεγουσιν (L) or λεγοντες (MN++
OL). In favor of και λεγουσιν is (a) the historical present
and (b) the freer translation. It may simply be, however, a
stylistic revision following the introductory verb Και παραγι-
νονται in the previous clause; if so, λεγοντες would be the OG,
reflecting the Palestinian text. If L preserves the OG, then
λεγοντες would be an early revision toward the 4Q texttype.

BAnvy and acx are two successive revisions toward a form
of the proto-Massoretic text (cf. the 8 variant mss): first,

BAnvy made the *koine* revision και ειπαν αυτω (= ויאמרו לו),
quoted by Cyril of Alexandria; then that revision was again revised in acx according to the Atticist preference for the second aorist ειπον (cf. Rahlfs, *SS III*, 176-177; and Brock, "The
Recensions," p. 234).

At any rate, no G ms reflects the fully developed (conflate?) M tradition. For this minus, $4Q = G\ C \neq M\ G_2$.

2 S 5:6		4Q	כי
		M	כי אם
		G	οτι (διοτι L)

2 S 5:10	*1 C 11:9*	4Q	ויהוה
		M	ויהוה אלהי
		G	και Κυριος
		Acx	και Κυριος ο θ͞ς
		C^M	ויהוה
		C^G	και Κυριος

2 S 6:2	*1 C 11:6*	4Q	[שם יהוה]
		M	שם שם יהוה צבאות
		OG	*το ονομα Κυριου
		G_2	το ονομα Κυριου των δυναμεων
		L	το ονομα Κυριου Σαβαωθ
		C^M	יהוה ... שם
		C^G	Κυριου ... ονομα αυτου
		C^{L+}	Κυριου ... το ονομα αυτου εκει

See the discussion on pages 194, 197, 201, and 204 for this
double minus.

2 S 6:3-4   1 C 13:7^{fin}

4Q	הֹעגלה $^{(4)}$ עֹ[ם]
M	העגלה חדשה: ^{4}וישאהו מבית אבינדב אשר בגבעה עם
G	την αμαξαν ^{4}συν
C^M	בעגלה
C^G	την αμαξαν

Cf. M note. Only M exhibits this long dittography.

2 S 7:23   1 C 17:21   VII.95˜

4Q   [ולע[שֹׁות ג[דולה]

M T P   ולעשות לכם הגדולה

G   του ποιησαι μεγαλωσυνην

C^M   גדלות

C^G   μεγα

J   και ποιμενος εις τηλικουτο μεγεθος

Cf. Well., Driver, Notes, NAB. There is considerable turbulence in the text of this verse. But the positioning of these words in 4Q is anchored by the final ואהלים *(sic)* in the line below (for this surprising reading in which the unanimous G tradition follows the 4Q tradition in a blatant error, cf. p. 71).

Palaeographically, the ג is practically certain. The only other (less likely) possibilities, due to the slant downward to the right, are א and י. The letter is certainly not ל (cf. לכם M), which would have required a slant in the opposite direction.

Further, from the point of view of textual witness, לעשות is followed only by לכם (in M T P), by גדלות (in C) and גדולה* (in G: μεγαλωσυνη always corresponds to גדל in S and C, not occurring in K). And note that only M T P add the definite article, omitted by G C^MG.

Thus, גדולה (and consequently the omission of לכם) is indicated by textual witness, palaeography, and a dramatic example of text affiliation at the end of the verse. For this omission, 4Q = G C ≠ M.

3. Variant

Five of the more striking variants shared by 4Q and G against M will serve to introduce this section:

1 S 2:29   V.350

4Q

ישרא[לֹ]ל[מה תבֹיט בזבחי ובמנחתי   ]

[להבֹיך מראֹש כול מנחֹות   ]

M T

ישראל ^29 למה תבעטו בזבחי ובמנחתי

אשר צויתי מעון ותכבד את בניך ממני להבריאכם מראשית כל מנחת

P

איסריל ²⁹למנא אעליתון בדבחי ובקורבני

דפקדת מן מדברא ויקרת בניך מני דתגבון מן ריש כולהון קורבנא

G

Ισραηλ εις βρωσιν. ²⁹και ινα τι επεβλεψας επι το θυμιαμα μου
και εις (επι LMN+) την θυσιαν μου αναιδει οφθαλμω; και
εδοξασας τους υιους σου υπερ εμε ενευλογεισθαι απαρχης
(-ην LMN++) πασης θυσιας

OL^{SV}

Israel, in escam. ²⁹Et ut quid respexisti in (ad v) incensum meum
et in (ad v) sacrificium meum impudenti oculo: et
glorificasti filios tuos super me, benedicere primitias
omnis sacrificii (ut benediceres a primordio in omnibus
sacrificiis v)

Cf. Well., Driver, Notes, NAB. The final word of 2:28 in
4Q is probably ישראל--the bottom trace of ל is visible just as
the leather breaks off, and εις βρωσιν is "a highly jejune
clarification" (Well.). 4Q = M T P ≠ G OL, but it is an entirely open question whether 4Q = G^V.

ולמה -- 4Q G OL add the conjunction against M T P.

חביט -- 4Q G OL again agree, this time preserving the correct reading; M's otherwise corrupt variant of this verse in
2:32a preserves the correct verb (cf. p. 59).

להבריך מראש -- T is a paraphrase of M for the whole verse
but interestingly has לאוכלותהון מריש here. It is also M
which P follows and from which it deviates, though here it
reads ש ריש מן דתגבון (נבא = "to choose" = Hb ברה, ברר, so Well.,
cf. 1 S 17:8: ברו/εκλεξασθε). For the apparently inferior
reading להבריך (ברך/ενευλογεισθαι/benedicere), 4Q = G OL ≠ M T
≠ P.

4Q has the support of T P for מראש; what of G OL? One is
tempted facilely to say that 4Q = M ≠ G, for απαρχη is frequently
ראשית, never ראש (H-R 118b,c). But απαρχη = רֵאשִׁית, not מֵראשית
(which would = απ(ο της) απαρχης cf. Dt 26:2). Rather, we must
treat this word with the problematical preceding word:

M	להבריאכם מראשית
G	ενευλογεισθαι απαρχης
G^V {	להבריך מֵראשית
	להבריך מראש (reading ΑΠ ΑΡΧΗΣ; *a primordio* OL^V!)
4Q	להבריך מראש

That G read ברך is certain (H-R 473a). G expresses no object
(though LMN++ later alter to απαρχην due to this problem). If
απαρχη were to = ראשית, then G would reflect neither of M's
mems (!), and απαρχης would be baselessly in the genitive
(whereas only the dative patterns with ενευλογεισθαι elsewhere). Mindful of the lack of word-division in ancient Gk
uncials, if we divide ΑΠ ΑΡΧΗΣ (απ αρχης = מראש Eccles 3:11;
Song 4:8; Is 48:16, 41:4 (?); απ αρχης = מראשית never), then we
solve both the problems of consonantal Vorlage and of syntax,
and, just as for להבריך, so too for מראש, 4Q = G OL ≠ M.

מנחות -- There is a vertical split in the leather at the
waw, but the ink traces almost surely form *waw*. However, the
3rd or early 2nd century Vorlage of 4QSam^a (contemporary with
G^V) may well have lacked the *waw*; note the defective orthography of 4QSam^b. Nonetheless, 4Q = OL^V P ≠ M G OL^S.

In fine, no pattern emerges for the three minor readings
εις βρωσιν (4Q = M [G^V?] ≠ G), ולמה (4Q = G ≠ M), and מנחות (4Q
≠ M G); but for the three more important words חביט and להבריך
מראש 4Q = G ≠ M.

1 S 10:27-11:1   VI.67-68

4Q	...ויהי כמו חדש ויעל	מנחה (vacat)
M	ויעל¹	מנחה ויהי כמחריש:
G OL	δωρα.	¹Και εγενηθη ως μετα μηνα και ανεβη
L	δωρα και εγενηθη ως κωφευων.	¹Και εγενετο μετα μηνα ημερων και ανεβη
J	δωρα....	.⁶⁸Μηνι δ᾿ υστερον

4Q has a major division (more than half of the remaining
line is left blank) after מנחה. The next line begins a 3½-line
section which is absent from every other ms and tradition--ex-
cept J! (see below, pp. 166-170). *After* this section and written intralinearly appears ויהי כמו חדש ויעל... .

L presents a doublet: Και εγενετο μετα μηνα (conforming
with OG OL$^{b(sv)}$ J, against M) is certainly the earlier; και
εγενηθη ως κωφευων (-υγων o) is a subsequent approximation

toward M. Shenkel presents in *Chronology*, pp. 114-115, the
evidence for κωφευειν as the characteristic KR translation of
חרש.

    J clearly follows a 4Q texttype (see pp. 165-173), and it
is not unlikely that he followed it in a Greek form: note that
he reads δωρα (pl! = Gk ≠ Hb).

    In both order and content for this variant, 4Q = G pL OL J
≠ M L$_2$.

2 S 4:12   4Q   מפיבשת
              M T P   אישבשת
              BAL+   Μεμφιβοσθε
              MN++ OL^b ⍍   Ιεβοσθε

For full discussion see above, pp. 42-45. BAL+ follow 4Q in a
clear error. This group either represents the OG (in which
case MN++ would be an early correction) or displays an early
erroneous revision (from OG which would be represented by MN++)
toward 4Q. The former is more likely, but in either case, an
early form of the G tradition clearly follows 4Q in an error.

2 S 5:9   *1 C 11:8*   *VII.65*
4Q   [ויבנה עיר]
M T P   ויבן דוד
G   και ωκοδομησεν αυτην πολιν
Lcfx   και ωκοδομησεν (+Δαδ b) την πολιν (+Κυριου cx)
C^M ויבן העיר
C^G και ωκοδομησεν   την πολιν
J   και αυτος ανοικοδομησας τα Ιεροσολυμα, πολιν αυτην

    Cf. Well., Driver. Well. considers G "correct with וִיבֶןָ,
since πολιν should be deleted as an addition from C." 4Q,
however, shows that πολιν is not to be deleted, or at least
that it has a Hb basis. Driver thinks that C^M may preserve the
original reading which underwent different word-division (ויבנה
עיר) to become the S^G reading. I agree with Driver, and 4Q
confirms that the erroneous word-division took place at the
Hebrew ms stage. G translates on the basis of an erroneous
Vorlage like 4Q, conclusively displaying intimate textual
affiliation.

    L changes αυτην to την either on the basis of C$^{G(M)}$ or

from sense; b adds Δᾱδ from M or for clarity, cx add Κυριου the
same way G omn have erroneously added Κυριου one line above
(5:8): הבית M, οικον Κυριου G.

   For וֹיבנה, 4Q = G ≠ M[SC]. For עיר (vs. דוד), 4Q = G J C[MG]
≠ M T P.

2 S 7:23   1 C 17:21 om   VII.95 om
4Q   ואהלים
M T P   ואלהיו
G OL[V]   και σκηνωματα

   Cf. Well., Driver, Notes. Here not only does G (without
variation) follow 4Q in root and lack of suffix, it follows
exactly in a clear and certain error, as OL[V] in turn clearly
follows G's error. This is again proof of the highest calibre
for close textual affiliation. 4Q = G OL[V] ≠ M T P ≠ C.

   Some of the more striking variants having been presented,
we may now review in order other variants shared by 4Q and G
against M.

1 S 1:23   4Q   [ויהו]ה היוצֿא מפֿיך
               M   יהוה את דברו
               G OL   Κυριος (+παν L+; +omne verbum OL[V]) το
                        εξελθον εκ του στοματος σου (eius OL[b])

1 S 1:24   4Q   ותעל אותו
               M   ותעלהו עמה
               G[V]   ותעל אתו
               G   και ανεβη μετ αυτου

See the fuller discussion above on pp. 48-49. G's translation,
pre-dating by at least a century the orthography of 4QSam[a], is
clearly following a 4Q texttype. Compare the similar phenomenon at 2 S 12:17 on p. 129.

1 S 1:24   4Q   [בפר בן] בקר משלש
               M   בפרים   שלשה
               G[V]   בפר   משלש
               G OL   εν μοσχω τριετιζοντι

See the fuller discussion above on pp. 48-49. בן בקר is probably a gloss in the 4Q tradition subsequent to the original G

translation.

1 S 1:25	4Q	[וי]שחט
	M	וישחטו
	G	και εσφαξεν

This variant is a part of a more complex reading (cf. p. 40 above), where 4Q and G preserve a long text lost by haplography in M.

1 S 2:4	4Q	חתה
	M	חתים (cf. M note)
	G	ησθενησεν

1 S 2:10	4Q	יחת
	M	יחתו
	G	ασθενη ποιησει

1 S 2:10	4Q	ויירעם
	M	ירעם
	G OL	και εβροντησεν

1 S 2:20	4Q	לאמר ישלם
	M	ואמר ישם
	G	λεγων Αποτισαι (Ανταποδωσει L)

G follows 4Q in both variants. λεγων is the customary rendering of לאמר (cf. p. 51). In 1 S 2:36 and 2 S 6:9 λεγων corresponds to ויאמר in M; but in both places 4Q reads לאמר, explaining the apparent exceptions (cf. pp. 74 and 84 below). αποτινειν reflects שלם 26 times, שים never; and ανταποδιδοναι reflects שלם 27 times, שים never.

1 S 2:20	4Q	השאי[ל]ת לי[ה]וה וילך האיש
	M	שאל ליהוה והלכו
	G	εχρησας τω Κυριω· και απηλθεν ο ανθρωπος

Cf. Driver, BASOR 22 and 26. Driver (p. 33) records as unacceptable some scholars' conjecture of השאילה, while "the Versions merely guess: LXX, Pesch., Vulg. 'which thou didst lend,' unsuitably...." In Ex 12:36, however, which is the only other instance of χραν = שאל, M has the Hiphil of שאל, as meaning would dictate.

Cross opts for [השאיל[ה. Either ה- (3rd sg. fem.) or ת-
(2nd sg. masc. or fem.) is morphologically and contextually
possible. Though Hannah is properly the one who asked for the
boy (1:27), I would opt for השאילת in the text of 4Q for two
reasons: (1) G reads εχρησας, and 4Q shares with G against M
one plus (האיש) and three other variants (וילך and, immediately
above, לאמר ישלם) in this single verse, with no examples to the
contrary. (2) The blessing is in fact addressed to Elkanah in
the second person (לך 4Q M, σοι G) and is followed (in 4Q G) by
"the man went to his home." At any rate, for this variant 4Q
agrees with G against M, at least closely (Hiphil) and maybe
perfectly (if ת-). Thus, within this single verse, 4Q = G ≠ M
in one plus and four variants.

1 S 2:21	4Q	ויפקד	
	M	כי פקד	(cf. M note)
	G	και επεσκεψατο	

1 S 2:22	4Q	[ועו]שׂיִׄם בניו לבני ישראל
	M	יעשׂון בניו לכל ישראל
	G	εποιουν οι υιοι αυτου τοις υιοις Ισραηλ

Cf. BASOR 22, note 26. In 4Q, the final *mem* of /יעשׂון
[ועו]שׂיִׄם] is clear; the second-to-last letter has a broad head,
more like the usual *yod* than like the usual *waw*. The reading,
עושׂים, obviates the necessity for Albright's rare "phonetic
assimilation before following *b (samdhi)*" in note 26 of BASOR
22. ע(ו)שׂים occurs frequently (cf. Mandelkern), including Gen
39:22, Ex 5:8, 1 S 8:8, Ezek 8:6--all of which are translated
(as here) with the 3 pl. indicative form by G, without parti-
cipial variant. Cf. also 1 S 2:23, 24 (p. 41 above), where 4Q
and M have participles, G the indicative ακουω. In confirmation, note the second variant לבני, shared by G.

1 S 2:25	4Q	אל יהוה	
	M	אלהים	
	G	προς Κυριον	

1 S 2:29	*V.350*	4Q	חבׄיט
		M	תבעטו
		G OL	επεβλεψας (-ατε A)

z(mg sin nom) απολακτιζετε

J   Ηλεις γαρ της εμης θεραπειας
                 μαλλον τους υιους...ηγαπησε.

επιβλεπειν is used to translate נבט 34x and is never used
for בעט. The anonymous reading in the margin of z is a correction toward M; απολακτιζειν is used only once in G, at Deut
32:15, and there it translates בעט. J unquestionably reflects
4Q G, not M. M's otherwise corrupt variant of this verse now
found in 2:32a preserves the correct verb והבטת; see pp. 58-59.

1 S 2:31-32	4Q	ביתי
	M	בביתך . . . בביתך
	G OL^S	εν οικω μου
	Acx	εν οικω μου . . . ων οικω σου
	L OL^V	εν τω οικω σου . . . εν τω οικω μου

Cf. the fuller discussion above, pp. 58-59. 4Q G OL^S preserve
the original reading, M is conflate and troubled, Acx and L OL^V
display varied forms of the conflation from M.

1 S 2:33	V.350 om	
4Q		יפולו בחרב אנשים
M P		אנשים ימותו
T		יתקטלון עולימין
G		πεσουνται εν ρομφαια ανδρων
L		πεσεται εν ρομφαια ανδρων
OL^sv		decidet (-dat v) in gladio virorum

Cf. M note, Notes, NAB. The leather of 4Q is shrunken and is
vertically split at the second *waw* of יפולו, an ink stroke like
waw being fairly clear (though perhaps continuing excessively
downward). The singular verb in L (followed by OL) is a gram-
matical correction of the synesis of [4Q] M G, correcting in
light of the singular collective subject πας περισσευων; it
says nothing about the Vorlage. For this variant, 4Q = G OL ≠
M T P.

1 S 2:36	4Q	לאמור
	M	ואמר
	G	λεγων (cf. above, p. 72)

1 S 5:10   4Q   למה הסבות[ם]

            M   הסבו

            G   Τι απεστρεψατε (απεσταλκατε L)

Cf. fuller discussions on pp. 122 and 123.

1 S 5:11   *VI.5*

4Q   [כבדה מאד כבוא ארון אלוהי ישראל ש]מֹה

M   שם   יד האלהים   כבדה מאד

G   βαρεια σφοδρα, ως εισηλθεν κιβωτος

        θεου Ισραηλ εκει (om εκει LNy)

J   συνεξεκομισε γαρ αυτη τα των Αζωτιων η κιβωτος παθη

Cf. Well. 4Q is reconstructed after G; see also M and G
in the preceding verse. That 4Q agreed essentially with G J is
demonstrated by its שֹׁ[מֹ]ה, which requires a verb of motion and
precludes a nominal clause such as כבדה ... יד ... . The spacing in 4Q clinches this hypothesis, since the line contains 43
spaces if reconstructed according to M, but 54 according to G.
The lines of this column average 50-52 spaces per line, the
shortest being 49.

The omission of εκει by LNy is anomalous, the single visible explanation being haplography due to the και which follows
(cf. Katz, *Philo's Bible*, pp. 53-54).

Well. attempts to explain G as a corruption of M and to
isolate the steps by which this came about. But his whole explanation is based on the false supposition that מות was original in the text (see p. 123f.).

J's statement that the ark (not God) carried the plagues
around with it, agrees with 4Q G, which describe the deathly
panic as very heavy when the ark (not God--"God" is only part
of the ark's epithet) moved thither. This contrasts with M's
statement that a deathly panic was in the city and that God's
hand was heavy there.

For both the ark and the motion, 4Q = G J ≠ M.

1 S 6:3   4Q   [ו]נכפר ל[כם]

           M   ונודע לכם

           G   και εξιλασθησεται υμιν

εξιλασκειν = כפר in the Octateuch, S, and K some 66 times,
without exception; cf. esp. Dt 21:8b and 1 S 3:14. Third-second

century palaeography and orthography might explain M's error:
‫ועט < ועיע‬ **<** ‫ועדיע‬   (‫ונודע < ונדע < ונכפר‬).

4Q's agreement with G on ‫ונכפר‬ coerces *(sensus causa)* the
reconstruction of the remainder of the verse with G against M
(though space would permit either):

    4Q   [‫הלוא חסור ידו מכם‬]

    M   ‫למה לא חסור ידו מכם‬

    G   μη ουκ αποσтζη χειρ αυτου αφ υμων;

For μη ουκ = ‫הלוא‬, see Judg 6:13; 9:38; 10:11; 15:2; 2 K 19:25;
Eccles 6:6.

1 S 8:16   4Q   ‫ועשׂוֹ‬

             M   ‫ועשה‬

             G   και αποδεκατωσει (= ‫ועשׂר‬*)

Cf. Well., Driver. Well. correctly chooses ‫ועשה‬ of M over
‫ועשׂר‬ of G. Driver follows him, adding the examples of Ezek
15:5 and Ex 38:24. Their choice is borne out by the syntax of
similar verbs in this passage and by the context: the king is
the subject of (‫ועשׂ‬) after ‫יקח‬, as he is of ‫יקח ושם‬ (8:11b),
‫יקח ונתן‬ (14b), and ‫יעשׂר ונתן‬ (15). Thus, ‫ועשׂוֹ‬ (4Q) as a
plural is ruled out. ‫ועשׂר‬ is a less objectionable error, since
that word occurs in both the preceding and the following verses.
Nonetheless, the king tithes only crops, vineyards, and flocks
(15, 17a); human beings he simply takes (11, 13, and esp. 17b
in contrast to 17a). Thus ‫ועשׂר‬* G is also rendered unlikely.

Further, it is hardly possible that ‫ועשׂ‬ is a "correction"
of ‫יעשה‬ ("he will take them, and *they* will do his work"), due
to the -‫ל‬ of ‫למלאכתו‬, clear in 4Q. Rather, 4Q is an error
based on the third-century palaeographic confusion of ‫ר/ו‬ (cf.
4QSam[b] and *BANE*, p. 175, line 4). For similar confusion of ‫ד/ר‬
with ‫ו/י‬, cf. 1 S 29:1 (‫בעירָן‬ M, εν Αεδδων B), 2 S 4:2 (of 4Q,
where the ‫ר‬ of ‫רמון‬ is still mistakable for ‫י‬), and 2 S 22:48
(‫ומריד‬* M, ‫ומרדַד‬ 4Q, see p. 91); note also the possibility
mentioned immediately above in 1 S 6:3 concerning the final ‫ר‬
of ‫ונכפר‬. Insofar as ‫ועשׂ‬ reflects an earlier ‫ועשׂר‬ in a third
century Vorlage, 4Q and G would agree in an error derived from
the same text type.

1 S 8:18^{fin} 4Q   [בימים /[בי]הֵם

M   ביום ההוא

G   εν ταις ημεραις εκειναις

fn^bsw ¢   εν τη ημερα εκεινη

G appends a gloss (cf. p. 141) not found in 4Q M, but this need
not reflect a Hb Vorlage. For the variant under discussion,
however, 4Q = G ≠ M.

1 S 9:18   4Q   [ויגש שאול א[ל שׁ]מואל בתוך הע[י]ר ויאמ]ר]

M   ויגש שאול את שמואל בתיך השער ויאמר

G   και προσηγαγεν Σαουλ προς Σαμουηλ

εις μεσον της πολεως και ειπεν

    Cf. Driver: "No doubt both here, *ch.* 30,21, and Nu. 4,9
(as Jud. 19,18b after הלך), את is merely an error for אל." In
4Q the top half of the ל in א]ל is clear and exactly in place.

    In the second variant (הע]י[ר) the letter before ר slants
downward from top right to middle left and therefore is probably י; though it could also be ד, ה, ר, it can by no means be
ע, which would slant in the opposite direction. For both variants, 4Q = G ≠ M.

1 S 9:19   VI.51   4Q   [אנכי ה[ו]א

M   אנכי הראה

G   Εγω ειμι αυτος

J   του δε Σαμουηλου αυτον ειναι φρασαντος

    4Q's final א is clear and is followed by עלֹה (= M G). The
ו is likewise almost certain, the only other possibilities being ה and ligatured י. By no stretch of Qumran orthography can
this reflect a form הראה, whereas G without variant solidly
grounds הוא.

    J's αυτον is all the more noteworthy since he (as do 4Q
and G) answers the question "Where is the prophet's *house*" with
"I am *he*." 4Q = G J ≠ M.

1 S 10:25   4Q   [וֹיֹלכוֹ איש למקוֹם[ו]

M   איש לביתו

G   και απηλθεν εκαστος εις τον τοπον αυτου

For both the plus and the variant, 4Q = G ≠ M.

1 S 10:26   4Q   יה[ו]ה̇ בלבבם

M   אלהים בלבם

G   Κυριος καρδιας αυτων

1 S 11:8   *VI.78*   4Q   שבעים אלף

M OL^b   שלשים אלף

G OL^v   εβδομηκοντα χιλιαδας

J   μυριαδες επτα

4Q = G OL^v J ≠ M OL^b.

1 S 14:32   *VI.120*   4Q   על

M   אל

G   εις

L   επι

J   επι

על is certainly reflected by επι. אל is frequently reflected
by προς, though εις = אל in 14:26. If εις = על here, 4Q = G L
J ≠ M; if εις = אל, 4Q = pL J ≠ M G.

1 S 14:47   *VI.129*   4Q   ובמלך צובה

M   ובמלכי צובה

G   και εις (+τον L) βασιλεα Σουβα

J   και τον βασιλεα της Σωβας

4Q = G J ≠ M.

1 S 14:50   *VI.130*   4Q   שר הצבא[ ]

M   שר צבאו

G   τω αρχιστρατηγω

efg+ A̶C̶E̶(vid)   τω αρχιστρατηγω αυτου

L   του αρχιστρατηγου αυτου

J   στρατηγον

4Q = G J ≠ M (G₂ L).

1 S 15:29   *VI.153*   4Q   [לא] ישוב

M   לא ישקר

G   ουκ αποστεψει (επισ- L)

J   στρεφειν

4Q = G J ≠ M.

1 S 17:4   *VI.171*   4Q   אַרבע

                         M   שש

                         Bvza₂L ₵₵ᵃ   τεσσαρων

                         N++   πεντε

                         Acx+ OLⱽ ₳₵ˢ   εξ

                         λ̥   τεσσαρων

                         σ'   εξ

                         J   τεσσαρων

                                                     4Q = G L λ̥ J ≠ M Gʰ.

1 S 24:20

4Q   הז[ה] ה̊י̊ו̊ם̊ ה[ה הזליה] עשית[ה] אשר התחת[

M   התחת היום הזה אשר עשיתי לי   (cf. M note)

G   καθως (+συ N++) πεποιηκας (+συ L; +μοι N) σημερον

        Both in the placement of היום הזה and in the omission of

לי, 4Q = G ≠ M.

1 S 25:3   *VI.296*   4Q   והאיש כלבו̇

                         M   והוא כלבו

                         G   και ο ανθρωπος κυνικος

                         J   κυνικης ασκησεως

                                  4Q = G ≠ M; and J = Gk ≠ Hb.

1 S 27:10   4Q [מ̇י̇ על אכיש אמר[ורי]

                         M   ויאמר אכיש אל פשטתם

                         G   και ειπεν Αγχους προς Δαυειδ Επι τινα επεθεσθε

        Well. suggests אן for אל; Driver prefers אן, though he be-
gins by suggesting אל מי. The scribe of 4Q had אל at first,
then partially erased the א and corrected *(prima manu)* to על,
indicating that here he may have had one reading like M and
another like G. προς Δαυειδ is a later expansion in G, as is
προς Αγχους later in the verse.   4Q = G ≠ M.

1 S 28:25   *VI.339*   4Q   [הוא]ה הלילה הליל[ורי]

                         M   וילכו בלילה ההוא

                         G   και απηλθον την νυκτα εκεινην

                         J   δια της νυκτος ηλθεν

That 4Q = G ≠ M in this prepositionless adverbial accusative
can be seen from:

1 S 31:12   VI.375   M   כל הלילה   (de 4Q)

G   ολην την νυκτα

J   δι ολης της νυκτος

Notice both J's insistence upon distinctive style and, nonetheless, his echoing of G.

1 S 30:29   4Q   הקנזי

M   הקיני

G   του Κενεζει

Acx   του Κειναιου (Κην- c[vid]x)

1 S 31:3   1 C 10:3   4Q C^M   עֳל שאול

M   אל שאול

G^SC   επι Σαουλ

The bottom half of 4Q's ע is clear: it is not א.   4Q = G C^MG ≠
M.

1 S 31:4   1 C 10:4   4Q C^M   שֳ[אור]ל̊ אל [נשא]

M   שאול   לנשא

G   Σαουλ προς τον αιροντα

C^G   Σαουλ   τω αιροντι

4Q = G C^M ≠ M C^G.

2 S 2:5   4Q   על

M   עם

G   επι

2 S 2:7   4Q   [   ]עֳ[ליהם ל]מלך

M T P   למלך עליהם

G   εφ εαυτους (-τον Βya₂) εις βασιλεα

Acex   εις βασιλεα εφ εαυτους

2 S 3:1 VII.20~   4Q   [הולך וֹד̊]ל

M T P   הלכים ודלים

G OL^m   επορευετο και ησθενει

Cf. Well. The subject of these verbs is שאול בית/o οικος Σαουλ;
thus, it is possible that M is plural *sensus causa*. This prevents the contrast from being conclusive, but the texts nonetheless stand so: 4Q = G ≠ M.

2 S 3:3	*1 C 3:1*	*VII.21*

4Q   דלו֯י֯ה֯ לאביגיל ה[כרמלית]

M T P   (P כלב מן א') כלאב לאביגל אשת נבל הכרמלי

G   Δαλουια της Αβειγαιας της Καρμηλιας

N   Δαλουιδ τη Αβιγαια

d++   Δαλουια τη Αβιγαια τη Καρμηλια

C^M דניאל לאביגיל הכרמלית

Bgc$_2$ Δαμνιηλ (Δαν- g) τη Αβειγαια τη Καρμηλια

ANrell   Δαλουια (-ας ny) τη Αβειγαια τη Καρμηλια

Syh   דלואילא

J   ο δε...εκ γυναικος Αβιγαιας Δαλουηλος (P; -ουιηλος S;
                  Δανιηλος ROME; Danihel Lat)

Cf. Driver. 4Q cannot possibly read דניאל; כלאב is within
the wide range of possibility but is quite unlikely; דלויה is
most probable: (1) The first letter can be identified as ד
with near certainty. The top half is clearly visible and has
the shape of a perfect ד (higher right shoulder, slanting tick
on left shoulder, deep depression between shoulders)--contrast
the medial *kaph* in מעכה in 4Q's following line. (2) The second
letter is ל (precludes דניאל). (3) Three traces, forming the
tops of letters, follow. The first is so faint that the most
one can say is that it indicates the presence of some letter.
The second includes a stroke slanting downward to the left,
very much like a *yod* or *pe*. It is highly unlikely that these
traces form *aleph* (cf. כלֲאַב M). The final trace could be the
tip of several types of letter, but its vertical slant nearly
rules out ב which needs a basically horizontal (though dipping)
stroke; it can be the right tip of ה.

Since the first letter forms a perfect *daleth* and looks
less like a *kaph*, and since the final traces favor -ויה more
than אב-, דלויה should be reconstructed. The subsequent words
in this reading, as well as the reading which follows (3:4),
support דלויה. דלויה has been reconstructed on the basis of G,
though דליהו is equally possible palaeographically and more
likely to have been the original. It also could help explain
the C and J readings, through its by-form, דליאל (cf. Syh of C).
See p. 188 for details of the J reading.

For דלויה, 4Q = G C^G (J) ≠ M ≠ C^M. Note also that in the omission of אשת נבל, 4Q = G C (J) ≠ M.

2 S 3:4	1 C 3:3	VII.21
4Q		לא̊[ב]י̊טל
M T P		בן אביטל
G		της Αβειταλ
L		της Αβειτααλ
c₂		της Αβεγγααλη (sic B-M)
cᴹ		לאביטל
B		της Σαβειταλ
ANrell		της Αβιταλ (-αμ be₂)
J		της Αβιταλης

4Q = G C (J) ≠ M.

2 S 3:23	VII.31	2 S 3:24	VII.32
4Q	אל דויד	de	
M T	אל המלך	אל המלך	
P	לות מלכא דויד	לות מלכא דויד	
G	προς Δαυειδ	προς τον βασιλεα (+δαδ cvx)	
J	[Δαυιδου ...] προς αυτον	προς τον βασιλεα	

A minor point, but a valid minor point: Except in the
references to kingship (VII.22, 24, 27), J calls David "David"
or "him" through this entire section (VII.21-31). In 2 S 3:23
(= VII.31) M introduces "the king," but 4Q G omn and J retain
"David" or "him." In 3:24 (= VII.32) G omn introduce "the
king," and J, who had begun his paragraph with "...Δαυιδου..."
and continued with "αυτον," now follows G *literatim* with προς
τον βασιλεα.   4Q = G J ≠ M.

2 S 3:29	4Q T P	ועל
	M	ואל
	G	και επι

2 S 3:33	4Q	על
	M	אל
	G	επι (τον fp; om Me₂*+)

2 S 3:34
4Q	[	כנב̊[ול
M		כנפול לפני בני עולה נפלת

G   ως Ναβαλ (ΝΑΦΑ Α) ενωπιον υιων (υιου ΙΜΝ++) αδικιας επεσας

σ'   αλλ ωσπερ πιπτουσιν εμπροσθεν αδικων επεσας j^{mg}

ο' ϑ'   ναφαλ ημαρτηται τα εχοντα ναβαλ j^{mg}

The third letter in 4Q can be א, ב, or ג and nothing else
(i.e., not פ). If 4Q does have כנבל, and insofar as j^{mg} is
correct, 4Q = G ≠ M in an error.

2 S 5:8   1 C 11:6 om   VII.63~

4Q   יגע

M   ויגע

G   απτεσθω

α'   και αψεται

σ'   και κρατηση (M; κατακρ- z; -σει j)

OL^b   occidet

For the jussive: 4Q = G ≠ M G^h.

2 S 5:13^b   1 C 14:3   VII.70~

4Q   לדויד עוֹד

M T P   עוד לדוד

G   τω Δαυειδ ετι

Acx OL^b   ετι τω Δαυειδ

c^M   דויד עוד

c^G   Δαυειδ (αυτω ΑΝ++; pr τω c₂) ετι (om be₂)

For the transposition, 4Q = G (C) ≠ M T P G^h OL^b.

2 S 6:3   1 C 13:7   4Q   [יהור]ה֯ עֹל

                            M   האלהים אל

                            G   Κυριου εφ

                            L   του θεου εφ

                            c^M   האלהים על

                            c^G   του θεου (κυ m) επι

(For this and the next three readings from 2 S 6, see the
fuller discussion in Chapter VII.)

Spacing and the letter traces in 4Q favor יהוה, though
האלוהים would be possible; L is revised toward M (or possibly
4Q). על = εφ clearly.

2 S 6:5   4Q   בֹּנֵי יִשְׂרָֽאֵל
                 M   בית ישראל
                 G   οι υιοι Ισραηλ
                 C   ישראל

2 S 6:9   *1 C 13:12*   4Q C   לאמֹֽר
                                M   ויאמר
                                G^SC   λεγων

Cf. pp. 51 and 72 above.

2 S 6:16   *1 C 15:29*   4Q C   ויהי
                                M   ויהיה   (cf. M note)
                                G^SC   και εγενετο

B.   The Pattern 4Q = G ≠ M in Section βγ

1.   Plus

Once again we shall present two striking examples of
pluses in which 4Q = G ≠ M, and then proceed with the remainder
of these readings.

2 S 13:21   *VII.173*

4Q   [כול] שמע אֵ֠ת [וידן דויד] והמלך   ]
    [ו]הדברים האלה ויחר לו מאד ולוא עצב את רוח אמנון בנו כי אה[בו כי בכור
                                                                    [הוא]

M T P   את כל והמלך דוד שמע
                                                הדברים האלה ויחר לו מאד

G OL^(sv)   και ηκουσεν ο βασιλευς Δαυειδ παντας τους λογους τουτους
             και εθυμωθη σφοδρα και ουκ ελυπησεν το πνευμα Αμνων του υιου
             αυτου οτι ηγαπα αυτον οτι πρωτοτοκος αυτου ην.

L OL^b   και ο βασιλευς Δαυειδ ηκουσεν παντας τους λογους τουτους
             και ηθυμησεν σφοδρα και ουκ ελυπησεν το πνευμα Αμνων του υιου
             αυτου οτι ηγαπα αυτον οτι πρωτοτοκος αυτου ην.

J   τοις μεν πεπραγμενοις ηχθετο, φιλων δε τον Αμνονα σφοδρα,
             πρεσβυτατος γαρ ην αυτω υιος, μη λυπειν αυτον ηναγκαζετο.

Cf. Well., Notes, NAB. Well. correctly concluded that the
plus in G should be in the text but could not determine why it
was missing from M. Cross concludes: "haplography: ולא...ולא
(*pace* Well.)."

4Q again preserves a plus of 2/3 line found in G OL J.
When reconstructed after G, 4Q's spacing falls perfectly into
order. 4Q = G J ≠ M.

Note that J's euphemistic ηχθετο ("carried away, moved,
weighed down") follows ηθυμησεν L $\mathcal{g}^j$ and *deficit animo* OL[b],
against ריחר/εθυμωθη [4Q] M G; just as in 2 S 6:8 his εδυσφορη-
σαν follows the euphemistic G L OL against M (cf. p. 233).

2 S 13:27   VII.174

4Q   אֵת אמנון ואת [כול] בני המלך   ]
            וריעש אבשלום משתה כמשתה ה[מֿ]ל[ך]יֿ[28וֿ]צֿיֿ אבשלום את נעריו לאמור

M T P   את אמנון ואת כל בני המלך:
            28ויצו אבשלום את נעריו לאמר

G OL   τον Αμνων και παντας τους υιους του βασιλεως και εποιησεν
            Αβεσσαλωμ ποτον κατα τον ποτον του βασιλεως 28και ενετειλατο...

J   προς αυτον εφ εστιασιν.

Cf. Notes; NAB; M note. Of the G OL plus only [ה][מֿ]ל[ך]
occurs on the leather. But there is a gap of ½ line in 4Q
which is perfectly filled with the plus as reconstructed from
G, and the המלך...המלך type of haplography is one of M's chief
characteristics (cf. immediately above in 13:21 for the identical pattern).

J's mention of the feast is not due to 13:28 (לב כטוב
ביין אמנון), for (a) no feast as such is mentioned there, and
(b) that is in the next section of M and G and is related in
the next section of J with the features of M and G there.
Rather, J's "feast" here is dependent upon the "feast" of 4Q G
here. A small piece of confirmation is J's προς αυτον; cf. אל
4Q, προς L OL; עם M, μετα Grell (13:24).

4Q and J again share a plus in G OL, lacking in M. 4Q = G
J ≠ M.

2 S 10:5   1 C 19:5   4Q   [לדויד על [האֿנשיֿם
                           M T P   לדוד
                           G   τω Δαυειδ υπερ των ανδρων
                           L   τω Δαυειδ περι των ανδρων
                           c[M]   לדויד על האנשים
                           c[G]   τω Δαυειδ περι των ανδρων

2 S 19:8(7)   VII.256   4Q Seb   [כי אֹם אי]נך]
                                  M T   אינך   כי (cf. M note)
                                  G   οτι ει (om ay*) μη
                                  J   αν επιμενης

This is frail evidence, since M displays a simple (haplo-
graphic?) omission. Nonetheless, especially since T follows
M, it is evidence, and the texts group themselves so: 4Q = G J
≠ M.

2 S 19:10(9)   4Q   [המלך דוֹי]ד]
                    M T P   המלך
                    G   Ο βασιλευς Δαυειδ

2 S 24:17   1 C 21:17   VII.328
4Q   ]ורא[נֹכי הרעֹה הֹרֹעתי
M T P   הערויתי   ואנכי
G   και εγω ειμι (om Ax) ο ποιμην εκακοποιησα (και ηδικησα a₂)
B(txt)   ηδικησα
B^ab(mg)   και εγω ειμι   ο ποιμην
L OL^S   και εγω   ο ποιμην εκακοποιησα
C^M   והרע הרעותי
C^G
                            κακοποιων εκακοποιησα
J   αυτος ειη κολασθηναι δικαιος ο ποιμην

Cf. Notes; NAB; Shenkel, "A Comparative Study," *HTR* 62
(1969) 81.

4Q probably preserves the original text (cf. the anti-
thetical ואלה הצאן which follows immediately). C^M seems to
present הרע as Hiphil infinitive absolute, and C^G certainly
understands it thus. M omits the word and displays הערויתי for
הרעתי, most likely a metathesis of ע/ר in the palaeography and
orthography of the time of the OG translation (see note on p.
76). That 4Q is not dependent on C is evident.

L probably presents the OG here, and Å∅B OL and J all echo
ποιμην. The characteristic KR usage of εγω ειμι for אנכי (cf.
DA, pp. 69-78, esp. p. 72) is virtually omnipresent in G rell
(A has εγω ειμι ηδικησα as its preceding clause). B(txt) has
undergone post-KR haplography, and B^ab(mg) have replaced the
omitted words.

For the plus הרעה, 4Q = G J (C^M) ≠ M T P (B*) (≠ C^MG).

For the variant הרעתי, we can conclude that G reflects 4Q, and Ba₂ reflect M. For αδικειν occurs 5 other times in S K C: = עוה 3x, = עשק 1x, = מעל 1x. αδικειν = רעע only once in the entire LXX (Is 65:25). On the other hand, κακοποιειν = רעע in all 4 of its clear occurrences in S K C (plus the double C witness here). κακοποιειν never = עוה elsewhere. Thus, for the variant, 4Q = G C^{MG} ≠ M Ba₂.

2. Minus

4Q and G share only one minus against M in section βγ:

2 S 22:39   *Ps 18(17):39*

4Q	אמח[צם]
M	ואכלם ואמחצם
G	και θλασω αυτους
L	εθλασα αυτους
A	και τελεσω αυτους και θλασω αυτους
Ps^M	אמחצם
Ps^G	εκθλιψω αυτους

See the fuller discussion on p. 109 below. For the lack of ואכלם, 4Q = G L ≠ M G^A.

3. Variant

2 S 11:5	*VII.131~*	4Q	אנוכי הרה
		M	הרה אנכי
		G	Εγω ειμι εν γαστρι εχω
		L OL	Συνειληφα εγω
		J	γενομενης δ' εγκυου

BAMN definitely show KR influence: εγω ειμι + finite verb for אנכי is one of the strongest signals of KR (*DA*, pp. 69-78). Barthélemy says that KR corrected toward the proto-Massoretic text; this may be such an example.

It is difficult to place L's συνειληφα εγω. Shenkel (*Chronology*, p. 116) finds συλλαμβανειν to be OG and εν γαστρι εχειν/λαμβανειν to be KR. The situation may be more complex. OG usage for הרה may include both συλλαμβανειν (16x in Gen, 9x in other books, including 1 S 1:20, 2:21, and 4:19, but never in βδ) and εν γαστρι εχειν (6x in Gen, 12x in other books, including the present reading and 2 K 8:12 and 15:16, but never

in α, ββ, or γγ). הרה is also reflected by the mixed εν γαστρι
λαμβενειν (6x), and earlier in the present verse we find [ר]ותח
4Q M, και εν γαστρι ελαβεν G, και συνελαβεν L OL. To appreci-
ate the ambiguity one may consider (1) Gen 16:4--כי ותרא ותחר
הרתה = και συνελαβεν και ιδεν οτι εν γαστρι εχει; (2) Aquila at
Is 7:14--where [εν γαστρι] συλλαμβανει and εν γαστρι εξει are
both attributed to α'; and (3) Mt 1:23 quoting Is 7:14--εν
γαστρι εξει // Lk 1:31: συλλημψη εν γαστρι. 4Q = G ≠ M.

2 S 15:2	4Q T	[כ]ול איש
	M P	כל האיש (cf. M note)
	G	πας ανηρ
	OL^S	si quem

2 S 15:31	4Q	[לדוי]ד[ ]
	M	לדוד (ודוד הגיד 2 mss; cf. M note)
	G	και ανηγγελη τω (om BAha₂) Δαυειδ
	L	και τω Δαυειδ απηγγειλαν

    Word order in 4Q is difficult to establish, but the entire
top of ל is clear. M variants include לדוד.
    G universally attests the dative for Δαυειδ. BAha₂,
though omitting τω (possibly after M) nonetheless show a passive verb, indicating that Δαυειδ is the indirect object, and
not the subject. Thus, as the mss stand, 4Q = G ≠ M.

2 S 18:9	VII.239	4Q	ריתל
		M	ויתן
		G	και εκρεμασθη
		L	και ανεκρεμασθη
		J	ανακρεμναται

See the other exposition of this reading on p. 178. 4Q = G J ≠
M.

2 S 19:7(6)	VII.255	4Q	[ ] [לו אבש]לום
		M	לא אבשלום (לו) Q; cf. M note)
		T	אלו אבשלום
		G	ει Αβεσσαλωμ
		J	ει γαρ Αψαλωμος

This is, of course, weak evidence, resulting from a simple

error in M not even shared by T. Nonetheless, the texts stand
so: 4Q = G J ≠ M.

2 S 19:11-12(10-11)   VII.259-260

4Q   [המלך ואת ל]שיב   ]
        [ואל ביתו ודבר כול ישראל בא אל המלך ¹²והמלך דויד שלח] אל צדוק הכו[הן]

M T   להשיב את המלך:
        ...¹²והמלך דוד שלח אל צדוק ואל
        אל ביתו ודבר כל ישראל בא אל המלך אל ביתו

G OL^S   του επιστρεψαι προς τον βασιλεα; και το ρημα παντος Ισραηλ ηλθεν
        προς τον βασιλεα. ¹²Και ο βασιλευς Δαυειδ απεστειλεν προς Σαδωκ
        και προς...

J   ταυτα... απηγγελλετο Δαυιδη˙ κακεινος... επεμψε προς Σαδωκον και...

        Cf. M note, Thenius, Well., Driver, NAB. With 4Q reading
as M, its line has approximately 29 characters; reading as G OL,
its line has approximately 62. 4Q must be reconstructed with
this plus in its proper place. J follows the 4Q G order.
Though M G L are all confused and conflate in these and the
following verses--and though for [הכו]הן 4Q ≠ M G J(vid)--for
the placement of the long plus here in this variant position,
4Q = G OL J ≠ M.

2 S 20:10   VII.284   4Q   על החמֹֿש
                            M   אל החמש
                            G   εις (επι Acx) την ψυαν (ψοαν B)
                            L   επι την λαγονα
                            OL^V   in utero
                            J   εις την γαστερα

Cf. p. 55 for a similar reading in 2 S 3:27. Both λαγων and
ψοα are possible renderings of the infrequent החמש; but for על,
4Q = L Acx ≠ M G^h.

2 S 20:10   VII.286   4Q   רדפו
                            M   רדף
                            BM++   εδιωξεν
                            AN++   εδιωξαν
                            L   κατεδιωκον
                            J   εδιωκε

Shenkel (*Chronology*, p. 113) lists καταδιωκειν as OG,
διωκειν as KR. Thus, OG/pL contained the imperfect tense of
the compound verb. KR, correcting toward M, shifted to the
singular and the more common aorist. AN++, while following the
aorist of KR, revert to the plural from syntax (to avoid synesis) and sense.

For his own reasons J does not reproduce the compound.
His verb is (unlike M BM+) necessarily in the singular, for he
leaves Abishai out of this clause. Accordingly, his reading
cannot help us on the number of the verb. Note, however, his
retention of the old imperfect from L.

For the plural verb, 4Q = OG/pL AN++ ≠ M BM+.

2 S 21:6	*VII.296~*
4Q	רנתחם ל]נו[
M^K	ינתן לנו
M^Q	יתן לנו
T	(w) וית-) יתיהבון לנא
P	נתלון לן
AMNrell $\not\!Z\not\!\!\!\!\!\not\!C$	δοτε (οτε a; da $\not\!Z$) ημιν
Bhx	δοτω ημιν
L $\not\!\!A$ Thdt	και (om $\not\!\!A$) δοθητωσαν ημιν

Cf. Driver, Notes. 4Q presents a plural, active command:
"And give u[s seven of his sons...]." Prescinding from the
initial *waw*, 4Q thus presents the Hb reading which lay behind
the OG (AMN++), the Peshitta, the Ethiopic (sing.), and the
Coptic. M^{K,Q} have a singular, passive jussive: "Let there be
given to us seven...," reflected in the hebraizing revision of
Bhx. The synesis occurring in M Bhx is smoothed in T L $\not\!\!A$.
Though 4Q prefixes an initial *waw*, for this variant, 4Q = OG P
$\not\!Z\;\not\!C$ ≠ M^{K,Q} G$_2$ ≠ T L $\not\!\!A$.

2 S 22:45-46	*Ps 18(17):45-46*
4Q	לשמ]ע ... בני נכר[
M	בני נכר ... לשמוע
BA	υιοι αλλοτριοι...εις ακοην
LMN++	εις ακοην... υιοι αλλοτριοι
Ps^M	לשמע ... בני נכר
Ps^G	εις ακοην... υιοι αλλοτριοι

See the fuller discussion on pp. 109-111.

2 S 22:48	Ps 18(17):48	4Q	ומרדד
		M	ומוריד
		G	παιδευων
		L	και εταπεινωσε
		Ps^M	וידבר
		Ps^G	υποταξας

Cf. Notes; NAB. 4Q probably has the original reading,
which would best explain both M and Ps^M. M's ומ(ו)ריד shows
both the palaeographic confusion of ד > י and the *lectio
facilior*. דבר of Ps^M is a synonymous variant for רדד:

Ps 18(17):48   וידבר עמים תחתי
                  και υποταξας λαους υπ εμε
Ps 47(46):4   ידבר עמים תחתינו
                  υπεταξεν λαους ημιν
Ps 144(143):2   הרודד עמי תחתי
                  ο υποτασσων τον λαον μου υπ εμε

The Gk witnesses also point to ומרדד. H-R lists only 2
translations for רדד: a questionable επακουειν once in Is 45:1,
and υποτασσειν once in Ps 144.(143):2 above. Ps^G thus testifies
to רדד/דבר in its Vorlage. Neither παιδευειν nor ταπεινουν
ever render ירד or רדד, so positive evidence is lacking; but
ירד in the Hiphil alone has 19 Gk correspondents in H-R, while
never receiving the services of παιδευειν or ταπεινουν (or
υποτασσειν). Thus, it is unlikely on a statistical basis that
these verbs are attempting to translate ירד; on a semantic
basis they are closer to מרדד; and υποταξας Ps^G is positive
evidence. The probable conclusion: 4Q = G L ≠ M.

2 S 24:16	1 C 21:15	4Q	עומד
		M	היה
		BAhxa$_2$	ην
		LMNrell ЖØЖ	ην εστηκως
		c^M	עמד
		c^G	εστως (ην εστως c$_2$)

2 S 24:17	1 C 21:17	4Q	הרעתי
		M	העויתי
		G	εκακοποιησα
		Ba$_2$(Ax)	ηδικησα
		C^M	הרעותי
		C^G	εκακοποιησα

See the larger discussion on p. 86.

C. Conclusion

Part A of this chapter is inordinately long. But that very length is eloquent testimony to the agreement of 4Q with the Old Greek Version. 4Q and G share against M 14 (or probably 15) striking readings: 6 (or 7) pluses, 3 minuses, and 5 variants. 4Q and G agree against M in 110 additional readings: 35 pluses, 20 minuses, and 55 variants. Thus, for the parts of Thackeray and Barthélemy's Old Greek sections of Samuel (α ββ) for which 4Q is extant, 4Q agrees with G against M in 124 readings.

Part B (for section βγ) lists 6 pluses (2 of which are striking specimens), 1 minus, and 13 variants for a total of 20 in which 4Q = G ≠ M.

Due to the random aspect of the surviving fragments, there can be no accuracy in statistics. But, though unfocused in details, the general picture provides a quite definite impression. Samuel fragments are extant for 29 chapters of α ββ and for 14 chapters of βγ, or approximately twice as many chapters in α ββ as in βγ. The ratio of 124 readings in the 29 chapters of α ββ to the 20 readings in the 14 chapters of βγ is roughly 3 to 1. G is three times closer to 4Q in α ββ than it is in βγ. Barthélemy's thesis, that G has undergone revision toward M in βγ, neatly explains this shift in the results.

As we recheck the readings in βγ, the two striking pluses show no signs of specific *kaige* revision, while OL and J attest to their origin in the OG substratum--and not the revisional stratum--of the *kaige* text.

Of the 18 remaining readings, only 5 show any indications of *kaige* revisional activity:

    2 S 24:17 εγω ειμι ο ποιμην εκακοποιησα (p. 86).

Here the use of εγω ειμι plus finite verb for אנכי should definitely be considered KR. But the *kaige* revisional activity
touches only εγω ειμι. Even Rahlfs (*Lucians*, p. 86) presumed
that ο ποιμην is OG/pL.

2 S 11:5 εγω ειμι εν γαστρι εχω (p. 87). Again, the
KR hand here is unmistakable. The revisor matched *εγω εν
γαστρι εχω of his OG base (= 4Q) against הרה אנכי of M and
simply inserted ειμι, because εγω ειμι was his exegetical translation of אנכי, without seeing a need to transpose the word
order. It is debatable whether this latter was the case or
whether the revisor had a Hb text like 4Q (thus a not fully developed Massoretic text). Nevertheless, whichever is the case,
the *kaige* revisional activity does not come in contact with,
much less conflict with, our main point, viz., that the Vorlage
of OG agreed with 4Q against M.

2 S 15:2 πας ανηρ (p. 88). The use of ανηρ for איש
is both an OG and a KR characteristic. ανηρ is a signal of
specifically KR activity only when איש is being used in the
sense of "chacun" (*DA*, pp. 48-54), which OG suitably renders
εκαστος. Since that is not the sense of איש here (*DA*, p. 50),
neither is ανηρ a signal of KR here.

2 S 20:10 εδιωξεν (p. 89). This is indeed an example
of *kaige* revision. But it all the more clearly demonstrates
the point, viz., that the OG/pL agreed with 4Q, while KR was a
revision precisely toward M!

2 S 21:6 δοτε (p. 90). Again the OG substratum
agrees with 4Q, while Bhx are revised to M.

Thus, none of the 20 agreements of 4Q G in section βγ
appear to be part of the *kaige* recensional stratum of the KR
text but rather part of the OG substratum of that text. This
means that the results from βγ can be combined with the results
from α ββ: the 4QSam[a] fragments agree with the Greek Version
in contrast to the Massoretic text in 144 readings.

Chapter III
THE AGREEMENT OF 4QSam^a WITH THE LUCIANIC TEXT

In this chapter we will deal with a specific subset of
readings in which 4QSam^a varies from the Massoretic text and
shows affiliation with Greek texts. 4Q frequently aligns itself with the Lucianic text against the majority of Greek mss,
and the frequency and strength of that alliance should be
tested.

A.   The Pattern 4Q = L ≠ M G in Section α ββ

The one plus, four minuses, and three variants for this
section will be simply listed in order.

1 S 5:9	*VI.5 om*
4Q	אֺ[חרי] סבו גתה
M T P	אחרי הסבו אתו
G	μετα το μετελθειν αυτην
L	εν τω μετελθειν την κιβωτον προς τους Γεθθαιους (προς Γεθ b')
OL^S	postquam translata est arca Dei

Cf. HTR 292, NAB. The OG read μετα το μετελθειν αυτην,
probably following its concise Egyptian Vorlage אחרי סבו*,
which would be the original reading here. The Palestinian text
characteristically included the explanatory גתה, and proto-
Lucian accordingly "corrected" toward it by adding προς (τους)
Γεθ(θαιους), after having rendered the ambiguous αυτην more specific with την κιβωτον.

Of the two Hb readings still preserved 4Q is the more correct with an infinitive construct plus subjective suffix (for
the masculine ארון), followed by the locative place name. The
M consonantal text suffered the *lectio facilior* corruption
גתה > אתו, both necessitating a transitive verb (Hiphil) and
forcing the Massoretes to point הסבו as a Hiphil perfect, 3rd
pl.--anomalously after אחרי (cf. GKC, 114a,d,e,r). Note that G
(both intransitive and with αυτην as subject) cannot be considered a translation of or a correction toward M.

This reading seems to be genuinely proto-Lucianic, for 4Q

95

= boc₂e₂ only, while OG differs both from them and from M, and
no revisional activity in G is evident. Thus, in a variant, 4Q
= pL ≠ OG ≠ M.

1 S 6:20	4Q	[לפני] יהוה הקדוש
	M	לפני יהוה האלהים הקדוש
	By Ʒ	ενωπιον του αγιου
	LN++	ενωπιον κυ του αγιου
	Acx+	ενωπιον κυ του (om cx) θυ του αγιου

4Q = G ≠ M Gʰ in lacking האלהים. By Ʒ should, according to
Rahlfs, represent OG. L would then be a proto-Lucianic revision toward a 4Q texttype which thoroughly (except for By)
penetrated the G tradition. Acx+ have characteristically revised toward M. Thus, in this minus, 4Q = pL ≠ OG ≠ M Gʰ.

1 S 14:32	*VI.120*	4Q	על
		M	אל
		G	εις
		L	επι
		J	επι

   This verse as well as the preceding and following verses
in Gᴮᴬᴺ are obviously OG. Note the frequent discrepancies from
M, the lack of any customary revisional characteristics, and
specifically the unusually free translation of prepositions:
συν for על twice! εις for על in BANrell fits the free pattern;
boc₂e₂ alone substitute επι for the unanimous εις, revising
toward the 4Q tradition. J's echoing επι and M's discordant אל
doubly indicate the pL stratum in L. Thus, the pL variant is a
revision of OG toward the 4Q tradition. Whether OG = M or not
does not matter here, for pL is obviously unaware of M but
aware only of OG and 4Q and revises OG toward its *hebraica veritas*, viz., the 4Q tradition.   4Q = pL J ≠ OG ≠ M.

2 S 3:28-29   VII.39~

4Q	⁽²⁹⁾ודם [אבנר בן נר י]וֹחוֹל	
M T P	מדמי אבנר בן נר ²⁹יחלו (מדמא) T; דמה (vid) מן (P	
G	απο των αιματων Αβεννηρ υιου Νηρ. ²⁹καταντησατωσαν (-ατω f)	
N	απο των αιματων αιματων Αβεννηρ. ²⁹καταντησατωσαν	
L Thdt	⁽²⁹⁾αιμα Αβεννηρ υιου Νηρ	
σ'	²⁹ελθετωσαν	

Cf. Notes, NAB. Cross believes 4Q to be original (*mem* being a dittograph: עַד עוֹלָם מַדְמִי). Though it has "no real parallel," still יחול finds a witness in f, and דם a witness in
(p)L.

A larger issue for text affiliation is: to which clause
does אבנר (מ)דמ(י) (מ) belong? Only 4Q and (p)L have it with the
following clause.

Thus, for יחול, 4Q = f only. For דם(ו) and sentence
structure, 4Q = (p)L only.

2 S 3:36	*VII. 43~*	
4Q	]בעיני כול הע[ם֯	
M T	בעיני כל העם טוב	
P	בעיני כלה עמא	
G	ενωπιον	του λαου
L	ενωπιον παντος του λαου	
Acx ℵ	ενωπιον	του λαου αγαθον (-θα cx)
o'a'θ'		+ ※ αγαθον
J	παρα του πληθους	

Just before ו֗[דע]ו֗ of 3:37, the top traces of final *mem*
can be seen on 4Q. That they represent *mem* and not *beth* (of
טוב) is reasonably certain: ב would have two shoulders, the
right lower than the left; here the left is lower, and the ink
continues to the right of the "right shoulder" forming a perfect top to a final *mem*. The line above has 47/48 characters,
the line below 46; this line has 46/48 without טוב, 50/52 with
טוב.

BMN++ represent OG here. L, the only Gk tradition with
παντος, must be proto-L, corrected according to the 4Q (P) tradition. If it were corrected toward M in the later stratum of
the L revision, it would have included αγαθον, as G^h shows.

J's πληθους cannot be used to distinguish between G and L;
nor can his silence on αγαθον be used to distinguish between
4Q G L and M G^h (though he appears to agree with 4Q G L against
M G^h), because the idea is also expressed by all in the first
half of the verse.

Thus, again in this minus, 4Q = pL ≠ OG ≠ M G^h.

2 S 4:10 4Q [לאמֹ]ר

M לאמר הנה

G οτι

L λεγων οτι

4Q probably lacks הנה, for its line is too long if הנה be inserted: the preceding line has 49 characters, the following 46; this line has 57 with הנה but 53 without.

No firm conclusion can be reached for this reading, for it is quite possible that G is not attempting to follow its Vorlage here but is rather reflecting 2 S 1:5 which is being quoted here: "οτι τεθνηκεν Σαουλ" (see also 2:7). But if G *is* reflecting its Vorlage, it agrees with the (probable) omission of הנה in 4Q, against M.

Further, L might possibly be a proto-Lucianic revision of OG toward a 4Q texttype, though the nature of the evidence here prevents anything like certainty. Only boc₂e₂ insert λεγων here, and their correction does not go as far as to include ιδου (as if from M). And, as can be seen from 2 S 1:16, 2:4, 5:6, etc., λεγων οτι often reflects לאמר without requiring כי in addition to לאמר in the Vorlage.

Keeping in mind the frailty of the evidence, this minus is classified: 4Q = pL ≠ M ≠ OG.

2 S 4:12 VII.52 4Q [אבנר בן] נר בח [ברון]

M T P אבנר   בחברון

G^BA Αβεννηρ υιου Νηρ

N Αβεννηρ   εν Χεβρων

LM++ OL^b 𝔄 Αβεννηρ υιου Νηρ εν Χεβρων

J Αβεννηρου

4Q spacing and the lack of ligature usually found in our scribe's writing of אבנר (cf. 3:30, 32bis, 37) indicate the full, conflated reading for 4Q.

G^BA should be judged OG here, with LM++ as subsequent, but early, conflation on the basis of 4Q (though the conflation could be on the basis of M). OL would then be translated from this pL correction toward 4Q, and M++ would customarily perpetuate the fuller text.

J never uses Νηρου παις after the initial mention of Abner in VII.9; thus, his lack of it here says nothing. His lack of

εν Χεβρων is likewise insignificant, for it is mentioned in the
more important topic sentence immediately following (VII.53 = 2
S 5:1).

   In this plus, 4Q = pL OL ≠ M ≠ OG.

2 S 5:11   *1 C 14:1*   *VII.66*

4Q   [וחרשי עץ]/ וחרשי קיר [ורי]בנו

M P   וחרשי עץ וחרשי אבן קיר ויבנו

BMN   και τεκτονας ξυλων και τεκτονας λιθων   και ωκοδομησαν

L OL   και τεκτονας ξυλων και τεκτονας τοιχου   και ωκοδομησαν

G^h ∅   και τεκτονας ξυλων και τεκτονας λιθων τοιχου και ωκοδομησαν

b   και τεκτονας ξυλων και τεκτονας τοιχου λιθων και ωκοδομησαν

c^M   וחרשי קיר   וחרשי עצים לבנות

c^B   και οικοδομους   και τεκτονας ξυλων του οικοδομησαι

be_2   και τεκτονας τοιχου   και τεκτονας ξυλων του οικοδομησαι

ANrell   και οικοδομους τοιχων και τεκτονας ξυλων του οικοδομησαι

J   και τεχνιτας ανδρας τεκτονας και οικοδομους

   Cf. HTR 293; also Talmon, *Textus* 1 (1960) 167:

         From the rendering of G in II Sam. v, 11 it may be
   deduced that the basic Hebrew reading in this verse was
   וחרשי עץ (עצים) וחרשי אבן (אבנים). But the copyist had
   before him also the reading וחרשי עץ וחרשי קיר, which had
   not yet been exclusively attached to the parallel in I
   Chron. xiv, l. Since he could see no good reason for pre-
   ferring one to the other he combined them, thus producing
   the doublet וחרשי אבן קיר.

   I concur fully with Talmon, though I should perhaps say "*a*
basic Hebrew reading." And I would classify that reading
(וחרשי אבן) as the Egyptian Hb, followed faithfully by BMN. On
the basis of a 4Q type of Vorlage, proto-Lucian corrected to
τοιχου.

   Just as (with Talmon) M conflated the Egyptian and the
Palestinian readings, G^h (Acx j^mg sub ※) conflated on the basis
of M. The conflation in b is late, trying to make sense of the
G^h conflation. Here again, there are three different Gk texts;
according to Lagarde's principle we should select the "freer
reading" as OG (λιθων pl.). 4Q L OL C side together against M
and against OG as well (although the whole context proves that

OG and L stand in a relationship of original-and-revision). It
is true that L could have derived its reading from the Hb of C
(C[G] is dependent upon S[G], not vice-versa), but there is no reason to posit this in the light of 4Q here and of this identical
pattern in other places which lack a C parallel. Furthermore,
it should not go unobserved that the C tradition transposed the
S order of וחרשי עץ / וחרשי (אבן) קיר.

J follows the S order, and, in the writer's view, his
οικοδομους reflects the 4Q L OL (C) reading, solidly establishing L here as pL. But in light of M/G at 1 C 22:15, only probability and not certainty can be maintained.

In sum, for this fourth minus, 4Q = pL OL (C) (J) ≠ OG ≠ M
G[h].

B. The Pattern 4Q = L ≠ M G in Section βγ

In contrast to the previous section, the pattern of 4Q L
agreement against M G in section βγ occurs frequently. We may
begin with two pluses (the first of which, as it happens, contains a minus as well) shared by 4Q and L which are lacking in
M G.

1. Plus

2 S 12:16	*VII.154*
4Q	[ורב]א̊ וישכב בשק ארצה
M	ובא ולן ושכב ארצה
Baya₂	και εισηλθεν και ηυλισθη επι της γης
A	και εισηλθεν και ηυλισθη και εκοιμηθη επι της γης
MNrell	και εισηλθεν και ηυλισθη (και εκοιμηθη) εν σακκω επι της γης
L	και εισελθων εκαθευδεν εν σακκω επι την γην
OL[V] Amb	et dormivit in cilicio
g[j]	om
J	πεσων επι σακκου κατα γης εκειτο

Cf. HTR 294. αυλιζειν, "to lie in the αυλα/courtyard, to
pass the night," is the characteristic KR correspondent for לון:
it is used for לון 3x in βγ (here, 17:16, 19:7(8); nowhere else
in Rgn). It occurs nowhere in the Pentateuch, 12x in B of
Judges (from 7 of which A dissents), and 3x in Ruth. It is
never used for שכב.

καθευδειν = שכב frequently, including 12x in α ββ, once in

βγ (12:3), once in γγ (1 K 18:27), never in γδ; = ישב once (1 S
19:9). It is never used for לון.

κοιμαν, the normal correspondent of שכב in βγ, is the characteristic revisional approximation for שכב (cf. above, p. 58).

Both ולן and בשק are unnecessary and are apparent expansions. The original Hb and subsequent developments may have
been as follows:

Original Hb:	ארצה	ושכב	*ובא
Pal. Hb:		וישכב בשק ארצה	ובא
M	ארצה ושכב ולן		ובא
OG	*και εισηλθεν	και εκαθευδεν	επι της γης
pL	και εισελθων	εκαθευδεν εν σακκω επι την γην	
KR	και εισηλθεν και ηυλισθη (και εκοιμηθη)		επι της γης
late confl.	και εισηλθεν και ηυλισθη και εκοιμηθη εν σακκω επι της γης		

J is obviously dependent upon L, and L alone = 4Q. This
combination evokes the verdict that L is pL. A(B+) are KR,
while MNrell follow upon both pL and KR.

The hypothetical character of the reconstructions labeled
"Original Hb" and "OG" does not affect the strength of the
later, demonstrable correspondences. Quite possibly, pL differs from OG. But, whatever the judgment on that, for this
combined plus and minus, 4Q = pL J ≠ M G^{KR}.

2 S 22:37   Ps 18(17):37   VII:305 (J omits 2 S 22:1--23:7)

4Q	[ולא מ֯עדו קרסלי
	[תר]חי[ב צעדי ול]א֯ עמדו קמי לי
M	תרחיב צעדי תחתני ולא מעדו קרסלי
BA+	εις πλατυσμον εις τα διαβηματα μου υποκατω μου
	και ουκ εσαλευθησαν τα σκελη μου
MN++	πλατυνεις τα διαβηματα μου υποκατω μου
	και ουκ εσαλευθησαν τα σκελη μου
L	και επλατυνας τα διαβηματα μου υποκατω μου
	και ουκ ησθενησα (-σαν ο) εν ταις τριβοις μου
	ολιγοτητες εξεστησαν με
	και ουχ υπεστησαν με οι υπεναντιοι.
Ps^M	תרחיב צעדי תחתי ולא מעדו קרסלי
Ps^G	επλατυνας τα διαβηματα μου υποκατω μου
	και ουκ ησθενησαν τα ιχνη μου

The right half (including the right margin) of the 4Q

column is preserved on this large fragment, making reconstruction according to space fairly certain. If the text of 4Q is
reconstructed according to S^{MG} and Ps^{MG}, the spacing fits well.

תחתני is omitted by 4Q against all traditions. But notice
that [תחנ[י] תֿחֿ occurs two lines directly underneath in 4Q at
22:40b, where boc$_2$e$_2$ alone omit against all traditions.

4Q has a supralinear addition, inserted by the original
scribe, over ולא of 37b. Since only תחתני is missing from 4Q,
since ולא אשוב fortunately appears in its proper place in the
following line, and since the supralinear [   ]מֿ ולא is
placed immediately over the ו[לא] in the text, it must be concluded that the supralinear addition is a doublet.

L also presents a doublet or even a triplet here. There
are too many variable Hb-Gk correspondences to reconstruct the
whole confidently, but at the very least it can be said that
the L reading forms not only the unique source but also a very
plausible source for the explanation of the doublet in 4Q:

και ουκ ησθενησα(ν) = ולא מעדו

και ουχ υπεστησαν   = ולא עמדו.

ασθενειν = מעד in the Ps reading here, and מעד occurs again in
Ps 26(25):1,   translated by ασθενειν in AS, with B variant
σαλευειν, as here. υφιστανται = עמד in 13 of its 16 occurrences, including 1 S 30:10 and 2 S 2:23 (where one also finds
υποκατω αυτου for תחתו).

The reconstruction listed above for 4Q is, of course,
questionable and proffered as suggestive. The less probably
correct reading and, at the same time, the *lectio facilior* may
have been in 4Q's text, reflected by L. Then the gloss either
from M or from Ps^M may have been inserted as a variant.

The person responsible for και ουχ υπεστησαν με οι υπεναντιοι may have been attempting to render *ולא עמדו קמי לי.
υπεναντιοι = קמי in Ex 15:7 and 32:25.   *קמי לי for קרסלי would
require (i) a confusion of the late Hasmonaean book hand's open
samekh for *mem* (cf. BANE, p. 176, line 3), (ii) a *yod-resh* confusion (cf. M's confusion of *yod-dalet* a few verses later in
22:48, described on p. 91), and (iii) a metathesis of ס/ר
(as in the metathesis in the preceding word: עמד/מעד).

Leaving this suggestion in the realm of suggestion, we can
nonetheless conclude that 4Q = L alone in presenting some

doublet here, and that possibly in the wording of that doublet,
4Q = L alone.

2. Minus

There are four minuses shared by 4Q and L against M and G
in the section βγ. The first we have seen just above in conjunction with the first plus at 2 S 12:16:   4Q and L lack וילן
found in M and G.   The other three follow:

2 S 13:32

4Q	‏[ ] היה [מיום] עֿ[נ]תֿוֿ‏ /[
M	‏על פי אבשלום היתה שומה מיום ענתוֿ‏
G	επι στοματος Αβεσσαλωμ ην κειμενος απο της ημερας ης εταπεινωσεν
L OL	εν οργη ην αυτω Αβεσσαλωμ αφ ης ημερας ης εταπεινωσεν
α' σ'	εν οργη ην αυτω Αβεσσαλωμ απο της ημερας

("α' σ' . . . parum probabiliter" - Field)

The point at issue here is ‏היתה שומה‏, not ‏על פי אבשלום‏,
since 4Q's reading there cannot be determined. 4Q has space
for only one of the two four-letter words. ‏מיום‏ is essential,
while ‏שומה‏ appears dubious, though Well. and Driver both presumed ‏שומה‏ (or some similar form) to be original.

No translation pattern can be established for κεισθαι,
since it occurs only 7x in LXX as a translation of a Hb expression, and each time the Hb is entirely different (H-R 758b,c).
Nonetheless, since κεισθαι is used as a passive to τιθεναι,
κειμενος is an exact reflection of ‏שומה‏--except that it is masculine (therefore indicating an original ‏היה‏ in the proto-M
text used by KR).

The subject of ‏היה‏ is probably Amnon. This is a causal
clause to explain why *only Amnon* is dead; thus, Amnon should
appear in it somewhere. In addition, Amnon is the subject of
‏מת‏ in the preceding clause and of ‏ענתו‏ in the following clause.
Amnon is also the subject of G's (KR's) κειμενος, indicating
that a scribe of M subsequently altered ‏היה‏* to ‏היתה‏, considering ‏שומה‏ genuine and feminine.

There is insufficient evidence for a confident reconstruction of the original, but 4Q L OL clearly agree against M G[KR]
in omitting ‏שומה‏:   4Q = L OL ≠ M G[KR].

2 S 22:43   Ps 18(17):43

4Q	[כעפר על]/ פני ארח [כ]טּיט חוצ[ו]ת ארקעם
M	כעפר ארץ כטיט חוצות אדקם ארקעם
G	ως χνουν γης˙ ως πηλον εξοδον ελεπτυνα αυτους
L	ως χνουν επι προσωπον ανεμου˙ ως πηλον των εξοδων λεανω αυτους
Ps^M	כעפר על פני רוח כטיט חוצות אריקם
Ps^G	ως χνουν κατα προσωπον ανεμου˙ ως πηλον πλατειων λεανω αυτους

Cf. M note 22:43a-a, Notes, NAB. כעפר על fits the lacuna
in 4Q very well. Prescinding from the question of whether ארח
or רוח is to be preferred, it is nonetheless clear in 43a that
4Q L Ps^{MG} are forms of one text tradition in contrast to M G.

In 43b it is also evident that אדקם, אריקם, and ארקעם are
simply three variants. The regular correspondent for λεπτυνειν
(G) is דקק (in 13 out of 15 occurrences; = רקע never); thus, G
= אדקם M.

λεαινειν (L Ps^G) occurs only 3x in LXX, though α' σ' θ'
use it in Prv 29:5 and Is 41:7 for מחליק. Those three occurrences are for שחק (at the beginning of this verse and in Job
14:19), and for רוק (here in Ps); λεαινειν is never used for
רקע. In fact, רקע in Qal is translated only by στερεουν 3x and
(επι)ψοφειν once.

Thus, first, it is fairly certain that G's ελεπτυνα reflects M's אדקם, while ignoring ארקעם. Secondly, on a semantic
basis it is probable that λεανω Ps^G ("rub smooth, pound in a
mortar") reflects not אריקם Ps^M ("empty out") but אדקם M
("crush, pulverize") or ארקעם 4Q M ("stamp, beat out"). It is
uncertain whether λεανω L reflects אדקם or ארקעם but, with
λεπτυνειν preempting דקק, it would seem that λεανω reflects
ארקעם. Since M is conflate, and since G has followed both ארץ
and אדקם, the conclusion becomes increasingly more probable
that M has inserted ארקעם from a Palestinian text and that L
has faithfully rendered that Palestinian text.

L alone has followed 4Q; it deviates with ανεμου (= רוח
consistently), but that deviation is from a 4Q texttype, not
from a M texttype. Ps^{MG} parallel the 4Q text, again deviating
with ανεμου (and אריקם), but ανεμου definitely (and אריקם possibly) deviates from a 4Q texttype and not from a M texttype.
Probably in both cola, 4Q = pL ≠ M G.

2 S 24:18	*1 C 21:18*
4Q	ויאמר עלה
M	ויאמר לו עלה
G	και ειπεν αυτω Αναβηθι
Lav	και ειπεν Αναβηθι
C^M	לאמר לדויד כי יעלה
C^G	του ειπειν προς Δαυειδ ινα αναβη

$$4Q = Lav \neq M\ G \neq C^{MG}.$$

3. Variant

2 S 12:15	4Q	אלוהים
	M T P	יהוה
	G	Κυριος
	L	ο θεος

Cf. HTR 294. It is impossible to determine whether pL reflects
the OG or is distinct from it. There seem to be no reasons
other than text affiliation for these correspondences. 4Q = pL
$\neq$ M G.

2 S 12:17	4Q	אליו
	M T	עליו
	G	επ αυτον
	L	προς αυτον

$4Q = L \neq M\ G.$

2 S 13:3	*VII.164*	4Q	[וי]הונתן
		M T P	יונדב
		G Å⊄⊯	Ιωναδαβ
		L g^j (txt)	Ιωναθαν
		OL^b (at 13:32)	Ionathab
		J	Ιωναθη

Cf. HTR 294. The G texts with Ιωναδαβ are B$^{a(vid)b}$AMNc$_2$
rell Thdt (-δαμ B*a$_2$; -δα c). Only boe$_2$ attest Ιωναθαν.

Jonadab occurs 5x in this story (11:3bis, 5, 32, 35; cf.
VII.166, 178). Neither Kennicott nor de Rossi shows any variants on the name (other than the occasional omission of the
matres ה or ו; cf. M 13:5). B-M, Field, and H-P list only
these variants: 13:5 Αμιναδαβ acx⊯; 13:32 Ιωναδαμ g*(vid),
-δαβ sup ras N^a (N* could have had -θαν); 13:35 Ιωναδαμ u*. OL
is lacking except for *Ionathab* at 13:32, which could be

interpreted either way.

J's Vorlage certainly read Ιωναθαν: his forms here (ο Ιωναθης, Ιωναθου, Ιωναθη VII.166, 178) parallel his forms of the prophet Nathan's name (ο Ναθας, τω Ναθα, τον Ναθαν VII.147, 150).

Mez (#123, p. 44) curiously lists Ιωναθαμ as the reading of his B text. Accordingly, he does not list this example among his proofs that J = L (p. 80). Should he have done so, 4Q would have offered him confirmation of the highest quality.

With the witness of 4Q and J, L should here be judged pL. But again, OG cannot be determined with confidence. The most that can be said is: 4Q = pL J ≠ M G.

2 S 13:24	*VII.174*	4Q	אל עבדו
		M	עם עבדך
		G	μετα του δουλου σου
		L OL	προς τον δουλον αυτου
		J	προς αυτον

Both the preposition and the suffix in M are superior, עבדך being standard courtly usage. It is difficult (cf. Brock, "Lucian *redivivus*," pp. 178-181) to determine whether G or L preserves the original translation. If G, then L is a pL revision (cf. 4Q OL J) toward 4Q in a pair of errors. If L is original, as seems more likely, then G is a subsequent correction (KR) toward M.

2 S 13:39	*VII.181*	
4Q	[רו]ח המלך	
M	דוד המלך	(cf. M note)
T	נפשא דדויד מלכא	
B+ P	ο βασιλευς Δαυειδ	
A+ Ⱬ	Δαυειδ ο βασιλευς	
LMN++	το π̅ν̅α του βασιλεως (+Δαυειδ L)	
OL^b	iratus regis	
OL^v	rex	
J	τα της οργης ... λελωφηκει	

Cf. Well., pp. 190-191 (the רוח deduction) and 223 (discovery of confirmation by L of that deduction); cf. also Driver, Notes, NAB (the latter two now confirming Well. on the further basis of 4Q).

4Q preserves the original Hb, and LMN (OL[b]) preserve the
faithful OG, though L later includes the conflation Δαυειδ. M
has the *lectio facilior* and *ad sensum* corruption רוח > דוד (sig-
naled by the preceding fem. ותכל), followed by (B)A+ P OL[v]. T
conflates 4Q and M. J clearly echoes the OG reading.

The jumbled "et requietus est iratus regis" of OL[b] makes
sense when an original ETREQUIETUSESTSPIRITUSREGIS (from OG και
εκοπασεν το πνευμα του βασιλεως) undergoes haplography
(ESTSPIRITUS > ESTIRITUS) and IRITUS is "corrected" to IRATUS.
4Q = OG L OL[b] J ≠ M BA OL[v].

2 S 15:2   VII.195

4Q	[ועמד]... רה[ויה]...	וקרא	
M	ועמד... ויהי...	ויקרא	
G	και εστη	και εγενετο... και εβοησεν (εβοα cx)...
L	και εφιστατο	και ην...	και εκαλει...
OL[s]	et stabat...	(et si...)	accedebat...
J	παρεγινετο...		ομιλων...

4Q is usually more consistent than M with modal verbs.
Note the imperfects of L OL J reflecting 4Q, the aorists of G
reflecting M. For these two variants, 4Q = L OL J ≠ M G.

2 S 15:2   4Q   וקרא לו אבשל[ום]
            M T   ויקרא אבשלום אליו
            G   και εβοησεν προς αυτον Αβεσσαλωμ
            Acx   και εβοησεν (εβοα cx) Αβεσσαλωμ προς αυτον
            L   και εκαλει αυτον Αβεσσαλωμ

4Q = L in both iterative verb and word order.

2 S 18:3   VII.234

4Q	[לא ישים לנו לב ... לא י[שׂ]י[ם] לנו לב
M	לא ישימו אלינו לב ... לא ישימו אלינו לב

G   ου θησουσιν εφ ημας καρδιαν...ου θησουσιν εφ ημας καρδιαν
L OL[b] ου στησεται εν ημιν καρδια...ου θησουσιν εις ημας καρδιαν
                                (non occident nobiscum   OL)

The first clause of M and of G is echoed exactly in the
second. 4Q's first clause is, accordingly, reconstructed after
its clear second clause.

G reflects M exactly in both clauses: plural verb, "heart"
as object, εφ ημας = עליכו/א. L's second clause agrees with
that of G, with the small exception of εις (= לכו??) vs. εφ (=
עליכו/א). But its first clause stands out startlingly from all
other traditions--except 4Q! L does not translate the intended
meaning of 4Q, but it does present an exact translation of
another possible interpretation of the 4Q text. OL^b agrees
with L in the first clause, while varying significantly from
the second clause, which nonetheless must have been similar to
G L's second clause (*occident* most likely reflects a form of
θνησκειν).

The pattern suggested by all this is that L attempts to
preserve two variants, the earlier in the first clause (= 4Q),
the later in the second clause (= M G^KR). OL, following L,
succeeded in the first clause and floundered on the second.

In fine, 4Q ≠ M G; if its first clause is to be reconstructed exactly as its second clause (which seems preferable),
then in that first clause (and originally for L in the second
clause as well?), 4Q = L ≠ M G.

2 S 18:9	4Q	וֹהוא
	M T P	ואבשלום
	G	και Αβεσσαλωμ
	L	και αυτος
	OL^b	et

The Vulgate *(cumque ingressus fuisset)* also omits the proper
name. 4Q = L (OL?) ≠ M G.

2 S 18:11	*VII.240*	
4Q	[ ] /[ם]שׁ[חם] לֹך לֹ[תוֹ]לֹ	
M T P	עשׁרה כסף לתת לך (+ סלעין עשׂרה/עסר post (T)
BA+	αν δεδωκειν σοι δεκα αργυριου	
LMN++	εδωκα (δεδ- N) αν σοι πεντηκοντα σικλους (om MN+) αργυριου	
J	πεντηκοντα σικλους αν αυτω δεδωκεναι	

Cf. Notes, NAB. 4Q has space for exactly four letters between the second ל and the ם; ע alone would leave an uncusto-
marily long gap, while חם (plus the space for word-division)
fits perfectly. The top half of the letter after ם is clear;
it can be an almost completely visible י (perfectly shaped) or

the top half of a fuller letter resembling פ; but the downward
slant of the left shoulder is too angled to be an admissible ר.
Palaeographically, the probable reading here must be given as
חמשים. J follows the OG/pL reading based on a Palestinian Hb
text. 4Q = OG L J ≠ M G.

2 S 22:33   *Ps 18(17):33*   *VII.305 om*

4Q   מאזרני

M   מעוזי

G   ο κραταιων με

L   περιτιθεις μοι

Ps^M   המאזרני

Ps^G   ο περιζωννυων με

Cf. M note 22:33a, Notes, NAB. 4Q = L (Ps^MG) ≠ M G.

2 S 22:39   Ps 18(17):39

4Q   אמח[צם]

M   ואכלם ואמחצם

G   και θλασω αυτους

L   εθλασα αυτους

A   και τελεσω αυτους και θλασω αυτους

Ps^M   אמחצם

Ps^G   εκθλιψω αυτους

    Cf. M note 22:39a-a; *SAYP*, pp. 270, 311-312 n.88; and
above p. 87. 4Q, with G Ps^MG, has preserved the shorter text.
A has characteristically corrected toward M, adding τελειν (=
כלה). In this minus, 4Q = G ≠ M G^h.

    Further, though the presence or lack of the initial *waw*/
και cannot be considered to reflect Vorlagen with total consistency (cf. *SAYP*, pp. 248-253, 325-338), it is interesting to
note both that L = 4Q in properly not adding και, and that L is
the only G witness which preserves the correct tense. Thus,
for the variant אמחצם, 4Q = L ≠ G ≠ M G^h.

2 S 22:45-46   Ps 18(17):45-46

4Q   גויים עם לא ידעתי יעבדני ⁴⁵לשמ]וע אזן ישמעו לי ⁴⁶בני נכר יתכחשו לי]
                              לא יחזרו ממסרותם ⁴⁷חי...

M   גוים עם לא ידעתי יעבדני ⁴⁵בני נכר יתכחשו לי לשמוע אזן ישמעו לי
      ⁴⁶בני נכר יבלו ויחגרו ממסגרותם ⁴⁷חי...

BA+   ⁴⁵υιοι αλλοτριοι εψευσαντο μοι εις ακοην ωτιου ηκουσαν μου
    ⁴⁶υιοι αλλοτριοι απορριφησονται και σφαλουσιν εκ των συγκλεισμων αυτων

MN++ ⁴⁵εις ακοην ωτιου υπηκουσεν μου και υιοι αλλοτριοι εψευσαντο μοι
    ⁴⁶υιοι αλλοτριοι απορριφησονται και σφαλουσιν εκ των συγκλεισμων αυτων

L   ⁴⁵εις ακοην ωτιου υπηκουσε μοι   διεψευσαντο με
    ακοη ωτιου εματαιωθησαν μοι
    ⁴⁶υιοι αλλοτριοι εασωσαν με ελυτρωθησαν εκ δεσμων αυτων

Ps^M S^P   גוים עם לא ידעתי יעבדוני ⁴⁵לשמע אזן ישמעו לי בני נכר יכחשו לי
    ⁴⁶בני נכר יבלו ויחרגו ממסגרותיהם ⁴⁷חי...

Ps^G   ⁴⁵εις ακοην ωτιου υπηκουσεν μοι και υιοι αλλοτριοι εψευσαντο μοι
    ⁴⁶υιοι αλλοτριοι   επαλαιωθησαν και εχωλαναν απο των τριβων αυτων

    Cf. NAB. Most of verses 45-46 has been lost from the 4Q
leather, and with so many variables in the mss it is too hazard-
ous to propose here a precise reconstruction of either 4Q or
the original text. The columnar arrangement above demonstrates
that, quantitatively, 4Q contains approximately the amount of
text as in the reconstruction. The average number of spaces
per line in this column is 58, and the line reconstructed for
4Q above tallies 60. Thus, 4Q probably lacks בני נכר יבלו.
    Stichometric arrangement, however, will further facilitate
our analysis:

M T BA+^V	4Q	MN++^V P; Ps^MG
⁴⁵בני נכר יתכחשו לי	לשמ]ע אזן ישמעו לי	⁴⁵לשמע אזן ישמעו לי
לשמוע אזן ישמעו לי		בני נכר יכחשו לי
⁴⁶בני נכר יבלו	בני נכר יתכחשו לי[	⁴⁶בני נכר יבלו
ויחגרו ממסגרותם	לא יחגרו ממסגרותם	ויחרגו ממסגרותיהם

    4Q affords us three positive bits of data:
1) The לשמע colon precedes the בני colon; thus, 4Q = LMN++ Ps^MG
≠ M BA.
2) ממסגרותם: 4Q = L ≠ M BAMN Ps^M ≠ Ps^G.
3) לא יחגרו: 4Q ≠ M BAMN ≠ Ps^M ≠ Ps^G. L has ελυτρωθησαν (=
יפדו?), which is unrelated to any of the many other readings
here. But since 4Q is alone and L is alone, and since L alone
followed 4Q's ממסגרותם, it is not unlikely that L, meeting the
textual turbulence visible in all mss here, followed 4Q, characteristically providing a smooth, sensible rendering of its

Vorlage. לא יחגרו ממסרותם ("they were ungirt from their bands")
became ελυτρωθησαν εκ δεσμων αυτων ("they were released from
their bands"). The two readings do in fact mean the same thing,
while no other reading comes close either to 4Q or to L.

But whence 4Q's לא? We noticed above that 4Q probably
lacks בני נכר יבלו. The occurrence of two doublets in L (εις
ακοην ωτιου/ ακοη ωτιου and εσωσαν με/ ελευτρωθησαν) while υιοι
αλλοτριοι is not repeated suggests that בני נכר is a doublet in
M and Ps^M, reflected in all G mss save L. Thus, 4Q = L ≠ M G
Ps^{MG}.

But יבלו remains. The textual data

4Q	לא יחגרו	
M	יבלו ויחגרו	
G	απορριφησονται και σφαλλουσιν	
L	εματαιωθησαν [= (ו)יבלו) cf. 2 K 17:15; Jer 2:5]	
Ps^G	επαλαιωθησαν [= (ו)יבלו) cf. Ps^M note; H-R]	

suggests that לא is a variant for an original or a supposed
(ו)בל*. Thus L would display a third doublet εματαιωθησαν (=
(ו)יבלו)/ελυτρωθησαν (= לְבַליחגרו), one element of which agrees with
M, the other with 4Q. Once the duplicate parts of L are removed, we notice:

L = 4Q

εις ακοην ωτιου υπηκουσε μοι   לשמ̇ע אזן ישמעו לי

διεψευσαντο με...υιοι αλλοτριοι   [בני נכר יתכחשו לי

...ελυτρωθησαν εκ δεσμων αυτων   לא יחגרו ממסרותם

In summary, for the three positive bits of data:
1) לשמע colon preceding בני colon: 4Q = L MN++ Ps^{MG} ≠ M BA;
2) the content of לא יחגרו: 4Q = L ≠ M BAMN ≠ Ps^M ≠ Ps^G;
3) ממסרותם: 4Q = L ≠ M BAMN Ps^M ≠ Ps^G;
and when the doublet-ridden L text is pruned, 4Q = L alone.

2 S 22:49   Ps 18(17):49

4Q	[הֹצרני]
M	חצילני
G	ρυση με
L	διετηρησας με (so B-M; Vann. silent)
Ps^M	חצילני
Ps^G	ρυση με

H-R lists 17 occurrences of διατηρειν with a Hb correspondent: = נצר 4x; = עמר 10x; = הלך, נטר, and עמד once each;
= נצל never.

On the other hand, ρυεσθαι = נצל frequently, = נצר only
once, in Ps 140(139):2 in the identical phrase found here:
מאיש חמסים תנצרני. The Hb phrase is repeated in 140(139):5,
rendered by εξελου BS, ρυσαι A.

Upon closer inspection, in fact, ρυεσθαι appears as the
characteristic revisional word of KR and α' for נצל. Note the
distribution of occurrences of ρυεσθαι = נצל in S K:

	α	0			
	ββ	0		βγ	5
	γγ	0		γδ	4

Note also in Judg 9:17:   and Judg 18:28:

M	ויצל	M	מציל
A	εξειλατο	A	εξαιρουμενος
B	ερρυσατο	B	ρυομενος

And lastly, Aquila prefers ρυεσθαι for נצל in:

1 S 30:22:   and Job 5:19:

M	הצלנו	M	יצילך
OG	εξειλαμεθα	G	σε εξελειται
L	εξηρημεθα	α'	ρυσεται σε
α'	ερρυσαμεθα		

Thus, we can say: (1) that G reflects M, while L reflects
4Q; (2) that G = KR; (3) that L = pL, because after the mid-
first century AD there was no possible basis for διετηρησας;
(4) that it is impossible to determine OG, since OG also employed ρυεσθαι for נצל occasionally (which correspondence KR
standardized), and since we cannot determine which Hb reading
OG had. If the Vorlage of OG had תצרני, OG probably had διετηρησας, and L = OG/pL. If the Vorlage of OG had תצילני, OG probably had ρυση and L = pL ≠ OG. The most we can say is: 4Q =
pL (OG?) ≠ MG^{KR}.

2 S 22:51	Ps 18(17):51	4Q	ישועת
		M	ישועות
		G	σωτηριας
		L	σωτηριαν

$$Ps^M \quad \text{ישועות}$$
$$Ps^G \quad \sigma\omega\tau\eta\rho\iota\alpha\varsigma$$

This is frail evidence. G could derive from 4Q as well as from
M. But the point is rather the opposite: L ≠ G, and L can derive only from the defective reading as found in 4Q. L can be
OG (if ות- is a later orthographic expression of an original
defective plural), or L can be pL revision--more likely the
former. 4Q = pL ≠ M G.

2 S 23:1

4Q	הגבר הקים אל
M	הגבר הקם על
T	גברא דמרבא למלכו
P	גברא דאקים נורא
G	(+o A) ανηρ ον ανεστησεν (+o M+) Κυριος επι
L OL^V	ανηρ ον ανεστησεν o θεος
g^j	om επι

אל is possibly the original word for God here; notice אל
further in verse 5:

M	אל
(OG?) L	θεου
BAMNrell	Ισχυρου (= KR; see *DA*, p. 83).

And for the Greek notice also four verses earlier, in 22:48:

M	האל
(OG?)	*Κυριος
L	Κυριος o θεος
BMNrell	Ισχυρος Κυριος (= KR)
A	υψηλος Κυριος (= העל?)

Whichever may be the Hb original, the OG (as in 22:48)
should probably be construed as Κυριος, since OG must have included some word for God and since Κυριος is otherwise unexplained. Only T fails to include a word for God precisely
here, and even T adds (ב)מימר immediately after the next word
משיח.

On the supposition that OG had Κυριος, all else fits characteristically into place: (p)L revised to o θεος on the basis
of a 4Q texttype (cf. 2 S 12:15: אלוהים 4Q, יהוה M T P, Κυριος
G, o θεος L). OL followed pL. T failed to understand M and
guessed with למלכו before משיח. KR failed to understand M and

in its literalism inserted into the OG text επι (for על) before
χριστον, thus distorting the meaning.

In summary, 4Q = L (≠ OG?) ≠ M G^KR.

2 S 23:3

4Q	[משל]/]צדי[ק באדם]וצדי[ק משל
M	מושל צדיק באדם מושל
G	Παραβολην ειπον Εν ανθρωπω πως κραταιωσητε
L ʂ^j	αρξον εν ανοις δικαιως αρχε (-χαι b)
OL^V	[*Parabolam loquere] hominibus iuste incipit

G follows neither 4Q nor M. It interprets the first משל
as a singular imperative but from משל "to speak a parable," and
OL^V (*e silentio* B-M) follows: G does not follow M. After a
confused πως in place of צדיק (≠ 4Q M), G interprets משל again
as an imperative, this time from משל "to rule," but in the
plural (≠ 4Q ≠ M). G, varying widely from M throughout this
verse and demonstrating no indication of KR activity, should be
judged OG.

L, followed by ʂ^j, interprets both verbs as singular im-
peratives from משל "to rule"--first in the aorist, then in the
present tense (= 4Q ≠ M). L properly translates אדם ("mankind,
men") with ανθρωποις, in contrast to G's ανθρωπω ("a human being").

OL^V follows L with *hominibus* as well as *iuste incipit*:
incipit, however, reflects αρχε(ι) in the sense of "begin" instead of "rule."

In summary, since L = 4Q while 4Q ≠ M ≠ G, L may be judged
a pL revision: 4Q = pL ≠ M ≠ G.

C.   4Q = M L ≠ G

2 S 18:3   *VII.234*

4Q	[ויאמר] העם]ל[א תצא
M T	ויאמר העם לא תצא
G	και ειπαν Ουκ εξελευση
L OL^b	και ειπεν ο λαος Ουκ εξελευση
J	συνεκστρατευειν αυτου ουκ ειασαν οι φιλοι

G should be the OG preserved here, since, if it had been
revised, ο λαος should have been inserted to correspond to the
4Q M gloss. L would then be a revision of OG toward either 4Q

or M. The witness of OL (and J?) tends to indicate an early
(pL) revision.

J's οι φιλοι, though fragile testimony, does positively
function exactly as ο λαος in L 4Q M, in contrast to G's omission.

See the reading from this same verse on p. 107 above. The
probability there that 4Q = L OL ≠ M G supports the pL suggestion posited for this reading: 4Q = pL OL J M ≠ G.

2 S 18:6	VII.236	4Q	ה]שדה
		M	השדה
		G	εις το δρυμον
		L OL[b]	εις το πεδιον
		J	εν πεδιω

Later in the verse, all mss agree (ביער M; de 4Q; εν τω δρυμω G
L OL; δρυμον J). But in this reading, 4Q = M L OL J ≠ G.

D. Conclusion

Part A of this chapter, analyzing section α ββ, presents 8
readings in which 4Q = L ≠ M G. There are one plus, four
minuses, and three variants in 4Q, relative to M.

The significance of this material lies not in the 4Q/M
disparity primarily, but in the evidence for proto-Lucianic revisional activity. The base for comparison, however, should be
OG, not 4Q or M. Let us, therefore, summarily review the eight
readings from the viewpoint of OG/pL.

1 S 5:9 προς τους Γεθθαιους. This is a pL plus inserted into the fundamental OG text, and its unique source is
the plus in the 4Q tradition. Neither OG nor pL was ever corrected toward either הסבו or אתו in M. 4Q = pL ≠ OG ≠ M.

1 S 6:20 κυριου. This is a pL plus inserted into
the basic OG text. The 4Q tradition is the catalyst of that
revision. M shows a more expanded text which is exactly reflected in G[h]. 4Q = pL ≠ OG ≠ M G[h].

1 S 14:32 εις/επι. boc$_2$e$_2$ alone substitute επι for
the unanimous εις in OG, revising toward על in the 4Q tradition. J's echoing επι and M's discordant אל doubly indicate
the pL stratum in L. Thus, the pL variant is a revision of OG
toward the 4Q tradition. 4Q = pL ≠ OG ≠ M.

2 S 3:28-29 αιμα Αβεννηρ. L departs from the unanimous G tradition, and the sole source for that departure is the
4Q tradition. Unfortunately, OG cannot be confidently isolated;
and so, either 4Q = pL, or 4Q = OG/pL. The most we can say is:
4Q = pL ≠ M G.

2 S 3:36 παντος. This is a uniquely pL revision inserted into the fundamental OG text on the basis of the 4Q tradition. M expands further with טוב and G[h] responds with αγαθον.
4Q = pL ≠ OG ≠ M G[h].

2 S 4:10 λεγων. This is a uniquely pL plus inserted
into the OG base text before οτι. It reflects לאמר in the 4Q
tradition but does not include the M expansion הנה.   4Q = pL ≠
OG ≠ M.

2 S 4:12 εν Χεβρων. This is a pL addition to the
fundamental OG υιου Νηρ. It reflects 4Q, with which alone it
agrees exactly. The 4Q pL conflation is continued in G[M++] and
OL[b].   4Q = pLM++ ≠ OG ≠ M

2 S 5:11 τεκτονας τοιχου. This is a pL revision of
the OG τεκτονας λιθων, due to the occurrence of קיר in the 4Q
tradition. M conflates with אבן קיר and G[h] imitates M.   4Q =
pL ≠ OG ≠ M G[h].

Thus, leaving out the possible but undemonstrable 4Q pL
reading in 2 S 3:28, seven readings from the 4Q fragments highlight pL revisions of the OG translation, where the 4Q pL, the
OG, and the M (G[h]) traditions are all three divergent. The OG
text is not in error for any of these readings; therefore,
there is no necessity for revision. But the early stratum of
the L tradition does nevertheless revise, and the consistent
basis for that revision was a Hebrew text tradition documented
in Palestine after the translation of OG but uninfluential
after the first century A.D.

Compared with the 124 readings from chapter II for which
4Q = G ≠ M in α ββ, these seven (or eight) pL revisions would
indicate that very roughly one out of every 19 (or 17) OG readings was corrected in the pL text.

This is light, not major, revisional activity. But it is
consistent (5 exact pluses and 2 exact variants) revisional
activity, and the closeness of 4Q to the Vorlage of OG (see
chapter II) leaves small scope for revision on the basis of

Hebrew Vorlage.

Parts B and C of this chapter, analyzing section βγ, present 27 readings in which 4Q = L ≠ M G. There are two pluses, four minuses, nineteen variants, and (in part C) two further variants for which L = 4Q and M, but due to the witness of OL J, it is argued that L depends on 4Q and not M.

The ratio of 27 readings in the 14 βγ chapters for which 4Q fragments survive to 8 readings in the 29 α ββ chapters is roughly 7 to 1. The frequency of 4Q L agreement against M G rises approximately 700% in section βγ as compared with section α ββ. This, plus the conclusion of the previous chapter, lends strong support to the Barthélemy-Cross hypothesis that G in βγ is the *kaige* recension of the OG/pL text, and that the OG/pL text there is to be sought basically in mss boc_2e_2.

Chapter IV

DISAGREEMENT OF 4QSam[a] WITH THE GREEK VERSION

We shall present in this chapter the evidence that is or
appears to be contrary to our main thesis, viz., that the Greek
version was originally translated from a Hebrew text much
closer to 4QSam[a] than to M. Thus, we will be dealing with readings opposed to the pattern 4Q = G ≠ M. These contrary readings will be subdivided into categories that will help elucidate the qualitative ways in which 4Q differs from G.

The basic, most important, and most consistent way in
which 4Q differs from G has been developed in the previous chapter. 4Q frequently agrees with the L text as opposed to M G,
and the reason for this has been demonstrated: L frequently,
especially in βγ, preserves the original Greek translation or
occasional revisions toward the 4Q texttype, while the majority
G text has undergone change--often in the direction of conformity with M.

There remain four other possibilities for 4Q divergence.
4Q can be a combination of M plus G, it can differ both from M
and from G, it can differ from the joint witness of M and G,
and it can align itself with M in opposition to G.

We shall, accordingly, classify under these four categories the readings contrary to the pattern 4Q = G ≠ M. All such
contrary readings will be listed, except for (a) those contrary
readings which are already presented and noted in other parts
of this study, and (b) those readings which were so highly
fragmentary or nebulous that they have surrendered nothing to
the siege of analysis.

A. The Pattern 4Q = M + G

1 S 2:8-9   V.347 om

4Q

נדב]ין   וכסא כבוד ינחלם כיא ליהוה מצקי ארץ וישת[

עליהם תֹבֹ]ל[9]ודרך חֹ]סידו ישמר   [

נתן נדֹ]ר לנוד]רֹ ויברך שֹ]ני צדיק 9b כיא לוא בכח יגבר איש[

10יהוה יחת מר]י[בו מי קֹ]דוש   [

M   נדיבים   וכסא כבוד ינחלם כי ליהוה מצקי ארץ וישת
                     עליהם תבל 9רגלי חסידו ישמר ורשעים בחשך ידמו
                 9bכי לא בכח יגבר איש
             10יהוה יחתו מריבו עלו בשמים

G^V

                     נדיבי עם וכסא כבוד ינחלם

         8bנתן נדר לנודר ויברך שני צדיק 9כי לא בכח יגבר איש
             10יהוה יחת מריבו יהוה קדוש

G OL   δυναστων λαων, και θρονον δοξης κατακληρονομων αυτοις.
        διδους ευχην τω ευχομενω, και ευλογησεν ετη δικαιου.
        οτι ουκ εν ισχυι δυνατος ανηρ·
        Κυριος ασθενη ποιησει αντιδικον αυτου· Κυριος αγιος

Cf. Notes, NAB. ודרך (4Q 2:9) appears in neither M nor G;
for 4Q's substitution of ודרך for רגלי, cf. ודרך חסידו ישמר Prv.
2:8.

After reading three (and possibly four) cola similar to
8b-9a in M (not in G), 4Q reads the next two cola with 8b in G
(not in M). The line which follows immediately in both M (9b)
and G (9), כי לא בכח יגבר איש, fits the space at the end of
4Q's line, and the next line of 4Q begins harmoniously with
verse 10 of both M and G.

What at first appears to be a 4Q conflation of M and G
will probably prove, especially in light of the much longer but
different texts of 4Q and G for 2:10 (see p. 49), to be due to
diverse haplographies in M and in G, and/or displacement of
stichoi.

1 S 1:28, 2:11   V.347 om
                    1 S 1:28
4Q   [   ]הֹר שם ותשתחו[ליהוה ותעזב]
M   וישתחו שם ליהוה   ליהוה
G   τω Κυριω.
LN+ א   τω Κυριω. και προσεκυνησαν (-σεν εκει Nb₂א) τω Κυριω
                    1 S 2:11
4Q   de
M   וילך אלקנה הרמתה
G   Και κατελιπον αυτον εκει ενωπιον Κυριου
                             και απηλθον εις Αρμαθαιμ

L   Και κατελιπον αυτον ενωπιον Κυριου εκει

Και προσεκυνησαν (-σεν ο) τω Κυριω και απηλθον εις Αρμαθαιμ

Cf. Well., Driver, BASOR 20. 4Q M and G each insert Hannah's prayer into the narrative at a different point, while Josephus customarily omits prayers and poems. The classification of this reading should perhaps be 4Q ≠ M ≠ G, since three different text traditions are obvious. For details, however, we note that (1) in placing ותשתחו before the prayer of Hannah, 4Q = M L$_2$ ≠ G pL; while (2) in the inclusion of ותעזבהו, 4Q = G ≠ M.

Perhaps most interesting is that, when the inserted prayer is removed and when the tautological gloss ενωπιον Κυριου (explaining εκει) is removed from G, then 4Q = pL ≠ M ≠ OG. The texts can be presented thus:

4Q	[	[ליהוה ותעזב]הו שם ותשתחו]
M	רישתחו שם ליהוה וילך אלקנה הרמתה	ליהוה
G^V	הרמתה וילכו שם	ליהוה ותעזבהו
pL^V	הרמתה ליהוה וילכו שם ותשתחו	ליהוה ותעזבהו

1 S 2:2   V.347 om

4Q	[כ]יא אין קד[ו]ש כיה[וה]]
	[ואין צדיק כאלוהינו ואין בלת]ך ואין צור כאלוהינו] [
M	אין קדוש כיהוה
	כי אין בלתך ואין צור כאלהינו
G^V	כי אין קדוש כיהוה
	ואין צדיק כאלהינו ואין קדוש בלתך

G   οτι ουκ εστιν αγιος ως Κυριος και ουκ εστιν δικαιος ως ο θεος ημων
    (+και L+) ουκ εστιν αγιος πλην σου

A   ουκ εστιν αγιος ως Κυριος και ουκ εστιν πλην σου
              και ουκ εστιν δικαιος ως ο θεος ημων

M and G each have three cola, differing in wording and order. 4Q spacing requires, and is perfectly filled by, a conflation of M and G:

M	4Q	G^V
אין קדוש כיהוה	[כ]יא אין קד[ו]ש כיה[וה]	כי אין קדוש כיהוה
	[ואין צדיק כאלוהינו]	ואין צדיק כאלוהינו
כי אין בלתך	[ואין (קדוש?) בלת]ך	ואין קדוש בלתך
ואין צור כאלוהינו	ואין צור כאלוהינו	ואין צור כאלוהינו

2 S 4:12 See p. 98, where, as in the three preceding readings, 4Q is a combination of M and G, and the pL text agrees with 4Q.

B.   The Pattern 4Q ≠ M ≠ G

The readings just presented could be viewed as one particular type of 4Q reading which agrees neither with M nor with G. But in addition to them there are readings which demonstrate that 4Q is more independent: that 4Q at times displays readings at variance with M where G likewise goes its separate way. We have in these readings then three independent, or independently reworked, text traditions.

1 S 2:13-16   See the numerous detailed agreements and disagreements discussed in BASOR 21-22. The text of 4Q displays an arrangement much different from M, while G in its present form, generally follows closer to M than to 4Q, though it also diverges from M.

1 S 5:8-10

4Q
```
[וי]סבו א[ת ארון א]להֹי ישֹ[אל אלינו ויסבו את ארון אלוהי]
[                              ] vac [              ]נה ג[דה
⁹ויהי א[חרי] סבו גתה ותהי [יד י]הוה [בעיר מהומה] גדולה
[מאד ריך א]ת אנשי העיר מקט[ן] ועד ג[דול           ]עפלים
¹⁰[וישל]חֹוֹ [א]ת ארון אלוהי ישראֹל עֹקרו[ן ויהי כבוא ארון]
[אלוהי ישראל עקרון ויזעקו העקרו]נֹים לא[מור] למה הסבותֹ[ם]
```

M
```
יסב ארון        אלהי ישראל        ויסבו את ארון אלהי
                    ס                                ישראל:
⁹ויהי אחרי  הסבו אתו ותהי  יד יהוה    בעיר מהומה  גדולה
מאד ריך  את אנשי העיר מקטן   ועד  גדול וישתרו להם עפלים:
¹⁰וישלחו        את  ארון האלהים      עקרון  ויהי כבוא ארון
האלהים          עקרון ויזעקו העקרנים  לאמר       הסבו
```

G^V   יסב ארון   האלהים   אלינו ויסב   ארון האלהים
       גתה

⁹ויהי אחרי   סבו   ותהי יד יהוה בעיר מהומה גדולה
מאד ויך   את אנשי העיר מקטן   ועד   גדול]   ?   [
¹⁰וישלחו   את ארון האלהים   אשקלון ויהי כבוא ארון
האלהים   אשקלון ויזעקו האשקלנים לאמר למה הסבותם

G   Μετελθετω (+δη η L) κιβωτος του θεου (+Ισραηλ LAN++) προς
ημας (+εις Γεθ LN+) και μετηλθεν (+η LAN+) κιβωτος του
θεου (+Ισραηλ LN+) εις Γεθθα (Γεθ LN+)
⁹και εγενηθη μετα το (εγενετο εν τω L) μετελθειν αυτην
(την κιβωτον προς τους Γεθθαιους L!) και γινεται χειρ
Κυριου εν (om B) τη πολει ταραχος μεγας (εν πληγη μεγαλη
L+) σφοδρα και επαταξεν τους ανδρας της πολεως απο μικρου
εως μεγαλου και επαταξεν αυτους (κ.ε.α. om L) εις τας
εδρας αυτων (om L) και εποιησαν εαυτοις (om bo, post Γεθθαιοι e₂A+) οι Γεθθαιοι εδρας (+χρυσας και εξεβρασαν εν
αυτοις μυες L+ OL)
¹⁰και εξαποστελλουσιν (+οι Γεθθαιοι L) την κιβωτον του θεου
(+Ισραηλ L) εις Ασκαλωνα και εγενηθη (εγενετο L) ως εισηλθεν η (om Bb₂) κιβωτος του (om B) θεου (+Ισραηλ N+) εις
Ασκαλωνα και εβοησαν (ανεβ- LN+) οι Ασκαλωνειται λεγοντες
Τι απεστρεψατε (απεσταλκατε L)

Overall, the classification of this passage must be: 4Q ≠
M ≠ G (cf. esp. 5:9 גתה).   4Q ≠ M G in (5:8) the transitive
[ה]סבו א[וי] and (5:10) אלוהי ישראׄל. 4Q = M ≠ G in (5:8)
[אל] ישׄ לוהי] א[, ואלוהי] ישראל, and (5:10) [ן]קרׄעׄ (note that
J = Gk ≠ Hb; cf. p. 181).   4Q = G ≠ M in (5:8) [אלינו], [נתח ג],
the intransitive סבו [אחרי], and (5:10) [ם]הסבותׄ למה. But
notice that, despite L's many inner expansions, 4Q = L in (5:8)
ישראל^{bis}+, (5:9) גתה !, ישראל+.

1 S 5:11   4Q   [ה]חמת יהו [מ] (or [ה]הומת[מ])
              M   מהומה מות
              Bya₂   συγχυσις
              LANrell   συγχυσις θανατου

Two possibilities appear: (1) G could be original, with

4Q and M (followed by G[h]) each expanding differently. It is also possible that (2) 4Q is original; cf. the only other example
of the use of the construct of מהומה (in Zech 14:13): מהומת
יהוה! The translator of G, with a Vorlage similar to 4Q, de-
clined on theological grounds to translate "the panic of the
LORD," and simply omitted יהוה (cf. other euphemistic changes
in OG on pp. 210-211, and M's omission of a word [מפיבשת] which
was erroneous in its Vorlage, pp. 42-44). M, either through
dittography, or motivated by an objection similar to G's, substituted מות for יהוה*. In favor of this second alternative is
the resultant textual disturbance in M at the end of this verse,
where G follows 4Q (cf. p. 75).

If the first alternative is verified, $4Q \neq M \neq G$. If the
second, $4Q = M^V G^V \neq M \neq G$.

1 S 9:7

4Q	[ויאמר ש[אול רה[נה]
M OL[qv]	ויאמר שאול לנערו והנה
G	και ειπεν Σαουλ τω παιδαριω αυτου τω μετ αυτου Και ιδου

4Q spacing seems to require this short, superior reading. M
adds לנערו, G adds אשר אתו*. $4Q \neq M \neq G$.

1 S 9:24   *VI.52~*

4Q	[השוק ה[עֿליוה ויש[ם]
M	השוק והעליה וישם
T	שקא וירכיה ושוי
P	שקא ועליתא וסם
G	την κωλεαν και παρεθηκεν
L G[h]	την κωλεαν και το επ αυτης και παρεθηκεν
J	παραθειναι τω Σαουλω μεριδα βασιλικην

Cf. Well., Driver; Notes: "ה[עֿליזה] ... festive." In my
view the penultimate letter is *waw* not *zayin*. Despite a speck
on the leather, traces of a head to the *left* can be seen,
whereas there is no trace at all to the *right* (which *zayin* need
not have but frequently does), and the vertical stroke curves
slightly so:), like *waw*, whereas *zayin* is straight or curves
slightly in the opposite direction. Compare the clear *zayin* in
ויאמר זה (1 S 8:11) on the same plate.

This clarification of the reading, however, remains unable

to advance our grasp of the meaning or the history of the text.
4Q ≠ G ≠ M G^h P Syh ≠ T.

J's βασιλικην is undoubtedly *ad sensum*, oblivious of the
presence (4Q or M) or absence (G) of a precise word in his Vorlage. His echo of G, however, is detectable in παραθειναι and
μεριδα (9:23).

1 S 10:3	*VI.55*	4Q	[ ]/ ככרות ////// שלוש		
		M	שלשת ככרות לחם		
		G^V	שלשת כלי לחם		
		G	τρια αγγεια αρτων (post οινου L)		
		J	τρεις αρτους		

4Q has an erasure of about 5 spaces after שלוש. (a) There
appears to be a clean, unused space after שלוש, probably elimi-
nating שלושת or שה- (but see next comment). (b) Next appears ג,
which is probably נ or כ, though it could also possibly be ב, מ,
or even ט, נ, פ, ע, or finally ת of שלושת. (c) The next letter
was certainly ל. (d) All ink traces have been erased from the
following space. (e) The top of a final *mem* is fairly clear in
the final space. Thus, palaeographically, the two leading possibilities are: שלוש כֹּלֹ[י]םֹ (preferably) and שלושֹתֹ לֹ[ה]םֹ.

Grammatically, שלשת ככרות (M) is incorrect, correct possibilities being שלוש ככרות (revised 4Q) and שלשת* כלי (G). Were
we to proceed deductively according to rigid rules of grammar,
we would say that the scribe of 4Q had already written שלוש and
therefore he already intended to write ככרות (and not לחם or
כלי). Thus, the erasure eradicates, *prima manu*, an immediately
recognized mistake. This mistake could have been either (1) a
simple error, or (2a) the incorporation into the text of
supralinear כלי in the Vorlage, or conversely (2b) the copying
of כלי from the text of the main Vorlage, when the scribe had
already intended to incorporate the reading from the M tradition. Notice that M is doing something similar: its "grammati-
cal error" is possibly not such but a convention for preserving
the awareness of a variant (cf. the same phenomenon in the following verse, discussed on p. 52 above).

The unreliability of such argumentation, however, can be
seen from comparing M and G at Lev 23:17; Judg 8:5; 1 S 2:32bis;
etc. At any rate, as the texts here stand, 4Q ≠ M ≠ G.

1 S 11:9

4Q	[ומיהוה התש̇[ועה]	
M T P	מחר תהיה לכם תשועה	
G	Αυριον υμιν η σωτηρια	
Acdpqtxz	Αυριον εσται υμιν σωτηρια	
*b*oc₂(sub ※·)e₂ OL	Αυριον υμιν εσται η σωτηρια	

b' omits the whole line through haplography: Ιαβεις -- Ιαβεις.
4Q ≠ G ≠ M G^h.

1 S 27:10   VI.324

4Q	[ויהוד]ה̇ ואל נגב ירח̇[מא]ל̇] ו̇ע̇ל נגב̇
M	יהודה ועל נגב הירחמאלי ואל נגב
G	Ιουδαιας και κατα νοτον Ιεσμεγα (Αερμων L) και κατα νοτον
J	τον νοτον των Ιουδαιων

This reading is included not because of the importance of
its contents, but to illustrate the minor independence of the
three texttypes. Out of the six words there are four disagreements, none with the same pattern as another: ואל (4Q ≠ M G);
om -ה (4Q ≠ M); ירחמאל (4Q = M ≠ G ≠ L); ועל (4Q = G ≠ M).

2 S 3:27, 29, 32

Another example of the minor independence of the three
texttypes can be seen by examining four readings occurring in
quick succession.

                    2 S 3:27   VII.36˜

4Q	עשאל אח̇יהו
M T P	עשהאל אחיו
G	Ασαηλ του αδελφου Ιωαβ
L	Ασσαηλ του αδελφου αυτου
J	Ασαηλω τω αδελφω

                    2 S 3:29   VII.39

4Q	ועל כ̇[ול] בית יואב
M	ואל כל בית אביו
T P	ועל (P ריש+) כל בית אבוהי
G	και επι παντα (εις b') τον οικον του πατρος αυτου
Thdt	τον οικον αυτου
J	τον οικον ολον αυτου

2 S 3:32   VII.42~

4Q	‏ועל קבר א[בנר
M T P	‏(על T P) אל קבר אבנר
G	επι του ταφου αυτου
cx	επι τον ταφον (του ταφου x) Αβεννηρ
L	επι τω ταφω Αβεννηρ
J	επι του ταφου

2 S 3:32[fin]   VII.42~

4Q	[	‏ויבכו כל העם[ ]
M		‏ויבכו כל העם
G		και εκλαυσεν πας ο λαος επι Αβεννηρ
L		και εκλαυσεν πας ο λαος

In 3:27 the proper name was substituted for the pronoun in the G text alone, after pL had gone its separate way.

In 3:29 it is possible that 4Q is original with ‏יואב. First, David's political (if not personal) anger, as well as his intent to pinpoint the blame emphatically and the curse explicitly, make the repetition of the name highly effective. Secondly, ‏בית יואב is repeated in the specification of the curse in the following clause. Thirdly, if David cursed the whole house of Joab's *father*, he would be cursing his own close relatives -- Zeruiah, for example, mother of Joab and sister of David (1 C 2:15-16)!

It is more likely, however -- according to Wellhausen's principle that a M vs. G variation on proper names usually indicates that neither was original -- that J and Thdt reflect OG/pL which preserved an original Hb ‏ביתו*. The 4Q tradition then would have later specified in one direction, while the M tradition would have specified in another, to be followed by the later G tradition.

Parenthetically, we can note that 4Q and G are doubtlessly correct with ‏ועל/και επι; cf. T P and, three words earlier in M: ‏על.

In 3:32 OG (J) reflect the original, while 4Q, M and, in their wake, T P G^h L substitute the proper name.

4Q should be reconstructed with ‏על (cf. T P G, and 3:29, 33, etc.). It is perhaps too risky to try to distinguish between the cases used with επι here. If there is intended nuance, notice should be called to Liddell-Scott s.v. επι with

Dative: "*upon*, just like the genitive, so that the Poets use
which ever case suits their metre, whereas in Prose the dative
is more frequent...." Also, the memory of another dead warrior
(επ' Ιφιδαμαντι, Iliad II.261) could have influenced the Lucianic editor. At any rate, BAMN, supported by J, are more than
likely the original OG; c can be a simple υ/ν error or can be
viewing the tears as falling *upon* the grave. Αβενηρ is hexaplaric in cx and probably hexaplaric in L, though it is possible that it is a pL correction toward a 4Q type of text.
Finally, J would not be expected to include either the name or
the pronoun (cf. the reading of 3:27 just above).

   In $3:32^{fin}$, though 4Q breaks off, spacing requires
that it read with M. Again, G alone has inserted the gloss
after the pL tradition had separated.

   Thus, in 2 S 3:27 and 3:32^{fin} G inserts the proper
name against 4Q M L. In 3:29 4Q and M G both add different explanatory insertions. In 3:32 4Q M G^h L insert the proper name
against G. This is the type of minor independence that is to
be expected between ms traditions.

2 S 4:4	4Q	ויהי
	M T	היה
	P	הוא
	G	και ουτος (-τως Mgm)

2 S 5:6, 8   1 C 11:5-6 om   VII.61 (64 om)

   The following three similar readings show no two ms traditions which pattern together consistently, and thus any significance is cancelled.

	2 S 5:6	1 C 11:5 om	VII.61
4Q	de		
M		העורים והפסחים	
T		חטאיא וחייביא	
P		עוירא וחגירא	
BA+ OL^b ʒ^j (vid)		οι τυφλοι και οι χωλοι	
MN++ OL^v		οι τυφλοι και οι χωλοι	
L		οι χωλοι και οι τυφλοι	
σ'		τους τυφλους και τους χωλους	
J		τους πεπηρωμενους τας οψεις και τας βασεις	

	2 S 5:8a	1 C 11:6 om	VII.64 om

4Q   ו[א]ת הע[ורים ואת]/ ה[פסחי]ם

M   ואת הפסחים ואת העורים

T   רית הטאיא רית חייביא

P   לעוירא ולהגירא

BA+ OL^b g^j (vid)   και τους χωλους και τους τυφλους

MN++ OL^v και τους τυφλους και τους χωλους

L   και τους χωλους και τους τυφλους

	2 S 5:8b	1 C 11:6 om	VII.64 om

4Q   עור ופסח

M P   עור ופסח

T   חטאיא וחייביא

G OL^b τυφλοι και χωλοι

L   τυφλος και χωλος

y Or-Gr   χωλος (-οι y) και τυφλος (-οι y)

When all three readings are considered together, 4Q ≠ M ≠ G.

2 S 12:17   4Q   [ול]א ברה אותם לחם

M   ולא ברא אתם לחם

T   ולא אכל עמהון לחמא

G   και ου συνεφαγεν αυτοις αρτον

L   ουδε συνεδειπνησεν αρτον μετ αυτων

ברא (M) is an error for ברה, just as אותם (4Q) is an error for
אָתָם. Our scribe (or his predecessor) has made a similar orthographic expansion in 1 S 1:24 (cf. pp. 48-49 above) where G =
4Q^v ≠ M.

2 S 13:31b   4Q   בגדיו

M   בגדים   (cf. M note)

T P   לבושיהון

G OL^b τα ιματια αυτων

L   τα ιματια

T P G OL all suggest בגדיהם. 4Q has the sg. suffix due to
attraction to בגדיו, 31a. L could be "corrected" toward M or,
more likely, polished Greek. 4Q ≠ M ≠ G.

There are two further ways in which the three texts show
their mutual independence or show ambiguity. First, just as 4Q
displays four combinations of M + G, so do both M and G display
conflations of 4Q + G^V and of 4Q + M, respectively. Secondly,
there are readings in which 4Q ≠ M, where the G reading is
ambiguous, capable of being derived from either 4Q or M.

First, for M as a conflation of 4Q + G^V, see the reading
of 2 S 22:43 on page 104 above. For G as a conflation of 4Q +
M, see the four doublets discussed below on pp. 197-201, and
the following:

1 S 10:5

4Q   [שם נציב פלש]חֹֽיֹ והיה

M T P   שם נצבי פלשתים ויהי

G ÅĊË   εκει (om Ae$_2$) το αναστεμα των αλλοφυλων

            εκει Νασειβ ο αλλοφυλος (om εκ. 2°--αλ. xÅ) και εσται
OL^b (om εκει 1°) resuscitatio Allophylorum (om εκει 2° -- αλλοφυλος)
OL^V [ubi] consistunt Allophyli et ibi sunt insidiae Allophylorum

4Q's singular reading is undoubtedly OG's αλλοφυλος,
against the plural found in M and in the G^h conflation prefixed
to OG. Cf. pp. 197-201 for the practice of prefixing the later
part of a G doublet to the 4Q-OG part. Though the prima facie
classification would be 4Q ≠ M ≠ G, on the basis of the parallels just referred to, 4Q = OG ≠ M G^h.

Secondly, we may conclude this section with those readings
in which 4Q ≠ M, where G is ambiguous:

2 S 2:6

4Q   אתכם   (cf. p. 71)

M   עמכם   (M uses אתכם later in this verse; de 4Q)

G   μεϑ υμων (G uses μετα for both את and עם)

2 S 2:8   4Q   שֹׁר הצבא

               M   שר צבא

               G   αρχιστρατηγος

M makes the small error of omitting the necessary -ה; G could
reflect either, since the translator would spontaneously correct such an error.

2 S 3:25   4Q   [ ] אל[בנׄר כי הלפתותך

            M T   אבנר בן נר כי לפתתך

            P   אבנר בן נר   למשדלותך

            G   Αβεννηρ υιου Νηρ οτι απατησαι σε

            cx ᵍʲ   Αβεννηρ   οτι απατησαι σε

Cf. Driver. The 4Q omission of בן נר is sure. The base
line of the *beth* running into the *nun* is clear, as is the absence of final *nun*. For this minus, 4Q = cx ᵍʲ ≠ M G.

The interrogative -ה following כי is not common, but cf. 1
K 8:27 // 2 C 6:18. Furthermore, notice M's lack of הלא at the
beginning of the verse, preceded by an anomalous הלוך (om G, de
4Q) whose first two letters and final letter are identical with
those of הלפתותך. G is ambiguous, since it is already a question, introduced by η ουκ (om M). Thus, 4Q ≠ M, where G is
ambiguous.

2 S 3:29   4Q   ולוא יכרת

            M   ואל יכרת

            G   και μη εκλιποι (εκλειποι oe₂++)

This reading in 4Q is not certain, but its traces cannot
represent ואל, while they do match those of other occurrences
of ולוא in this scroll (2 S 22:38, 13:25; cf. 5:9 and 11:10).
For לא with the imperfect for emphasis (note the emphatic repetition of יואב as the immediately preceding word), see GKC
§§107o, 109d and:

1 S 14:36		2 S 17:12		Josh 9:23(29)
4Q de		4Q de		
M ולא נשאר		M ולא נותר		M ולא יכרת
G και μη υπολειπωμεν		G και ουχ υπολειψομεθα		G ου μη εκλιπη

2 S 3:32   4Q   המלך קולו

            M   המלך את קולו

            G   ο βασιλευς την (om v) φωνην αυτου

OG would add την spontaneously, even if it were lacking in the
Vorlage, while KR would add it due to את.

2 S 3:34
4Q   ורגליך/ בנחש[תי]ם לא הג/ש
M T P   ורגליך לא לנחשתים   הגשו

G   οι ποδες σου ουκ εν πεδαις ου προσηγαγες (-γεν ΒΑ+)

L gʲ   ουδε (οι δε ο) οι ποδες σου εν πεδαις ου προσηγαγες

G is ambiguous, since ου can be "not" (= 4Q) or "when" (=
M?). According to the stichometric arrangement and the non-
aspirated form in B-M for ου προσηγαγες, 4Q = G ≠ M. A case
for the opposite, however, could also be made. Thus, perhaps
we should rest with: 4Q ≠ M (G ambiguous). Neither the context within this colon or the content of the contiguous cola
will help decide. Note that 4Q ≠ M = G for לא of M, while 4Q =
G ≠ M for (בנחשתים)בְ in this colon. The previous colon (cf. p.
135) indicates 4Q ≠ M = G, while the following colon (cf. p.
82) indicates 4Q = G ≠ M.

2 S 18:5   4Q   הֺעֹ[ם] שמעים

            M T   העם שמעו

            G   ο λαος ηκουσεν

G is singular, to avoid synesis, and could reflect either the
finite verb of M or the participle of 4Q (cf. p. 73 above).

2 S 20:11   4Q   ומי לד[ויד]

            M   ומי אשר לדד

            T   ומן דלדויד

            G   και τις του (τω L) Δαυειδ

2 S 22:48   *Ps 18(17):48*   4Q   נתן /[   ]

                             M   הנתן

                             G   ο διδους

                             L   ος εδωκεν

                             Ps^M   הנותן

                             Ps^G   ο διδους

C. The Pattern 4Q ≠ M G

There are approximately two dozen instances in the scroll
where M and G share a reading against 4Q; two dozen, that is,
in addition to the instances that appear in other sections of
this study. We may begin with two clear examples of 4Q's independence from the combined M G witness.

1 S 2:22   V.339 om

4Q   [ושמונה שנים] וׄעלי זׁקׁן מאד בן תשעים שנה

M   ועלי זקן מאד

G   Και Ηλει πρεσβυτης σφοδρα

For fuller discussion, cf. BASOR 22, and above, pp. 57-58.
At the death of Eli (1 S 4:15 = V.359), his age is noted as
ninety-eight (M G$_2$ L J; de 4Q), though G had ninety (possibly
by haplography, as Cross suggests). In this expansion at 2:22,
4Q ≠ M G J.

1 S 11:9-10   4Q   [וׄיׄהורה התשׁׄ[וׄעה]   ]   M G   תהיה לכם תשועה
                      ]   [לׄכם פתחו הׄ]   [
                      ]   וׄ[יׄאמרׄ[וׄ] אׄנׄשׄ[יׄ]   ויאמרו אנשי

The spacing of this fragment clearly suggests that one complete
line is present in 4Q which is not found in M G, etc. There is
no clue in any biblical ms to indicate what is here contained.
T is nearly identical with M; and P, though it has a slightly
longer text, does not have enough to amount to a full line, nor
does it contain anything resembling פתחו. Nor does J (VI.76)
mention anything about "opening," "entrances," etc. 4Q ≠ M G.

Having seen two clear examples of readings of 4Q against
the combined M G witness, we may review the remainder of such
readings in order.

1 S 1:11   4Q   ]   וׄ[מׄורה לא יעבור
                  M   ומורה לא יעלה
                  G   και σιδηρος ουκ αναβησεται

Cf. Judg 13:5:

                  M   ומורה לא יעלה
                  G   και σιδηρος ουκ αναβησεται (trp AMN+)

and Judg 16:17:

                  M   (מורה) לא עלה
                  G^B ουκ ανεβη (αναβησεται AGM[txt]++)

αναβαινειν should normally reflect עלה (over 400x: H-R
70-72). But it does reflect עבר 3x (Num 32:7 G^A; 2 K 8:21;
Amos 5:5 G^A). To use διαβαινειν, however, the normal

translation of עבר, to describe the movement of a razor vis-à-
vis the head might be to indulge in misplaced humor.

More importantly, the whole נזיר motif with its phraseology is influenced by the Samson story in Judg 13--16, where the
two parallel texts listed above are found. The source for G of
Samuel may possibly be G of Judg 13:5, rather than M or 4Q of
S. Notice that the source for G^{A++} (OG in Judg) at Judg 16:17
may well have been G of Judg 13:5, since the former quotes
αναβησεται of Judg 13:5 exactly even though the tense should
have been changed from future to aorist. G^{B} (KR in Judg) has
revised toward M.

Even though the texts stand as 4Q ≠ M G, this testimony is
weakened by the double possibility of (1) the unsuitability of
διαβαινειν and (2) the influence from G of Judg.

1 S 1:22

4Q contains a noticeably longer reading than that in M G;
cf. the discussion on pp. 165-166 below. The fact that Josephus knew this reading although it appears in no other extant
text demonstrates that his Vorlage definitely contained the
reading of 4Q. To the extent that it be demonstrated in chapter VIII and *passim* that J's primary Vorlage was OG/pL, this
reading does not prove that the OG was similar to M and different from 4Q, but rather that the received G of 1 S 1:22 is secondary -- revised from a longer OG/pL, similar to 4Q and used
by J, toward the shorter, "ascending" M tradition.

1 S 2:18	4Q	חורג
	M	חגור
	G	περιεζωσμενον

Cf. BASOR 22. A *lapsus calami* by the scribe of 4Q (cf. חגור in
4Q at 2 S 6:14), thus pointless.

1 S 2:21

4Q	[הוה י]לפני /[הנער] שמ ל[דגניו]
M	יהוה עם שמואל הנער וידגל
G	και εμεγαλυνθη το παιδαριον Σαμουηλ ενωπιον Κυριου

Cf. BASOR 22. Cross's reconstruction, [ראל]שמ וידגל would
be preferable if we had only the leather of the scroll. The

leather now breaks off in the middle of the *mem*; accordingly,
one would judge that הנער is an addition and 4Q, with שמואל
alone, would preserve the superior reading.

But an early photograph, taken before the leather had re-
ceded a millimeter or two at the margin, shows the clear top of
a final, not medial, *mem*. הנער (with M G) probably fills the
remaining space; certainly 4Q does not have space for הנער
שמואל. Thus 4Q ≠ M G for this reading. But note that within
this verse 4Q = G ≠ M 3x: ויפקד, ותלד עוד, and לפני יהוה (cf.
respectively, pp. 73, 50, and here).

1 S 2:25	4Q	[ל]קֹוֹל כיא
	M	לקול אביהם כי
	G	της φωνης του πατρος αυτων οτι (γαρ L)
	x	της φωνης αυτου οτι

4Q's halting text probably betrays a simple error of omission.

1 S 26:11	*VI.313*	4Q	[א]ת חנִיֹתֹוֹ
		M	את החנית
		G	το δορυ
		J	αυτου το δορυ

Literally, 4Q = J alone ≠ M G. But the mercurial character of
Josephan style weakens somewhat the significance for that for-
mula. On the other hand, one notices (see pp. 170-171) that
J's whole line from which this phrase is taken is copied from
G! Our final judgment for this reading thus is 4Q ≠ M G.

1 S 28:2	4Q	אכֹיֹ[ש] אֹל [דויד]
	M	אכיש אל דוד
	G	Αγχους προς Δαυειδ

The spacing in 4Q can be tightly controlled here, and there is
not room for both the א of אל and the subsequent space between
words. 4Q ≠ M G.

2 S 3:34	4Q	א]סורות ידיך לא] בזקים
	M T P	ידך לא אסרות
	G	αι χειρες σου ουκ εδεθησαν

In this plus, 4Q ≠ M G.

2 S 3:34   4Q   כל

                   M   כל העם

                   G   πας (om cx) ο λαος

The omission of העם is probably by simple inadvertence in
4QSam^a alone (cf. כל העם 5 words later in 4Q) and would have
been supplied by any other scribes of the 4Q tradition.

2 S 5:8   *1 C 11:6 om*   *VII.61-64 om*

4Q   שנאה

M   שנאו K; שנאי Q

T   רחיקת

P   סנא

G   (+και ΒΑ+) τους μισουντας

OL^b   omnes qui oderunt

    Cf. M note 5:8b, Driver, Notes. Only 4Q T P have David's
soul hating the blind and the lame; M^{K,Q} G OL reverse the
hatred. Notice that και τους (B+) is a logical extension of
the error caused by the hebraizing revision of G toward M.
Even more specifically, G follows M^Q in an error, while for the
superior variant of 4Q, 4Q ≠ M G.

2 S 6:13   *1 C 15:26*

4Q   שב[עה] פרי͘ם ושבע͘[ה אילים]

M   שור   ומריא

G   μοσχος και αρνα (for the multiple G variants, cf. B-M)

C^M   שבעה   פרים   ושבעה   אילים

C^G   (+αν Bc_2) επτα μοσχους και (+αν BS^Ic_2) επτα κριους

4Q is to be reconstructed after C; 4Q = C ≠ M G. For fuller
presentation and significance of this pattern, cf. pp. 152-160
below.

2 S 10:5 ˅ *1 C 19:5*   4Q   שבו יר͘ח͘ו

                                  M^SC   שבו בירחו

                                  G^SC   Καθισατε εν Ιερειχω

It is difficult to decide whether this variant should be classified here or in the preceding section as "4Q ≠ M where G is
ambiguous." For how else would G translate 4Q? At Num 36:13 G
translates ירחו with <u>κατα</u> Ιερειχω.

2 S 11:4   VII.130 om

4Q   מתקדשת   ותב̊[ורא]

M T   מתקדשת מטמאתה ותשב

G   αγιαζομενη απο ακαθαρσιας αυτης   και απεστρεψεν

L   ην λελουμενη εξ αφεδρου αυτης   και απηλθεν

OL^b   lota erat post purgationem   et intravit

OL^v   erat dismissa (abluta OL^v[2]) excelso loco

Cf. Notes. The emphasis in this reading is on מטמאתה, present in all texts save 4Q. But ותב̊[ורא] also merits attention on a smaller scale. This is the reading most plausible for 4Q--the lower horizontal bar of ב is nearly unmistakable. It is impossible to read ש as the third letter. απερχεσθαι = הלך normally, but = בוא in 1 S 25:5 and 2 S 3:24 (A; εισ- B); it never corresponds to שוב in S or K (though it does in other books). ותבוא is also supported by both OL^b and OL^h. For this word, 4Q = L OL ≠ M G. The OL readings further attest to L (λελουμενη) as OG: lota, abluta = λελου-; dismissa = λελυ-.

For the main reading (the מטמאתה minus), 4Q ≠ M G.

2 S 11:16   VII.136-7~

4Q   [ו]י[הי בשור̊[ו]י[הי בשור̊

M   ויהי בשמור יואב אל העיר

T   והוה כד צר יואב על קרתא

P   וכד שרא יואב על קריתא

G   και εγενηθη εν τω φυλασσειν Ιωαβ επι την πολιν

L ǵ^j(vid) και εγενετο εν τω περικαθησθαι τον Ιωαβ επι την πολιν

OL^b   cum obsidit Ioab civitatem

4Q cannot be reconstructed with any certainty. The final letter could be מ as well as ר. But all traditions go against M's אל, and all traditions except G are allied against בשמור as well (and for the שמר...אל connection, see 1 S 26:15). Note that T L OL P ǵ^j(vid) all have some form of "encamping against" or "besieging," as opposed to M's *lectio facilior* followed by G. περικαθησθαι = צור the only three times it is used with Hb correspondent: Judg 9:31, 1 K 15:27, and 2 K 6:25. φυλασσειν, however, occurs over 60x in S K, always reflecting שמר, with only three exceptions. In 1 K 11:38 (תשמע את כל אשר אצוך) it reflects שמע, followed later in the same verse by לשמור חקותי, also translated by φυλασσειν! And in 2 K 17:9 and 18:8 it reflects נצר!

Just as M is probably an error, so should 4Q probably be understood as an error for בצור (cf. T L OL 𝔖ʲ) or בשרות (cf. P).

2 S 12:14	4Q	אֵ֯ת דְּבר יהוה
	M	את איבי יהוה
	T	דסנאי עמא דיוי
	G α'σ'ο'	τους εχθρους κυριου
	L	εν τοις υπεναντιοις/τον Κυριον (trp o)
	ϑ' MN	τοις εναντιοις Κυριου
	c	τω Κυριω
	OLᵛ	contrarios Domini
	∅	verbum Domini

All texts here (except c) are euphemistic. Only ∅ agrees with 4Q for this variant, while 4Q ≠ M G.

2 S 12:15	VII.154
4Q	לדויד
M T P	לדוד ויאנש
G	τω Δαυειδ και ηρρωστησεν (-ωστει L)
J	νοσον...χαλεπην

This is a simple haplography in 4Q (ריאנש ויבקש). 4Q ≠ M G J.

2 S 12:16	4Q	ויבק[ש/ דוי]ד֯ מן האלוהים
	M	ויבקש דוד את האלהים
	T	ובעא דויד רחמין מן קדם יוי
	P	ובעא דויד מן אלהא
	G	και εζητησεν Δαυειδ τον θεον
	L	και ηξιου Δαυειδ τον θεον (K͞ν̄ b+)

T P agree with 4Q against M for מן. G at first appears to reflect M, but this is possibly a question of Gk style only. Cf. Dan 1:8:

| M | ויבקש משר הסריסים |
| LXX ϑ' | και ηξιωσε τον αρχιευνουχον |

Thus, supported by T P in this variant, 4Q ≠ M G (or 4Q ≠ M, while G is ambiguous).

2 S 13:32   4Q   ‏[את כול] הֹנֹעֹדים כול בני‏

M   ‏את כל הנערים בני‏

G   παντα τα παιδαρια   τους υιους

L   παντα τα παιδαρια   οι υιοι

This is possibly a doublet in all traditions. 4Q alone has repeated ‏כול‏ as well here. Note ‏כל בני המלך‏ in all traditions in
the similar sentence of the next verse. For the plus, 4Q ≠ M G.

2 S 15:2   VII.195   4Q   ‏על יד הדרך‏

M   ‏על יד דרך השער‏

T   ‏על כיבש אורח תרעא‏

P   ‏תרעא דמלכא   על גב‏

G   ανα χειρα της οδου της πυλης

L   επι   της οδου της πυλης

OL[S]   ante portam in via

J   προς τα βασιλεια

Roughly, the text traditions align themselves so:

4Q   ‏על יד הדרך‏

M T G   ‏על יד דרך השער‏

L OL   ‏על   דרך השער‏

P (J?)   ‏על יד   שער המלך‏

For the minus, 4Q ≠ M G.

2 S 18:10   VII.240~   4Q P   ‏איש ויגד‏

M T   ‏איש אחד ויגד‏

G   ανηρ εις (om a₂) και ανηγγειλεν

J   τουτο τις ιδων...εδηλωσεν

The exact literal equivalence of G to M, including ανηρ
(instead of τις) for ‏איש‏ (cf. DA, pp. 48-54, esp. p. 54, note
2) classify G as KR, which in this passage has influenced the
entire later tradition, including L.

Since this is a case of Hb and biblical Gk style and
translation, the testimony of J unfortunately cannot help us.
He would render τις (or an equivalent) regardless of the presence or absence of ‏אחד‏/εις in his Vorlage. For the minus, 4Q ≠
M G.

2 S 22:36   Ps 18(17):36

4Q	ועזרתך תרבני
M	וע[נתך תרבני

G   και υπακοη σου επληθυνεν με

L   και ταπεινωσεις επληθυναν μοι

και η δεξια σου αντελαβετο μου

και η παιδια σου ανωρθωσε με

Ps^M רימינך תסעדני ועניתך תרבני

Ps^G και η δεξια σου αντελαβετο μου

και η παιδεια σου ανωρθωσεν με εις τελος

και η παιδεια σου αυτη με διδαξει (εις--διδαξει om G^ℵ)

Cf. M note; Notes; NAB; *SAYP*, pp. 269 and 310 nn. 82, 83. The first element of the repetitive parallelism, ימינך(ו), תסעדני, was probably in the Hb text of S and Ps originally, then lost from S through haplography.

The Vorlage of (OG)/pL still had the reading which was translated και η δεξια -- ανωρθωσε με. L does not simply borrow this from Ps^G; rather, both L and Ps^G (cf. Ps$^{G ℵ}$) had this translation. L$_2$ prefixes to the early translation the revisional approximation toward M (και ταπεινωσεις...; for this procedure, see below, pp. 197-201), while Ps^G adds the doublet και η παιδεια σου αυτη με διδαξει and gathers the gloss εις τελος.

ימינך(ו) תסעדני was lost by haplography in the Hb of S, and the וענתך/ועזרתך variants developed, possibly through loss of understanding of the original word (cf. *SAYP*, p. 310 n. 83, and NAB).

At the level of Hb-Gk equivalents, all Gk witnesses indicate ועניתך. Though υπακοη = LXX *hapax leg.*, υπακοειν = ענה 14x, including 22:42 (= עזר never). Also, ταπεινωσις = ענה regularly (= עזר never). παιδ(ε)ια = מוסר regularly, = ענוה only here.

For the texts as they now stand, 4Q ≠ M G$_2$ ≠ L Ps^G ≠ Ps^M.

D.   The Pattern 4Q = M ≠ G

Finally, there is a series of readings in which 4Q aligns itself with M in opposition to G, showing the distinctiveness of the G tradition from the 4Q tradition.

1 S 1:12   *V.345*   4Q   ‏ו ע[ל י שמֹר‏]

M   ‏ו ע ל י שמר‏

G   Ηλει ο ιερευς εφυλαξεν

J   Ηλεις ο αρχιερευς

This expansionist gloss in G is another example of the phenomenon discussed on pp. 126-128 above.   4Q = M ≠ G J.

1 S 8:18ᶠⁱⁿ   *VI.42*

4Q   vac   ‏הֹהֹם‏

M   ‏ההוא‏:

G   εκειναις οτι υμεις εξελεξασθε εαυτοις βασιλεα

J   εασει δικην υποσχειν υμας της αυτων κακοβουλιας

G adds a clause explaining why God will not listen when
the people cry out against their king's oppression.   J's more
general "punishment because of your own bad counsel" (similarly
concluding Samuel's warning speech) undoubtedly reflects the G
plus.   4Q = M ≠ G J.

1 S 10:12   4Q   ‏אביהם‏

M   ‏אביהם‏

T   ‏רבונהון) רבֹון‏ (dw)

P   ‏אבוהי‏

G L OL   πατερ αυτου (+ου Κεις AN++ ⱦ OL)

In the narrative's final stage, G's singular suffix (= Saul) is
superior; thus, an *ad sensum* correction in G, deviating from
its Vorlage?

1 S 10:26   *VI.67~*

4Q   vac   ‏בלבבם הֹ[ו]ה יהֹ נגע א[שר]החיל בני[עמו‏ /‏וילכו]‏

M   ‏בלבם אלהים נגע אשר‏   ‏החיל עמו‏   ‏וילכו‏:

G OLᵇᵛ   και επορευθησαν υιοι δυναμεων ων ηψατο Κυριος
καρδιας αυτων μετα Σαουλ (om αυτων--Σαουλ OL)

J   Σαουλω δε απερχομενω...συνηρχοντο πολλοι μεν αγαθοι

It is difficult to determine 4Q's reading prior to ‏בני‏.
There is room for one short word at the beginning of this line,
and the end of the preceding line has a ±4 word lacuna.   M G J
all contain some word for "with," only OLᵇᵛ lack it.   Since 4Q
(= M) lacks G's ‏עם שאול‏* at the end of the verse, it is best to
presume that ‏עמו‏ is the first word of 4Q's line, M possibly

having lost בני by haplography due to homoioteleuton (the ligatured final *yod* of בני resembles *waw*, and the ligatured final
waw of עמו resembles *yod*). J is too paraphrastic to be deci-
sive here.   4Q = M ≠ G.   Note, however, that 4Q = G ≠ M for בני
and יהוה.

1 S 15:29   VI.153

4Q	[ה]וֹא לֹהֹ[נחם]
M	הוא להנחם
Bacx+	εστιν του μετανοησαι αυτος.
L Thdt	εστιν του μετανοησαι.
N++	εστιν του μετανοησαι αυτος (om Nav) απειλησει και
	ουκ εμμενει
J	εμμενειν γαρ τον θεον..., ανθρωπινου παθους οντος
	ουχι θειας ισχυος

The Hb tradition is sound. OG had the expansion, as in
N++. Word order shows that, as often, εστιν = הוא; αυτος obviously refers to ανθρωπος and is the subject of the two following verbs ("For not like man is He, to change His mind; *he* [=
man] makes threats and does not abide [by them]"). The αυτος
in BAcx+ is thus the truncated remains of an erstwhile plus;
one would not simply add αυτος alone here, and it is not coincidental that αυτος is the subject of the addition inserted
precisely here! J read the plus and incorporated it (εμμενειν
and the whole positive clause about human inconstancy), thus
confirming its age.

The plus was later excised in revision toward M--but the
cut was not clean, BAcx+ carelessly retaining αυτος (erroneously for הוא). The late Lucianic edition did the final, clean
surgery, yielding a text carefully revised back to M. (Note
the marginal censure in j^mg against the L₂ addition "ο αγιος
του Iηλ" earlier in the verse: το ο αγιος του Iηλ παρ ουδενι
κειται εν τω εξαπλω.) In omitting the G plus, 4Q = M L (G^h) ≠
OG J.

1 S 15:30

4Q	[נ]גֹד זקני עמֹ[י ונגד יש]רֹאל שו[ב]
M	נגד זקני עמי ונגד ישראל ושוב
BN+	ενωπιον πρεσβυτερων Ισραηλ και ενωπιον λαου μου και αναστρεψον
LAcx+	ενωπιον πρεσβυτερων του λαου μου και ενωπιον του Ισραηλ και αν.

This is either an erroneous transposition in OG (= BN+) or a tendentious change placing "Israel" before "Saul's people." Whichever, pL then corrected toward 4Q, or G^h corrected toward M. 4Q = M $G^{h,L}$ ≠ OG.

1 S 24:18	4Q		ויאמר אל
	M		ויאמר אל
	G		και ειπεν Σαουλ προς
	L Thdt ∅		και ειπεν προς

1 S 25:5	*VI.297˜*	4Q	[ים]ויאמר דּוִֹד אל הנער[ים]
		M	ויאמר דוד לנערים
		G	και ειπεν τοις παιδαριοις
		A	και ειπεν Δαδ τοις παιδαριοις
		L	και ειπεν προς τα παιδαρια
		cx	και ειπεν αυτοις

Note that for אל 4Q = L ≠ M G^{BAN++}. But this is weakened by the presence of the explanatory gloss דויד, for which 4Q = M A ≠ G.

1 S 26:12	4Q	[ ] כִֹי מקי[ץ]
	M	מקיץ כי
	G	ο εξεγειρομενος

Against this plus (כי) in the Hb tradition, G maintains a superior, short reading. 4Q = M ≠ G.

2 S 3:1	*VII.20˜*	4Q	ודויד
		M P	ודוד
		T	ובית דוד (ודוד) a,d)
		G	και ο οικος Δαυειδ
		o OL^m	και Δαυειδ
		J	των μεν μετα Δαυιδου

Cf. Well. It is impossible to say which was original. The parallel would seem to require ובית דויד; but David himself was becoming greater, whereas, since Saul was now dead, the parallel (or opponent) to David was *de facto* the house, or party, of Saul. 4Q = M o OL ≠ G.

2 S 3:24   4Q   [   ] זֹה למה

                  M   למה זה

                  G   και ινα τι (+ τουτο L)

G is probably OG freely translating a Vorlage exactly like 4Q
M, whose זה is superfluous. L adds τουτο (-ον e$_2$) for literal
fidelity.

2 S 3:28   *VII.39*

4Q   מעם יהוה עד עולם

M T P   מעם יהוה עד עולם

Bya$_2$Acx+   απο Κυριου και (om cx; απο νυν g) εως αιωνος

M++ ℊ^j απο Κυριου απο νυν και εως αιωνος

LN+ Thdt   απο Κυριου (om απο K. io*) απο του νυν και εως του αιωνος

OL^s amodo et usque in aeternum

    Cf. Driver. The variation in G could derive from a double
tradition or confusion in the Hb (מעם/מעתה יהוה), or from an *ad
sensum* Gk addition (απο Κυριου <u>και</u> εως αιωνος would tempt a
scribe to insert απο νυν before και, for και should not be
there unless it followed another time expression, as in 1 C
16:36, for example).

    OL suggests that the double Hb tradition underlay our vari-
ants. 4Q and M, followed by Bya$_2$Acx+, read מעם יהוה. The Vorlage of OL (cf. io*) read απο νυν (= מעתה), shared by LMN ℊ^j.
The OG Vorlage should thus be reconstructed as מעתה*; OG read
απο νυν (cf. LMN++ ℊ^j OL); subsequent corrections toward Hb
texts (starting either with pL or with οι γ′ or o′) produced
the conflation (LMN) and the anomalous απο Κυριου και... (BA++).
    4Q = M G^{BA} ≠ OG^V LMN++ OL.

2 S 3:34   4Q   [ו]יספר

                  M   ויספר

                  BA+   και συνηχθη (-θησαν cx)

                  L   και συνηλθεν

                  MN++   και προσεθετο

4Q and M are defectively written (1. ויאספו). BA+ are trans-
lating אסף, L is probably a variation from BA+ (X > Λ), and
MN++ are "corrected" back to the mistaken יסף of 4Q M. 4Q + M
≠ G.

2 S 4:2   VII.47~

4Q	[ן] תחש[ל]עלבנימי[תחשב]
M	(תחשב) על בנימן
T	על דבית בנימין
G	τοις υιοις Βενιαμειν
J	το μεν γενος Βενιαμιται

4Q has no space between ל and בנימין, suggesting that -ל and
not על be read. But just as the fragment begins, there can be
seen a trace of ink which could be either the tail of the base
line of ב or the tail of ע. If the former, 4Q = G ≠ M; if the
latter, 4Q = M ≠ G. In either case, 4Q = M ≠ G in omitting בני
(cf. the opposite phenomenon on p. 54).

2 S 4:12   4Q   הן]נَّעֹרים]
             M T   הנערים
             G   τοις παιδαριοις αυτου

2 S 11:4   4Q   ותבוא אליו
             M   ותבוא אליו
             G   και εισηλθεν προς αυτην (-ον s*^vid)
             cx   και   ηλθε   προς αυτον

Cf. 12:24: G possibly preserves the original text here.   4Q =
M cx ≠ G.

2 S 19:8(7)   VII.256~

4Q	ורע]ה לך זאת[
M T P	ורעה לך זאת
G	και επιγνωθι σεαυτω και (οτι MN++) κακον σοι τουτο
L	και επιγνωθι τουτο σεαυτω οτι χειρον σοι εσται τουτο
J	πικροτερον

Cf. DA, pp. 121-122. Barthélemy considers και επιγνωθι
τουτο σεαυτω to be the (erroneous: = ורד) OG, και κακον σοι
τουτο to be the KR correction, and οτι χειρον... to be the L
form of KR.

I would agree that και επιγνωθι τουτο σεαυτω is the OG and
that και κακον σοι τουτο and οτι χειρον σοι εσται τουτο are
hebraizing revisions. But there is no compelling reason to
allege specifically KR revision here. This looks rather like
the early type of hebraizing revision which is responsible for
the many G doublets in the non-KR as well as the KR sections of

1-2 Rgn. In confirmation, J (who nowhere else shows influence
specifically from KR) includes the revisional addition. He
would have the comparative, no matter what his Vorlage had; it
is impossible to determine whether his Vorlage included ἐπιγ-
νωθι.

In sum, 4Q = M ≠ G, where G errs from the common 4Q M tradition.

2 S 22:36	*Ps 18(17):36*	4Q	ישעך
		M	ישעך
		G	σωτηριας μου (om Nv)
		Ps^M	ישעך
		Ps^G	σωτηριας μου

The common Hb tradition is to be preferred here.   4Q = M^{S,Ps} ≠
G^{S,Ps}.

E. Conclusion

In this chapter we have presented the evidence that is or
appears to be contrary to our main hypothesis, that the Old
Greek translation was made from a Hebrew Vorlage much closer to
4QSam^a than to M, and that a branch of the early Greek tradition shows some revision of OG toward the 4Q tradition. What
is the amount and strength of the evidence that distinguishes
the 4Q tradition from the G tradition?

In chapter III we isolated 35 instances of 4Q = (OG)/pL
agreement which can be added to the 144 instances of 4Q = OG/
(pL) agreement marshalled in chapter II, for a total of 179
readings in which 4Q agrees with the pre-KR form of the Greek
Version.

In part A of this chapter, four readings are presented in
which 4Q = M + G. Though this formula at first suggests 4Q
conflation, in none of the four cases can we be confident of
actual conflation. In 1 S 2:8-9, 4Q probably preserves a
fuller text which has been shortened by haplography in M and in
G and rearranged by displacement of stichoi. In 1 S 1:28, conflation is possible, but double haplography is perhaps more
likely. In 1 S 2:2, however, haplography is less likely; the
4Q tradition probably developed a simple צור/צדיק variant and
expanded it. Finally, 2 S 4:12 is a simple 4Q explanatory

gloss (rather than a real conflation) and was mirrored in the
pL revision.

These 4 readings do distinguish the 4Q tradition from the
G tradition. But, if we ask what the source of the shorter G
readings is, the answer is: the same text tradition as 4Q, as
opposed to M. Furthermore, two of the readings show pL in
sharper agreement with 4Q, further distinguishing the partial
OG and fuller pL dependence on the 4Q tradition. Thus, these 4
readings in G show dependence upon the 4Q tradition as opposed
to M, raising the total to 183.

In part B are listed 5 composite and 7 simple readings
which illustrate the independence of the three traditions. The
corrective value of these readings teaches us that OG is not
directly translated from the 4QSam^a tradition and that pL is
not directly based on the examplar 4QSam^a. The comparatively
small number of readings as well as the content of many of the
readings suggest that the divergences stem from original independence of OG^V (the Egyptian Hebrew text tradition) from the
Palestinian tradition plus independent reworking of the texts
subsequent to their mutual contact.

Fifteen additional readings were discussed in part B: one
M conflation, five G conflations, and nine 4Q/M discrepancies
where G is ambiguous. The M conflation of 4Q + G demonstrates
4Q/G disagreement and is therefore strong evidence. The G conflations of 4Q + M demonstrate 4Q G agreement and are therefore
not contrary evidence. The ambiguity of G in the final nine
readings prevents us from forming a judgment on them. Part B,
accordingly, isolates 13 readings contrary to the pattern 4Q =
G ≠ M.

Part C considers 23 readings in which G agrees with M
rather than with 4Q. After assessment of their significance,
6 emerge as truly contrary evidence, and 17 do not really speak
to our problem.

4Q exhibits five pluses (1 S 1:22; 2 S 3:34; 13:32;
and strikingly, 1 S 2:22 and 11:9-10) shared by no other biblical ms.

4Q displays one minor variant (1 S 26:11) shared by no
other biblical ms. J agrees with 4Q in this reading (and in 1
S 1:22 just above). In both cases J = 4Q alone. Three other

J = 4Q alone readings are discussed on pp. 165-172, and for 3
of the 5 (including the present reading), J shows dependence on
a Greek medium.

4Q makes one simple slip (1 S 2:8) and 3 simple omis-
sions (1 S 2:25; 2 S 3:34; 12:15) which would not be reflected
in any other Hb or Gk text dependent upon it.

4Q makes another probable error (2 S 11:16) where M
also errs in another way; G (in the KR section) agrees with M,
while L OL T P 𝔤ʲ appear to support the fundamental reading of
the 4Q tradition.

Three further readings (2 S 12:14; 15:2; 18:10) occur
in the KR section which seem to be part of the later revisional
stratum.

G is ambiguous in 3 readings (1 S 1:11; 2 S 10:5; 12:10).
None of the above readings constitute truly contrary evidence but either are peculiarities of 4Q specifically (just as
4Q M and G each showed minor peculiarities in part B) or are
useless from the G side, due to KR revision or to ambiguity.

G does, however, agree with M against 4Q in 6 readings.

One variant reading (2 S 6:13) 4Q shares with C, while
J repeats exactly the OG OL reading. This is solid and strong
contrary evidence (just as the J OG agreement is solid and
strong evidence for the second part of our hypothesis).

4Q contains a superior reading (2 S 5:8) and G follows
M in the inferior reading.

The following seem to be genuine agreements of G with M
against 4Q: 1 S 2:21; 28:2; 2 S 11:4; 22:36. But 1 S 2:21 includes a word in which 4Q = G ≠ M; 1 S 28:2 is a minor variant;
and 2 S 11:4 and 22:36 occur within the *kaige* section, though
probably not in the revisional stratum of KR.

Part C thus isolates 6 readings (two of which are strong
examples) contrary to the pattern 4Q = G ≠ M.

Part D presents 18 readings in which 4Q = M ≠ G.

G includes 8 expansionist glosses: 1 S 1:12; 8:18; 10:26;
15:29; 24:18; 2 S 3:1; 4:2; 4:12. (In three of these J is
ambiguous, in none does he disagree with G, and in four he follows the plus displayed by G only.)

G errs twice: 1 S 15:30; 2 S 22:36.

G corrects the common Hb: 1 S 10:12; 2 S 3:34.

The G translation once (2 S 3:24) presupposes a Vorlage identical with 4Q and M.

G contains a doublet (see below), one element of which agrees with 4Q M.

None of these readings really runs contrary to our hypothesis, viz., that the Vorlage of G was closely related to 4Q. But 5 further readings do marshal truly contrary evidence:

G presents a doublet (2 S 19:8), one element of which presupposes a variant Hb Vorlage (or a misreading of its Vorlage).

The G translation at one point (2 S 3:28) presupposes a Vorlage at variance with 4Q M.

G once (2 S 11:4) presents a superior variant.

Finally, G preserves the original reading twice (1 S 25:5 and 26:12) where the common Hb tradition includes expansionist glosses.

These last 5 readings do highlight readings in the G text which presuppose a Hb Vorlage different from the 4Q tradition.

Thus, from the several categories of contrary evidence collected in this chapter, OG/pL appears independent of the 4Q tradition in 24 readings. This contrasts with the 183 readings in which 4Q = OG/pL $\neq$ M, yielding a ratio of roughly 7.6 to 1. The Hebrew text tradition which provided the Vorlage in Egypt for the pristine Greek translation of 1-2 Samuel is distinct from the Palestinian Hebrew text tradition. That divergence, however, is quite small when compared with either the 4Q or the OG divergence from the M tradition.

Chapter V

THE AGREEMENT OF 4QSam[a] WITH CHRONICLES

Due to the interrelatedness of the several goals of this
study, much of the material which properly lies within the
boundaries of 4QSam[a]-Chronicles investigation is treated in
other chapters. That material will not be repeated here but
will be summarized in classified lists, and only the significant 4Q-C material which is not discussed in other chapters
will be analyzed in detail here.

A. Systematic Comparison Through 2 S 6

First, for a comprehensive comparison of 4Q, M for Samuel,
and Chronicles through a continuous chapter, see pp. 193-221
which analyze 2 S 6 // 1 C 13:1--14; 15:25--16:3. The results of
that analysis which illumine the 4Q-C relationship can be summarized here.

The Hb texts of 4Q, M, and C were compared for those parts
of 2 S 6 in which 4Q was both extant and at variance with
either M or C. 4Q emerged as the best of the Hb texts, followed closely by C and distantly by M. 4Q agreed with M against
C in 11 readings, all supported by G. This pattern, of course,
was to be expected. The significant pattern appeared when 4Q
agreed with C against M in 13 readings. Possible 4Q dependence
on C for these readings was ruled out when it was seen that (1)
4Q was independent of both M and C in 8 further readings (4Q ≠
M ≠ C); (2) G (OL) continued in the main to ally itself with 4Q
(4Q = G C ≠ M), thus grounding the readings as old S readings,
incorporated like much else of S-K into C; and (3) indications
from G, M, and C pointed in favor of C dependence on the 4Q
tradition in 10 (or possibly 12) of the 13 readings. Only one
reading proved ambiguous or possibly contrary. There was no
clear evidence indicating 4Q dependence on C.

This means that, in addition to the genuine, old Samuel
material preserved by the congruence of 4Q M G (OL), other
genuine, old Samuel material can at times be discovered by the
combined testimony of 4Q G (OL) C, whether M agrees or disagrees.

That combined testimony becomes yet more weighty if supported
by Josephus, who is tabulated (cf. p. 216) as demonstrating an
astounding 92% agreement with the extant portions of 4Q for 2
S 6 (and 96% with the hypothetical Gk form of 4Q). The group
4Q G OL C J, in contrast to M, is referred to as the "Palestinian" text of Samuel.

B.   The Pattern 4Q = C ≠ M G

Secondly, we may begin to analyze readings in which 4Q
agrees with C against the M tradition, where G follows M.

1.   Plus

2 S 10:6-7   1 C 19:6-8   VII.121

4Q

]   בני עמון] אלף כֹּבֹר כסףֿ

]   [לשכור להם מן ארם נהרים ומן ארם מ[עֹלֹֿה]   ומצובֹה[ֿ רכב ופרשיט

]   ? שנים שלורשׁ[ם אֹלף רכֹב]ואת מלך מעכה וא[יֹשׁטוב

]   ֹהֹ[ובני] עמורֹן נֹאֹספו מן ה[עֹדים

[רישֿמע דויד ויש[לֹֹֿח]אֹ[תֹ] יראֹ[ֹב

M T P   וישלחו בני עמון

וישכרו את ארם בית רחוב ואת ארם   צובא

עשרים אלף רגלי   ואת מלך מעכה אלף איש ואיש טוב

שנים עשר אלף איש

[7]וישמע דוד וישלח   את יואב

C^MG   וישלח חנון ובני עמון אלף ככר כסף

לשכר להם מן ארם נהרים ומן ארם מעכה   ומצובה רכב ופרשים

[7]וישכרו להם   שנים ושלשים אלף רכב ואת מלך מעכה ואת עמו ויבאו

ויחנו לפני מידבא   ובני עמון נאספו מעריהם   ויבאו למלחמה

[8]וישמע דויד וישלח   את יואב

G   και απεστειλαν οι υιοι Αμμων και εμισθωσαντο την Συριαν
         και Ροωβ και την Συριαν Σουβα (om και 4°–Σουβα B+ ⅍ℤ)
         εικοσι χιλιαδας πεζων και τον βασιλεα Αμαληκ (Μααχα[ν] AMN+)
         χιλιους ανδρας και Ειστωβ δωδεκα χιλιαδας ανδρων.
         [7]και ηκουσεν Δαυειδ και απεστειλεν τον Ιωαβ

L   και αποστελλουσιν οι υιοι Αμμων και μισθουνται τον Συρον
         και Βαιθρααμ και τον Συρον Σουβα (και την Συριαν Σουβα sub ⁛ c₂)
         εικοσι χιλιαδας πεζων και τον βασιλεα Μααχα
         χιλιους ανδρας και τον Ειστωβ δωδεκα χιλιαδας ανδρων.
         [7]και ηκουσεν Δαυειδ και απεστειλεν τον Ιωαβ

J   και πεμψαντες προς Συρον τον των Μεσοποταμιτων βασιλεα

       χιλια ταλαντα συμμαχον αυτον επι τουτω γενεσθαι τω μισθω

       παρεκαλεσαν και Σουβαν· ησαν δε τοις βασιλευσι τουτοις

       πεζου δυο μυριαδες. προσεμισθωσαντο δε

       και τον εκ της Μιχας καλουμενης χωρας βασιλεα

       και τεταρτον Ιστοβον ονομα, και τουτους εχοντας

       μυριους και δισχιλιους οπλιτας. [122]Ου κατεπλαγη δε

       την συμμαχιαν και την των Αμμανιτων δυναμιν ο Δαυιδης

   Cf. 2 S 8:3-6 // 1 C 18:3-6 = VII.99-100; Ps 60(59):2;
also Well., Driver, Notes, and above, p. 56. Two separate fragments contribute to the 4Q reconstruction above. The first,
exhibiting both top and left margins, comprises the ends of the
first four lines. The second is a medial section in lines two
to five. The precise spatial relation of the second fragment
to the first is not certain, but it can hardly be far from the
position given above. The many lines extant at the bottom of
this column range approximately from 54 to 60.

   The present text appears to have been a glossators' carni-
val, influenced by the parallel sources noted above. A full
reconstruction is beyond our present purpose, which is to chart
4Q's relation to M and C, and to show whatever dependence J may
demonstrate. The C relationship can be seen more strikingly
from the following list of the words that appear on the 4Q
leather:

M G L	4Q	C^M	C^G	J
--	אלף	אלף	χιλια	χιλια
--	ככר	ככר	ταλαντα	ταλαντα
--	כסף	כסף	αργυριου	--
*--	[מ]עֹכה	מעכה	Μοοχα	--*
--	רכב	רכב	αρματα	--
--	ופרשים	ופרשים	και ιππεις	--
20,000	[ו]שנים	שנים	32,000	20,000
πεζων/רגלי	ושלושי[ם]	רשלשים		πεζου
+1,000	אלף	אלף		--
ανδρας/איש	רכב	רכב	αρματων	--
+12,000	--	--		12,000
ανδρων/איש	--	--		οπλιτας
ראיש טוב Ειστωβ	[וא]יש[ˢ]טוב	--	--	Ιστοβον
--	[ובני]	רבני	και οι υιοι	την των Αμμανιτων
--	עמון	עמון	Αμμων	δυναμιν
--	נאספר	נאספר	συνηχθησαν	την συμμαχιαν
--	מן		εκ των	--
--	ה[ערים]	מעריהם	πολεων αυτων	--

(*M has מעכה and J has Μιχας later in the verse where all traditions include it. Apparently, only 4Q and C^{MG} have it at
this point.)

The strikingly close relation of C to 4Q is obvious here.
From this specific text in isolation it cannot be proved either
that 4Q is a conflation of M and C or that C is dependent on
4Q. To answer that question it is necessary to examine the
consistent, general patterns of 4Q vis-à-vis M and G.

What this specific text does demonstrate is that, during
the first century before and the first century of the Christian
era, texts of Samuel were extant which at points were much
closer to our present C than to our present M.

As we examine the Greek text of Samuel, we notice that it
falls within the area considered by Shenkel to have undergone
KR revision, and we notice that it clings very closely to M.
We do find in G an error not made in M: Ειστωβ vs. איש טוב
("the men of Tob"). G, however, is not responsible for the
error but is merely faithfully following its Hb Vorlage, as 4Q
witnesses. We have noted other errors in 4Q followed by G (cf.

pp. 42-45, 70-71ter, 76, 82f.).

M, on the other hand, errs with the immediately preceding
איש אלף (ואיש טוב). איש may be dittographic (cf. שם שם in 2 S
6:2, discussed on pp. 194, 197), and אלף may be inserted from
several possible marginal glosses (שנים עשר אלף איש [אלף איש, אלף רכב
אלף ככר כסף, etc.). For this error, however, G omn depend on M.

An attempt to solve this anomaly according to the hypothesis of recensional development would run thus: אישטוב (= 4Q)
was in the Hb Vorlage, the OG/pL rendered Ειστωβ, KR took over
this error from its OG basis because it was not a clear *corri-
gendum* relative to the proto-M ms; אלף איש, however, was glar-
ing in proto-M and thus was rendered χιλιους ανδρας.

Suspicions might arise that this reasoning is wantonly
speculative and that the process could as easily have happened
in just the opposite way. But the suspicions may be assuaged
as we shift our gaze to Josephus. J's Vorlage, dating approximately from the turn of the era, seems throughout to show agreement with OG/pL, unaffected by KR. If our hypothesis above is
correct, his witness should include Ειστωβ and not χιλιους
ανδρας -- and this is precisely what we find. J includes Ιστοβον (as a person) and his total (20,000 + 12,000) explicitly
rules out the "1000 men" of M G^{KR} L$_2$. J thus follows G in one
error dependent ultimately on the 4Q tradition, and he (with
OG/pL) does not commit the subsequent error for which G^{KR} L$_2$
depend on M.

Furthermore, J makes a parallel error, treating Σουρον as
a person, the king of the Mesopotamians. The Gk masc. Σουρος/ν
must have been in his Vorlage (cf. L). It is inconceivable
that he would mistake ארם for a person and then name him Σουρος!
Thus, that Vorlage was in Greek and contained Σουρος/ν. It
could not have been M or G^{KR}, for neither have נהרים/Μεσοποταμια.
And it is no longer easy to be persuaded toward C by Rahlfs'
argument (*Lucians*, p. 87): "for only C speaks of Μεσοποταμια
and names the land, as Josephus does, in the first place, and
only C mentions the price of 1000 talents, whereas in S it
merely says that they had bought the help of the Syrians." For
the text of 4Q demonstrates that "1000 talents" was definitely
in one texttype of the Samuel narrative a century before J
wrote, and precisely in that texttype upon which J depends for

a nearby error (Ιστοβον). As a corollary, one may plausibly
posit that ארם נהרים as well was in the 4Q tradition.

In addition to Ιστοβον, J also agrees with S against C for
his expression of the totals: 20,000 + 12,000 as opposed to
32,000 (omitting the erroneous, extra, late "1000 men" of M G^{KR}
L$_2$).

Finally, J mentions four persons hired by the Ammonites:
Syros for 1000 talents, Suba, the King of Micha, and Istobos;
the first two command 20,000 infantry and the latter two 12,000
armed men. As we attempt to ascertain J's overall Vorlage we
may array his details and the possibility of his deriving those
details from the individual texts we have extant:

J	M	G	L	4Q	C^M	C^G
Συρον	/	/	=	/	/	/
τον των Μεσοπ. βασ.	/	/	/	[=]	=	=
χιλια ταλαντα	/	/	/	=	=	=
και Σουβαν	=	=	=	[=]	=	=
πεζου 20,000	=	=(?)	=	?	/	/
τον...Μιχας...βασ.	=	=	=	=	=	=
και Ιστοβον	/	=	=	=	/	/
12,000 οπλιτας	=	=	=	?	/	/

(See p. 207f. for explanation of the sigla.)

For Συρον we have seen that a Greek Vorlage was necessary.
χιλια ταλαντα definitely and Μεσοποταμιτων probably could have
been derived from the 4Q tradition of S or from the C tradition.
Since it is possible that the 20,000 infantry and the 12,000
armed men could be found in the 4Q lacunae in addition to the
32,000 (?) רכב, J's totals could be derived definitely from M G
L or possibly from 4Q. Istobos must be derived from the 4Q G
L tradition (not M or C).

The clues afforded by J point most closely and economi-
cally to a Greek form of 4Q and/or to L.

2 S 24:16^{fin} 1 C 21:15-16   VII.327

4Q   ומלאך י[הוה עומד ע]ום גרן א[ר]נא ה[ניב]ו[ס]י ו[ש]א ו[דויד]   ]

[את עיניו... בין[הארץ ובין [הש]מ[וי]ם ו[ח]ר[ב]ו[שלופה בידו [נטויה]

[על ירושלים...   והזקנים על פנ[יהם מכ]וסים ב[ש]קים ולאמר דויד אל יהוה

M T P   ומלאך יהוה היה עם גרן האורנה היבסי:

ויאמר דוד אל יהוה

G   και ο αγγελος Κ̄ῡ ην (+εστηκως ΙΜΝ+) παρα τω αλω Ορνα του Ιεβουσαιου.

^{17}και ειπεν Δαυειδ προς Κυριον

C^M ומלאך יהוה עמד עם גרן ארנן היבוסי ^{16}וישא דויד
את עיניו וירא את מלאך יהוה עמד בין הארץ ובין השמים וחרבו שלופה בידו נטויה
על ירושלם ויפל דויד והזקנים מכסים בשקים על פניהם ^{17}ויאמר דויד אל האלהים

C^G και ο αγγελος Κυριου εστως εν τω αλω Ορνα του Ιεβουσαιου.
^{16}και επηρεν Δαυειδ τους οφθαλμους αυτου και ειδεν τον αγγελον
Κυριου εστωτα ανα μεσον της γης και ανα μεσον του ουρανου
και η ρομφαια αυτου εσπασμενη εν τη χειρι αυτου εκτεταμενη
επι Ιερουσαλημ και επεσεν Δαυειδ και οι πρεσβυτεροι
περιβεβλημενοι εν σακκοις επι προσωπον αυτων.
^{17}και ειπεν Δαυειδ προς τον θεον

J   ο δε βασιλευς σακκον ενδεδυμενος εκειτο κατα της γης...
αναβλεψας δ' εις τον αερα ο βασιλευς και θεασαμενος τον αγγελον
δι' αυτου φερομενον επι τα Ιεροσολυμα και μαχαιραν εσπασμενον
ειπε προς τον θεον

Cf. Notes, NAB. 4Q preserves two full lines that have
dropped out of M through haplography (homoioarchton): ...וישא
ויאמר. C also preserves these lines, though it should be empha-
sized, with four more indications, that 4Q is not dependent on
C: (1) 4Q preserves the correct name of Orna (= G^{SC} ≠ M ≠ C^M).
(2) C^{MG} have transposed על פניהם/מחכסים בשקים. (3) 4Q exhibits
the Hithpael of מחכסים, whereas C uses the Hophal. (4) 4Q
agrees with M G for אל יהוה, against C^{MG} אל האלהים.

J's Vorlage also preserved the full reading. Insofar as
it be established that he was using a Greek Vorlage, this may
be viewed as another example of a reading in the original Hb of
S, preserved in the 4Q tradition, taken over by C, translated
in OG, incorporated by J, lost in M, and finally excised from G
in revision because it had no basis in M.

2 S 24:20   1 C 21:20   VII.330

4Q   [ורירא את המלך ואת עבדיו עוברים עליו מתכסים] בשקים וארנא דש הטּ֯ים
M T P   וירא את המלך ואת עבדיו עברים עליו

G   και ειδεν τον βασιλεα και τους παιδας αυτου
       παραπορευομενους επανω αυτου (διαπορευομενους επ αυτου L)

C^M   וארנן דש חטים   וארבעת בניו עמו מתחבאים   וירא את המלאך

C^G   και ειδεν τον βασιλεα (αγγελον p^b)
       και τεσσαρες υιοι (-ρας υιους BL+) αυτου μετ αυτου μεθαχαβειν
       (κρυβομενοι AN++) και Ορνα ην αλων πυρους

J   Ορωννας δε τον σιτον αλων
       επει τον βασιλεα προσιοντα και τους παιδας αυτου παντας εθεασατο

Cf. Well., Notes, NAB, and M note at 1 C 21:20: Kennicott
ms 587 contains המלך for המלאך.

The 4Q reading documented here is line 7 of a large fragment most of which we have already seen. Lines 1-3 form the
immediately preceding reading of 2 S 24:16^{fin}. Line 4 contains
the reading discussed on pp. 86 and 92, and line 5 the reading
on p. 105. Line 6 preserves [כא]שר צוה יהוה וישקׂף of 2 S 24:19-
20 in agreement with M, against אשר דבר בשם יהוה וישב of 1 C
21:19-20.

Despite the apodictic statement of Well., it is unclear
whether וארנא דש חטים is original or an expansion; it does fit
smoothly as the setting for the meeting of 2 S 24:18-25.
בשקים [מתכסים], however, probably is a gloss, repeated (מתכ[סים]
בשקים) in the following, final line of this fragment where
again no other tradition mentions sackcloth. The corruption in
C (המלאך for המלך, וארבעת for ואת עבדיו, עמו for עליו, and
finally:) מתחבאים seems to presuppose מתכסים.

The partial correspondence of this 4Q plus with C blends
harmoniously with the character of the remainder of the fragment, which agrees largely with C J against M. It differs from
C in minor ways even within the words shared with C and maintains loyalty to the S tradition--preserving short, superior
readings (expanded differently by M and by C), preserving the
proper spelling of ארנא (against the different misspellings of
M and of C), preserving the literary balance (*pace* Well.) of
אנכי הרעה with ואלה הצאן (against M and against C), etc.

Finally, it may be pointed out that J reproduces the detail of Orna's threshing (= 4Q C ≠ M) in combination with that
of the king's servants (= S ≠ C), while lightly echoing Septuagintal phraseology. The combined clues suggest a Greek form of

the 4QSam tradition as his source--a suggestion supported by
the J witness for the other lines of this fragment. For this
plus, 4Q = C J ≠ M G.

We may conclude this section by listing two more pluses:
2 S 6:2 (see p. 194)   -היא קרית יערים אשר ל
2 S 6:7 (see p. 195)   שלח ידו אל הארון.

2. Minus

There are but two minuses shared by 4Q and C against M G.
The first occurs at 2 S 5:4-5 and is discussed on pp. 60-62.
It fits prima facie the pattern 4Q = C ≠ M G, but the Old Latin
of Samuel agrees with 4QSam, and as the details of the analysis
unfold, the most cogent solution appears as follows: 4Q (OG)
OL C J preserve the original short text; M adds a long chronological gloss, and in its wake T P G_2 add the material on the
basis of M. This reading, consequently, does not belong in
this category, but--as a clue to our whole thesis--should be
classified under the pattern 4Q = OG OL C J ≠ M T P G_2.

The second minus is a minor reading, occurring at:

2 S 8:6	*1 C 18:6*	*VII.104~*
4Q	לדו[יד עבדים]	
M T	לדוד לעבדים	
P	לדויד עבדים	
G	τω Δαυειδ εις δουλους	
C^M	לדויד עבדים	
C^G	τω Δαυειδ εις παιδας (δουλους be$_2$)	
J	Δαυιδης ... υπηκοον εποιησατο	

$$4Q = C P ≠ M T (G^{SC}).$$

3. Variant

Similarly, there are two variants fitting the classification 4Q = C ≠ M G. The first is 2 S 6:13 (see p. 196): שבעה
פרים ושבעה אילים.

The second is a minor reading, occurring at:

2 S 8:2	*1 C 18:2*	4Q	ויה[י](ו) [ ]
		M	ויהי
		G	και εγενετο

$$c^M \qquad \text{ויהיו}$$
$$c^G \qquad \text{και ησαν}$$

C. The Pattern 4Q = G C ≠ M

These readings, contained under the more general classification 4Q = G ≠ M, occur *passim* through chapter II, where their problems and probabilities are discussed. They will be collected systematically here for convenience.

1. Plus

2 S 6:6	(see p. 56)	4Q = G C J	≠ M	את ידו
2 S 8:4	(p. 56)	4Q = G C J	≠ M	רכב
2 S 8:7-8	(p. 45)	[4Q = G L OL J	≠ M C	long plus 1°]
		(4Q?) = G L OL C J	≠ M	long plus 2°
2 S 10:5	(p. 85)	4Q = G L C	≠ M	על האנשים
2 S 24:17	(p. 86)	4Q = G (C) J	≠ M	הרעה

2. Minus

2 S 3:3	(p. 64)	4Q = G C	≠ M	אשת נבל
2 S 5:1	(p. 65)	4Q = G C	≠ M G_2	ויאמר
2 S 5:4-5	(p. 60)	4Q = OG OL C J	≠ M G_2	chronological notice
2 S 5:10	(p. 66)	4Q = G C	≠ M G^h	אלהי
2 S 6:2	(p. 66)	4Q = OG (C)	≠ M G^{KR}	2° שם, צבאות
2 S 6:3-4	(p. 66)	4Q = G C	≠ M	חדשה וישאהו מבית...
2 S 7:23	(p. 67)	4Q = G C	≠ M	לכם ה-

3. Variant

1 S 31:3	(p. 80)	4Q = G C	≠ M	על
1 S 31:4	(p. 80)	4Q = G C^M	≠ M C^G	אל
2 S 3:3	(p. 81)	4Q = G C	≠ M	הכרמלית
2 S 3:3	(p. 81)	4Q = G C^{AN++} (J)	≠ M ≠ C^{MB+}	דלויה
2 S 3:4	(p. 82)	4Q = G C (J)	≠ M	לאביטל
2 S 5:9	(p. 70)	4Q = G (C) J	≠ M	ויבנה עיר
2 S 5:13	(p. 83)	4Q = G (C)	≠ M G^h	לדויד עוד
2 S 6:3	(p. 83)	4Q = G C	≠ M	על
2 S 6:9	(p. 84)	4Q = G C	≠ M	לאמר
2 S 6:16	(p. 84)	4Q = G C	≠ M	ויהי
2 S 24:16	(p. 91)	4Q = OG/pL C	≠ M G^h	עומד
2 S 24:17	(p. 92)	4Q = G C	≠ M G^B	הרעתי

D. The Pattern 4Q = G ≠ C ≠ M

1. 4Q = G (C) ≠ C ≠ M

This group of readings constitutes a refinement of the
preceding section. Included are readings just listed under the
broader classification 4Q = G C ≠ M which, within the broader
agreement of 4Q-G-C against M, show minor disagreements between
4Q-G and C.

2 S 5:9	ויבנה עיר	4Q G		2 S 5:13	לדויד עוד	4Q G
	ויבן העיר	C			דויד עוד	C
	ויבן דוד	M			עוד לדוד	M

2 S 6:2	שם...יהוה	4Q G		2 S 8:7-8	(see immediately
	שם...יהוה.	C			above, p. 160,
	שם שם...יהוה צבאות	M			under "1. Plus")

2 S 24:17	הרעה הרעתי	4Q G
	הרע הרעותי	C^{MG}
	העויתי	M

To this group, we may add an even further refined example:

2 S 5:11 (pp. 99f.):

וחרשי עץ וחרשי קיר ויבנו	4Q pL (J)
וחרשי עץ וחרשי אבן ויבנו	OG^V
וחרשי קיר וחרשי עצים לבנות	C
וחרשי עץ וחרשי אבן קיר ויבנו	M G^h

For this M conflation, 4Q = pL (J) ≠ OG ≠ C ≠ M G^h.

2. 4Q = G ≠ C ≠ M

There are three further readings which show a distinctive
4Q G agreement against C and against M:

2 S 6:5	(p. 84)	בני ישראל	4Q G
		ישראל	C
		בית ישראל	M
2 S 7:23	(p. 71)	ואהלים	4Q G OL
		om	C
		ואלהיו	M

The original S text undoubtedly contained "gods," becoming

"tents" in 4Q either by simple metathesis or by monotheistic
Tendenz. C lacks this word only, again either by simple omission or by monotheistic *Tendenz*. It is difficult not to conclude that the C omission is due to its Palestinian Samuel Vorlage, which in the 6th-5th century included either "gods" and
thus C omitted the polytheistic reference, or "tents" and thus
C omitted the nonsense.

The final reading is closely parallel to the final reading
(2 S 5:11) of the preceding section:

2 S 24:18   (p. 105)   ויאמר   4Q (OG) pL
                          לאמר לדויד כי   C
                          ויאמר לו   M G^h
                  For this M expansion, 4Q = (OG)/pL $\neq$ C $\neq$ M G^h.

E. Remaining Patterns

Since 4Q is a Samuel scroll, the pattern 4Q = S $\neq$ C is to
be presumed as the dominant pattern. In addition to the above
variations from that pattern there remain three minor readings,
each of which varies in its own way.

2 S 3:2   *1 C 3:1*   *VII.21~*   4Q   ויולד
                                       M T P   וילדו
                                       G   και ετεχθησαν
                                       C^M אשר נולד
                                       C^G οι τεχθεντες
                                       J   εγενοντο δε

In the structure of this entire genealogy 4Q is closer to
M than to C, and this reading constitutes the first word after
a passage in 4Q M, omitted from C. But that conversely means
that C must introduce this new passage, and the introduction is
supplied in accord with the introduction of the preceding,
parallel genealogy in 1 C 2:50:

                              אלה היו בני כלב ...   1 C 2:50
        ואלה היו בני דויד   אשר נולד לו בחברון הבכור אמנן   1 C 3:1
    א[מנן   ויולד לדויד בנים בחברון ו]1   4Q
    בכורו אמנן   וילדו לדוד בנים בחברון ויהי   M

C has taken this text from S and incorporated it within

the C genealogical system. For uniformity the introduction has been rearranged. Notice, however, that among the visible variants, C shares the orthography of 4Q (אמנן--less characteristic for both 4Q and C) and the singular verb (נולד) despite a plural subject. This occurs together with a set of three readings in as many lines shared by 4Q and C against M.

Nonetheless, for the variant in isolation, 4Q ≠ M ≠ C.

Secondly, at 2 S 10:5 (see p. 136) the prepositionless ירחו in 4Q varies from בירחו of M C (G is ambiguous). Thus, 4Q ≠ M = C.

Thirdly, at 2 S 5:13 (see p. 182), 4Q and M preserve the original עוד פלגשים ונשים. G transposes, perhaps for protocol, and J follows G. C has deleted פלגשים to maintain the pure pedigree of the Davidic line (cf. 1 C 3:9). Thus, 4Q = M G^h ≠ G J ≠ C.

F. Conclusion

In previous chapters we have seen that 4Q is a Samuel text of a tradition different from M, and that OG/pL are significantly closer to the 4Q tradition than to the M tradition.

In this chapter we have seen C join the 4Q G tradition against M. C never agrees with M against 4Q, except for the addition of the preposition in בירחו (2 S 10:5; see also pp. 194-197). On the other hand, C agrees with 4Q against M in 42 readings, some of which are quite striking.

Searching for the root of this 4Q C agreement, we are impressed with two observations. First, the 4Q C agreements are mostly original S readings corrupt in M, or narrative expansions typical of the Palestinian text tradition, e.g., the Samaritan Pentateuch. The 4Q C agreements are thus a subset of the larger pattern 4Q = OG/pL OL C ≠ M. Secondly, none of the 4Q C agreements either betrays characteristics commonly associated with the Chronicler's specific interests (Levitical, genealogical, cultic, etc.) or displays new types of variation from M due to the fact that C now provides a parallel.

This combination of observations points to the Samuel tradition, not the Chronicles tradition, as the source of the 4Q C similarity. 4Q is not a late conflation of an old S text corrected and supplemented by C readings, but C is rather what has

been believed all along, viz., a retelling of the S K history.
The contribution of 4Q is that it provides us with an exemplar
much closer than M to the Samuel textual basis used by the
Chronicler.

Chapter VI

THE AGREEMENT OF JOSEPHUS WITH 4QSam[a]

The reading of "Jezreel" as the locale for the Philistine battle of 1 S 28:1 is "a rare instance when 4Q Sam and Josephus stand together against all other traditions," published by Cross in the *Harvard Theological Review* 57 (1964) 292-293. Among his unpublished notes Cross mentions two additional attestations by Josephus of unique readings in 4QSam[a]: 1 S 11:1 and 2 S 11:3 (cf. NAB).

Since the ms 4QSam[a] and the priest and general Josephus were in neighboring environs during the First Jewish Revolt, and since at Titus' bidding Josephus took some ιερα βιβλια (*Vita*, 416-418) from Jerusalem to Rome where he composed the *Jewish Antiquities*, it would seem a promising endeavor to compare Josephus' narrative with the Samuel scroll. It is not, of course, suggested that Josephus knew our specific ms, but it is quite possible that his text of Samuel would be closer to 4QSam[a] than to the Massoretic Samuel. Chapter VI will study that possibility.

A. The Agreement of J with 4QSam[a]

1. J = 4Q alone

1 S 1:22	*V.347*	4Q	ונת]חֿיהו נזיר עד עולם
		M T P	om
		G OL[b]	om
		J	ανατιθεισα τω θεω προφητην

Cf. BASOR 18 and n. 5; NAB; and above, pp. 39-40.

4Q displays a reading of approximately one line not found in other biblical mss. M[S] never uses נזיר, nor does G[S] ever translate נזיר, with the ambiguous exception of δοτον in 1:11 (in the entire LXX δοτος occurs only there, and without Hb correspondent).

J relates the προφητης feature in perfect order at 1 S 1:22, after the birth and naming of Samuel (1:20 = V.346) and the bringing of sacrifices and tithes (1:21 = V.346).

That προφητης is J's equivalent for נזיר (4Q) is to be expected, since J never uses ναζιραιος in the sg. and only twice
in the pl.: in *Ant*. IV.72 as a parenthetical curiosity, pre-
supposing that his audience is unfamiliar with the term, and in
XIX.294 as an unemphasized item in a list of Agrippa's religious acts. In the other two places where one would look seriously for its mention, J is likewise silent: (1) the law of
the Nazirite (Num 6:13-21) is absent from *Ant*., except for the
aside in IV.72 mentioned above; and (2) the Nazirite κατ'
εξοχην, Samson, though he is presented throughout the detailed
narrative of V.276-317 as a Nazirite (cf. 285, 306, 312), is
never labeled a "Nazirite" (cf. Judg 13:5,7; 16:17) but rather
a "prophet" (285)!

Although this reading must be considered in conjunction
with 1:11 (see pp. 39-40), we nonetheless have here a solid
plus in which J = 4Q alone.

1 S 11:1^{init} *VI.68-69*

4Q	J
[נ]ח̊ש מלך בני עמ̊ון	Ναασην ... τον των Αμμανιτων βασιλεα·
הוא לחץ	ουτος γαρ πολλα κακα
את בני גד	τους περαν του Ιορδανου ποταμου
ואת בני ראובן	κατωκημενους των Ιουδαιων διατιθησι ...
בחזקה	ισχυι μεν και βια ...
ונקר להם כ[ו]ל/[	των ... λαμβανομενων τους
[עי]ן ימין	δεξιους οφθαλμους εξεκοπτεν.

Cf. Notes, NAB, and p. 69 above. 4Q contains 3½ lines of
text not found in M G OL T P 𝔄 ₵ 𝔏. There is a paragraph break
in the ms after מנחה, the last word of 1 S 10. Then begins 1 S
11:1 with the text cited above, constituting line 1 and the beginning of line 2 of the 4Q narrative. Then, inserted intralinearly above line 4 appears ... ויהי כמו חדש ויעל. It is
only with this ויעל that the truncated Massoretic chapter 11
begins.

Especially since J rearranges his text so liberally elsewhere, it is strikingly noteworthy here that every phrase of
4Q is reproduced by J in exact order. Furthermore, the 4Q
paragraph is original, not an insertion. It is impossible that

either 4Q or J could have derived this from elsewhere in a
Massoretic or Septuagintal type of text. This can be proved
from the following points:

מלך -- Nahash is never termed מלך in this chapter in M
or G (see below).

לחץ -- 4Q and J carefully distinguish between the past
fact of oppression against Reuben and Gad and the present threat
against Jabesh. The former is entirely lacking in M G.

גד ... ראובן -- It is admittedly difficult to divide
Jabesh-gilead sharply from Gad (cf. the troubled text of Josh
13:7-8, the conflicting statements of 13:25, 31; also *IDB* II,
p. 397), but Gilead was recorded with Manasseh (the territory
is eponymously named after the grandson of Manasseh in Num
26:29) and not with Gad (Num 26:15-18). More importantly for
our present textual considerations, J distinguishes clearly
between τους περαν του Ιορδανου [= בני גד ובני ראובן] and τους
Γαλαδηνους [= יבש גלעד] (VI.71), where he also distinguishes
between the past fact and the present threat. M G have nothing
about Reuben and Gad.

בחזקה -- M G have no similar expression.

ונקר -- Again, M G do not speak of the accomplished
mutilation.

The passage must, therefore, be considered original and
not a later summary compiled from various facts related elsewhere and inserted here. Furthermore, it can be argued on
stylistic grounds that the passage is original and that the M G
tradition probably also had it at an earlier stage.

Nahash is termed מלך twice: in 1 C 19:1 (= 2 S 10:1) and
in 1 S 12:12. In 1 C 19:1 we find נחש מלך בני עמון; we are
told that he has died, וימלך בנו. After verse 1, Hanun is
never termed מלך but rather in 2a חנון בן נחש, and thereafter
simply חנון. The pattern is identical in 2 S 10: the proper
name נחש is not used in verse 1, but the identifying title is
given: מלך בני עמון; we are told that he has died, וימלך חנון
בנו. After verse 1, Hanun is never termed מלך but rather in 2a
חנון בן נחש, and thereafter simply חנון.

Returning to 4Q at 11:1, we note the identical pattern.
Nahash is identified in the first phrase as נחש מלך בני עמון.
Subsequently מלך never appears on the three-fourths complete

fragment. Rather, 4Q reads [נח[ש once and then נחש העמוני with
M as M begins its narrative (ויעל נחש העמוני). As the 4Q fragment breaks off, M G continue their narrative, never once telling the reader that נחש is מלך.

Thus, if 4Q is taken as original, the stylistic pattern
unfolds exactly as in the other Ammonite passage in 2 S 10 //
1 C 19. If not, the pattern is all there except for the identifying first piece.

The remaining occurrence of נחש מלך בני עמון is in 1 S
12:12, appearing exactly as in 4Q and 1 C 19:1. Did 4Q possibly cull the phrase from 12:12? Just the opposite. The entire chapter 1 S 12 is a Deuteronomistic summary whose termin-
ology is heavily derivative from 1 S 7--11 (for this analysis
I am gratefully indebted to the research (see Bibliog.) of my
Finnish colleague, Dr. Timo Veijola, at Göttingen). Thus, the
epithet in 12:12 should be presumed to derive from 1 S 11 (and
it does -- from a 4Q type of text!), and not vice-versa. This
is another example confirming Cross's statement that "the text
of the Deuteronomic history used by the Chronicler...was by no
means identical with the received text. Yet it is equally
clear that the Chronicler used the Old Palestinian text current
in Jerusalem in his day" (*HTR* 57 [1964] 294).

Two final points should be appended. First, J, though
exhibiting considerable fidelity to 4Q's order as we have just
seen, does invert the order of Mηνι δ᾽ ὕστερον [ויהי כמו חדש].
In 4Q it follows the section on the mutilation by Nahash of
Reuben and Gad, whereas in J it precedes that section. J has
simply drawn this datum from its original situation and used it
as part of his topic sentence, keeping the reader's mind on the
main thread of his story (Saul's rise to kingship). He has
done this often; cf. V.338, 341; VI.18; VII.162; etc. His
meaning, however, is not altered, and he still agrees with 4Q G
pL OL against M L$_2$ in keeping it with 11:1.

Secondly, 4Q may provide a clue to the absence of this
section in M G. Above and evidently intended as prior to
ויאמרו כול אנשי יביש אל נחש (11:1b) is 4Q's supralinear insertion (*prima manu*): ויהי כמו חדש ויעל נחש העורמי ויחן על יביש
[גלעד]. Either 4Q's Vorlage contained the entire reading and
the scribe at first omitted the supralinear insertion through

homoioteleuton (immediately preceding is אֶל [י]בֵשׁ גִּלְעָד) and--
fortunately for us!--subsequently corrected the omission; or
the insertion is simply a variant preserved between the lines.
The former is more likely: (a) on a simply visual level, the
grounds for such a haplography are strong. (b) Since ויהי כמו
חדש does not occur at the end of 1 S 10 (or elsewhere) in 4Q^{txt},
its occurrence only in 4Q^{mg} indicates that this should be part
of 4Q's normal text. (c) The different spellings of יב(י)ש do
not indicate two different sources, for both are found side by
side in 4Q^{txt} and in M as well. (d) Nothing in the insertion
is similar enough to the text to be labeled a variant, except
perhaps [גלעד] ויחן על יביש, but this can be a variant for
ויבאו אל [י]בש גִּלְעָד only if the preceding [בני עמון   ]
is taken as subject, to prove which there is scarcely any evidence. Finally, (e) our scribe has also corrected himself
supralinearly (ליהוָֹה > ליהוה) at 2 S 6:2 (see pp. 194 and 197).

Thus, 4Q correctly preserves an entire narrative section
lost from all other biblical mss, though its scribe has slipped
and then found it necessary to incorporate part of the text
supralinearly. M had not only lost these several lines of text
but even conspicuously erred with the residue, placing a confused ויהי כמחריש at the end of chapter 10 instead of the beginning of chapter 11. T P, derived from M, probably never
knew the section.

We must raise the question, however, whether OG originally
contained the reading. (a) The late L conflation, influenced
by KR (see p. 70), brings one form of the G text into conformity
with M T P. (b) At an earlier stage (G OL), the G text was
free of that M corruption but still lacked the Reuben and Gad
section. (c) J faithfully repeated his biblical source (*contra*
Marcus, Loeb, p. 201, note c on 1 S 11:1) from the 4Q tradition,
and δωρα indicates (see p. 70) that that biblical source was in
Greek. We have seen numerous other examples of 4Q pluses
shared with G J against M, and we have seen examples of exci-
sions from G on the basis of M: cf. especially 1 S 15:29 (p.
142) where OG contained a plus which was repeated by J but subsequently deleted from BAL+, leaving an error in the hexaplaric
text not unlike the ויהי כמחריש phenomenon! It is plausible,
therefore, to posit that the OG originally contained this

reading.

In sum, for a long, original plus, J = 4Q (OG?) alone.

1 S 26:11	*VI.313*	4Q	א[ת חניתוֹ
		M T P	את החנית
		G	το δορυ
		J	αυτου το δορυ

For this variant, J = 4Q alone, although the reading is
admittedly fragile. But on the one hand, it gains importance
from the other readings in this section, and on the other, if
it is argued that J is too close to M G for 4Q-J significance,
then the following evidence must be considered:

G (26:11)   λαβε δη   το δορυ... και τον φακον του υδατος
G (26:12)   ελαβεν Δαυειδ το δορυ   και τον φακον του υδατος
J   λαβων αυτου το δορυ   και τον φακον του υδατος
G   απηλθον... και ουκ ην ο βλεπων... παντες υπνουντες....   και διεβη
J   εξηλθεν... μηδενος αισθομενου... παντων δε κατακοιμωμενων... διαβας δε

It is remarkable that φακος is used for צפחת only in this
chapter (26:11, 12, 16) in the entire LXX. φακος is used in
its primary meaning for עדשה, "lentil," four times (Gen 25:34;
2 S 17:28; 23:11; and Ezek 4:9) and for פך three times (1 S
10:1 and 2 K 9:1,3). Conversely, צפחת is translated by καψακης
four times (1 K 17:12, 14, 16; 19:6) and by φακος only for its
triple occurrence in this chapter.

Thus, the possibility that J may have arrived at his
translation independently of G should strain our credulity. If
yet more proof is sought, we may glance forward to the slightly
altered text in the next occurrence (26:16-17 = VI.315-316) and
notice the effect on J:

G   το δορυ του βασιλεως και ο φακος του υδατος που εστιν...
            και επεγνω Σαουλ   την φωνην του Δαυειδ

J   ζητησον ουν το δορυ του βασιλεως και τον φακον του υδατος....
            Σαουλος δε γνωρισας την του Δαυιδου φωνην

And we may glance backward at the first mention of the δορυ
(26:7 = VI.312):

        M   וחניתו מעוכה
        G   και το δορυ αυτου ενπεπηγος

J   του δορατος, τουτο γαρ αυτω παρεπεπηγει

Again, both מעך (3x) and εμπηγνυναι (8x) are rare words, and
the only time they ever correspond to each other is in this
verse. Furthermore, J's diction is magnificently derivative
from G throughout this entire passage.

Thus, as the texts stand for the variant, J = 4Q alone,
but much more impressive is J's dependence on a Vorlage in
Greek.

1 S 28:1^{fin}   VI.325

4Q   [ויד] דו אמר[ורי]²אל יזרע לחמה[למ שיך ואנ אתה   ]
M   דוד ויאמר²   :שיך ואנ אתה במחנה
G   εις (+τον LA+) πολεμον συ και οι ανδρες σου.
J   εις τον πολεμον εις Ρεγαν ... συμμαχησαι τον Δαυιδην αυτω
        μετα των ιδιων οπλιτων

      (ΡΕΓΑΝ RE,Zon; ΡΙΓΑΝ O; ΡΕΓΓΑΝ MSP; Rella Lat.)

    Cf. HTR 293, NAB. This reading is from a fragment 13
lines long, allowing more than sufficient basis to establish
יזרעאל למלחמה as a plus appended to the final words of M G at
28:1. There appears to be, however, no room for the ה-locative
which Cross reconstructs (יזרעאל[ה]), since there is space
enough for only two normal letters between the ל of יזרעאל and
the א of ויאמר. These letters are on the same portion of the
fragment, and there are no clues of shrivelled or distorted
leather. The slightly narrower size of the *waw* and *yod* afford
the space required for word division.

    J's Vorlage must have had approximately ΕΙΣ (ΤΟΝ) ΠΟΛΕΜΟΝ
ΕΙΣΡ(Α)ΕΛ; see p. 14 for the strength of J-Lat. J saw and
reproduced Λ (and not Γ), for Λ is solidly in the J text-
tradition. The double (Λ and Γ) text-tradition is not explainable if Γ was original -- unless either (a) a second corruption
is posited which by chance happens to yield the correct reading,
or (b) the Latin has been corrected. But the latter is impossible, since only J-Lat and 4Q (lying hidden during the entire
existence of J-Lat) contain the correct reading.

    That "Jezreel" was the correct reading is not a conjec-
ture. 4Q documents it, and M G explicitly certify it at 28:4
and 29:1 (note that at 29:1 as well B+ ₡ err on this frequently
corrupted name).

Mez (pp. 32-33) had attempted to explain ΕΙΣ ΡΕΓ(Γ)ΑΝ as a corruption of εις φαραγγα, which he deduced as "die altlucianische Lesart." He argued that J is based "ganz auf vorlucianischen Texten." P often agrees with pL, and P has נחלא. נחלא = φαραγξ in Jer 7:31, 32; 40:4; etc. Since J and P both agree with pL often, and since they both err here, φαραγξ may be the *medium tertium*.

But how does Mez explain φαραγξ, especially when it is not attested? He speaks vaguely of "Hilfe eines Targums," plausibly suggesting: הצבא (M) > חילא (T) [= both "strength" and "valley"].

But Wellhausen (p. 8, n.) may be closer to the mark, viewing the P error as a problem of inner-Syriac palaeography (سلل > سلل). And 4Q provides a much closer basis for ΕΙΣ ΤΟΝ ΠΟΛΕΜΟΝ ΕΙΣ ΡΕΓΑΝ with למלחמה יזרעאל, which has the added advantage of being the correct reading.

Three further observations prove helpful. First, G often confuses the name Jezreel (1 S 25:43; 27:3; 29:1, 11; 30:5, etc.). Secondly, Josh 15:9 offers an example of our specific type of error, though this time in reverse: בעלה M; ΕΙΣ ΒΑΑΛ AGNΘrell OL ΑΖΖΑ; ΙΕΒΑΑΛ Bqr.

Finally, Josephus himself (and not just the later, corrupted J text) did not recognize that in his Vorlage Jezreel was meant (though something quite similar was present), because he habitually (VIII.346, 355, 407; IX.105; etc.) identifies it for his foreign readers by appending "πολις" to it, whereas here he does not append "πολις." Thus the 4Q texttype had יזרעאל correctly, G frequently errs on the name, G[B+] of Josh 15:9 displays a similar type of error, and Josephus' Vorlage contained a form quite close to ΙΕΣΡΑΕΛ but already corrupt. That "corruption already in the Vorlage of J" is a specifically Greek language corruption: יזר- > ΙΕΖΡ- (or ΙΕΣΡ-) > ΕΙΣ Ρ-.

The most cogent conclusion is that J used a Greek Vorlage erring at this point, erring from its own 4Q-type Hebrew Vorlage which contained the plus in correct form. Subsequent "correction" of G toward M excised all clues to this detail until the discovery of the Qumran Samuel scroll.

2 S 11:3   *1 C 20:1 om*   *VII.131*

4Q   ‏[אוריה החתי נ]ושא כלי יואב‏

M T P   ‏אוריה החתי:‏

G   Ουρειου του Χετταιου;

J   τον Ιωαβου μεν οπλοφορον ... Ουριαν

Cf. Notes, NAB. In this plus, 4Q and J alone agree in
calling Uriah Joab's armor bearer. Uriah the Hittite is named
20x in this chapter and 6x elsewhere (12:9, 10, 15; 23:39 // 1
C 11:41; and 1 K 15:5), yet no other ms preserves this detail
here or elsewhere.

Since C omits the entire interlude, this reading in which
4Q = J alone lends weight to our general hypothesis that, where
4Q or J agree with C (with or without G^S) against M, they are
dependent not on C but on a Palestinian text of Samuel.

Furthermore, to the extent that J can be demonstrated as
dependent on a Vorlage in Gk, this explanatory gloss can be
considered another proto-Lucianic plus, based on a Palestinian
Hebrew ms, present when J wrote, and excised from the text in
the post-hexaplaric reworking of the L text. It is impossible
now to determine whether the OG contained the plus (thus, J =
OG/pL) or lacked it (thus, J = pL ≠ OG).

Again for this plus, J = 4Q alone.

2. J = 4Q G ≠ M

Most of the remaining readings in which 4Q and J intersect
have already been discussed under various other rubrics. Thus,
as they are here regrouped according to J categories, they will
be only briefly noted. For economy of space, however, in order
to avoid repeating most of this material in chapter VIII when
discussing the Vorlage of J, attention will be drawn in the
present chapter to the relationship of J to the Hebrew and the
Greek. When considering that relationship, we should keep in
mind that the aim of Josephus was not to reproduce the biblical
ms tradition faithfully but to narrate the stories after the
fashion of the Hellenistic historiographers.

a. Plus

1 S 1:11 = V.344,347 (see pp. 39-40)   J = 4Q G OL ≠ M
G   και οινον και μεθυσμα ου πιεται
J   και ποτον ην υδωρ

2 S 8:7-8 = 1 C 18:7-8 (pp. 45-48)   J = 4Q G OL (C) ≠ M
G^L και παντα τα οπλα τα χρυσα... και ελαβεν αυτα Σουσακειμ
βασιλευς Αιγυπτου εν τω αναβηναι...Ροβοαμ υιου Σολομωντος...
εκ των...πολεων του Αδρααζαρ...
εποιησεν Σολομων την θαλασσαν την χαλκην...τα σκευη

J   χρυσας...και τας πανοπλιας... ας υστερον ο των Αιγυπτιων βασιλευς
Σουσακος στρατευσας επι τον υιονον αυτου Ροβοαμον ελαβε...
των Αδραζαρου πολεων...
και χαλκος...εξ ου και Σολομων το...σκευος θαλασσαν...εποιησε

Most of this G^L J material is taken from two long pluses,
both of which are absent from M, the first absent from C though
present in 4Q, and the second present in C and presumably in 4Q
as well. Some of the material listed as G^L is shared by OL but
omitted or confused in G^B. J is farthest from M and closest to
L.

2 S 13:21 = VII.173 (p. 84)   J = L OL (4Q G) ≠ M
G^L και ηθυμησεν σφοδρα και ουκ ελυπησεν το πνευμα Αμνων του
υιου αυτου οτι ηγαπα αυτον οτι πρωτοτοκος αυτου ην.

J   ηχθετο, φιλων δε τον Αμνωνα σφοδρα,
πρεσβυτατος γαρ ην αυτω υιος, μη λυπειν αυτον ηναγκαζετο.

J 4Q G OL share the plus omitted by M within a passage
lacking in C. J agrees with L OL against 4Q M G in the mollified ηχθετο.

2 S 13:27 = VII.174 (p. 85)   J = 4Q G OL ≠ M
G   ποτον κατα ποτον του βασιλεως
J   εφ εστιασιν

2 S 24:17 = 1 C 21:17 = VII.328 (p. 86)   J = 4Q G OL ≠ C ≠ M
G   ο ποιμην
C^G κακοποιων
J   ο ποιμην

The remaining pluses shared by J 4Q G against M follow now
in order:

1 S 6:2 = VI.8-10   (p. 51)   J = 4Q G OL ≠ M

4Q G OL add a third group to the two mentioned by M. J
greatly expands his narrative at this point by presenting the
contents of the alternate groups' proposals. Perhaps for his
own reasons (cf. Loeb, note a, pp. 168-169), or perhaps due to
his Vorlage, J distinguishes three groups.

1 S 12:8 = VI.89   (p. 53)   J = 4Q G ≠ M

Here J shares two pluses with 4Q G.

1 S 14:29 = VI.119   J = G (4Q?) ≠ M

4Q   ‏[העם וידע]/וֹיֹאמר יהונתן‎

M   ‏ויאמר יונתן   :העם‎

G   ο λαος. και εγνω Ιωναθαν και ειπεν

J   μεταξυ δε γνους ... εφη δε

The text of this whole section shows disturbance in all
traditions. 4Q's lines appear to be averaging about 55 characters per line in this column; with ‏וידע‎ (cf. G J) the count
is 54; without it (as M), 49. Thus, despite G's transposition
of Ιωναθαν, there is some probability that 4Q should be reconstructed with ‏וידע‎.

J's γνους can be an inference from the fellow soldier's
apprising Jonathan (14:28) of the curse, but the use of the
identical root in the identical spot must be judged: J = G
(4Q?) ≠ M.

1 S 15:27 = VI.152   (p. 54)   J = 4Q L (G) OL ≠ M

J adds Σαουλος with 4Q G L OL, but he further imitates L's
επελαβετο, not G's εκρατησεν.

2 S 3:7 = VII.23   (p. 55)

4Q contains the wrong name here. G followed 4Q in this
error, but M lacks any name. J agrees with 4Q G in presenting
the name, but as a historian, he presents the correct name.

2 S 6:6 = 1 C 13:9 = VII.81 (p. 56) J = 4Q G C ≠ M

G[SC] και εξετεινεν Οζα την χειρα αυτου

J Οζα ... εκτειναντα την χειρα

2 S 8:4 = 1 C 18:4 = VII.99 (p. 56) J = 4Q G OL C ≠ M

G αυτου χιλια αρματα

J αυτου αρματα χιλια

2 S 13:37 = VII.180 J = 4Q G OL[b] ≠ M OL[v]

4Q	גשור בֹּאֹ[רץ]
M T P	גשור
G	Γεσσειρ (-σσουρ BA+) εις γην (την Bo*)
OL[bv]	Gessur (+terram OL[b])
J	Γεσσουραν ... χωρας

J follows the 4Q G OL[b] plus. B shows a simple uncial error Γ > T, copied by o*, but corrected to γην by o[a].

2 S 19:8(7) = VII.256 (p. 86) J = 4Q G ≠ M

b. Minus

Due to the evanescent character of minuses and the eclectic character of Josephus' narrative, it is infrequent that one can confidently posit a minus in J as causally dependent upon a minus in his Vorlage. One such case, however, can be confidently presented.

The M tradition, followed by T P and the present form of G, added a two-verse chronological gloss about David (2 S 5:4-5; cf. pp. 60-62). The 4Q tradition, followed by C and OG, did not contain the gloss. OG was followed in its shorter text by OL and J. All traditions contain the chronological data somewhere, but J's notice at VII.65 is dependent not on M G_2 at 2 S 5:4-5 but on G at 2 S 2:11, where the dependence is evident in content, word order, and syntax.

c. Variant

Three variants shared by J 4Q G against M deserve special notice:

1 S 10:27--11:1 = VI.67-68 (pp. 69, 166) J = 4Q G OL ≠ M

In addition to placing ויהי כמו חדש (with 4Q G OL) properly

in chapter 11, and in addition to narrating (with 4Q alone) the
paragraph now lost from all S texts, J agrees with G OL against
the Hb mss 4Q and M for the plural δωρα.

The second variant is not in itself striking, but it
assumes much greater importance when seen with three more readings of the same nature:

1 S 11:8 = VI.78   (p. 78)   "70,000" J 4Q G OL^V ≠ "30,000" M OL^b
1 S 17:4 = VI.171 (p. 79)   "4" J 4Q G   ≠   "6" M G^h OL^V
2 S 6:13 = VII.85 (p. 196)   "7" J 4Q G OL C ≠   "6" M
2 S 18:11 = VII.240 (p. 108)   "50" J 4Q OG L   ≠   "10" M G^h

2 S 10:6 = 1 C 19:6 = VII.121 (pp. 152-6)   J = 4Q G ≠ M ≠ C

4Q errs with אישטוב for איש טוב. G agrees with the error
in 4Q, making it a man's name, and J copies the G error. C
fully omits the detail.

The remaining variants shared by J 4Q G follow now in
order:

1 S 2:29 = V.350   (p. 73)   J = 4Q G OL ≠ M
    επεβλεψας G OL; επιβλεπειν J.

1 S 9:19 = VI.51   (p. 77)   J = 4Q G ≠ M
    Εγω ειμι αυτος G; αυτον ειναι J.

1 S 14:47 = VI.129   (p. 78)   J = 4Q G ≠ M
    βασιλεα G J.

1 S 14:50 = VI.129   (p. 78)   J = 4Q G ≠ M G$_2$
    αρχιστρατηγω G; στρατηγον J.

1 S 15:29 = VI.153   (p. 78)   J = 4Q G OL ≠ M
    αποστρεψει G; επισ- L; στρεφειν J.

2 S 3:4 = 1 C 3:3 = VII.21   (p. 82)   J = 4Q G C ≠ M
    της Αβειταλ G; της Αβιταλης J.

2 S 5:9 = 1 C 11:8 = VII.65   (p. 70)   J = 4Q G C ≠ M
    και ωκοδομησεν αυτην πολιν G^{SC};
    και αυτος ανοικοδομησας τα Ιεροσολυμα, πολιν αυτην J.

2 S 13:39 = VII.181   (p. 106)   J = 4Q OG L OL^b
      το πνευμα G; τα της οργης J.   ≠ M BA OL^v

2 S 18:9 = VII.239   (p. 88)   J = 4Q G ≠ M
      εκρεμασθη G; ανεκρεμασθη L; ανακρεμναται J.

2 S 19:7(6) = VII.255   (p. 88)   J = 4Q G ≠ M
      ει G J.

2 S 19:11-12 = VII.259-260   (p. 89)   J = 4Q G OL ≠ M

      J follows 4Q G in placing this long reading in its correct
order.

3. J = 4Q L ≠ M G

      In addition to the six readings in the previous section
which showed special L influence on J, there are six (or probably eight) further readings for which J is dependent upon 4Q
L.

2 S 12:16 = VII.154   (p. 100)   J = 4Q L OL ≠ M G^{KR}
      και εισελθων   εκαθευδεν εν σακκω επι την γην L
      και εισηλθεν και ηυλισθη   επι της γης G^{KR}
            πεσων   επι σακκου κατα γης εκειτο   J.

2 S 13:3 = VII.164   (p. 105)   J = 4Q L ≠ M G
      Ιωναθαν L; Ιωναθη J.

1 S 14:32 = VI.120   (p. 78)   J = 4Q L ≠ M G
      επι L J.

2 S 5:11 = 1 C 14:1 = VII.66   (p. 99)   J = 4Q L OL ≠ OG ≠ M G^h ≠ C
ξυλα κεδρινα και τεκτονας ξυλων και τεκτονας τοιχου και ωκοδομησαν L
ξυλα κεδρινα και οικοδομους τοιχων και τεκτονας ξυλων του οικοδομησαι C^G
ξυλα κεδρινα και τεχνιτας ανδρας τεκτονας και οικοδομους οι κατασκευασαν J.

2 S 13:24 = VII.174   (p. 106)   J = 4Q L OL ≠ M G
      προς L J.

2 S 15:2 = VII.195   (p. 107)   J = 4Q L OL ≠ M G

      J agrees with the tense of 4Q L in two verbs.

Two additional readings for which J is probably dependent upon 4Q L appear below, under the pattern J = 4Q M L OL ≠ G (p. 180).

4. J = 4Q C ≠ M G

The following five readings show striking agreement among J 4Q C against M G:

2 S 6:2 = 1 C 13:6 = VII.78   (pp. 194, 230)   J = 4Q C^{ML} ≠ M G ≠ C^G
Καριαθιαρειμ C^L; Καριαθιαριμα J, in a four-word plus by 4Q.

2 S 6:7 = 1 C 13:10 = VII.81   (pp. 195, 233)   J = 4Q C ≠ M G
Only J 4Q C^{MG} repeat the reason why Oza died, in another four-word plus by 4Q.

2 S 10:6 = 1 C 19:6 = VII.121   (pp. 152-156)   J = 4Q C ≠ M G
χιλια ταλαντα αργυριου C^G; χιλια ταλαντα J. Adjacent readings show patterns of J = S ≠ C and J = Gk ≠ Hb.

2 S 24:16 = 1 C 21:15-16 = VII.327   (pp. 156f.)   J = 4Q C ≠ M G
και ειδεν τον αγγελον... και η ρομφαια αυτου εσπασμενη...
    επι Ιερουσαλημ... εν σακκοις... και ειπεν Δαυειδ προς τον θεον C^G
σακκον... και θεασαμενος τον αγγελον... επι τα Ιεροσολυμα
και μαχαιραν εσπασμενον ειπε προς τον θεον J.

All this material is from a two-line plus in J 4Q C. Further in this same sentence J mentions ο ποιμην, found in G (*literatim*) and OL, reflecting a 4Q plus which is absent from M and confused in C.

2 S 24:20 = 1 C 21:20 = VII.330   (pp. 157ff.)   J = 4Q C ≠ M G
και ειδεν τον βασιλεα και τους παιδους αυτου
    παραπορευομενους επανω αυτου G
και ειδεν τον βασιλεα και τεσσαρες υιοι αυτου μετ αυτου
    μεθαχαβειν και Ορνα ην αλων πυρους C^G
Οροννας δε τον σιτον αλων
    επει τον βασιλεα προσιοντα και τους παιδας αυτου παντας εθεασατο J.

J incorporates the 4Q C plus about Orna's threshing, while in the adjacent clause he agrees with S against the multiple C corruption. The pattern is identical with that of the two preceding readings: J is dependent upon a Samuel text of the 4Q tradition.

5. J = 4Q M L OL ≠ G

There are only two readings in which J = 4Q M ≠ G:

2 S 18:3 = VII.234   (p. 114)   J = 4Q L OL M ≠ G

G omits o λαος against all other traditions. It is either
an error in OG corrected by the early stratum of L (cf. 4Q OL
J) or possibly the original short reading filled in by the
early stratum of L.

2 S 18:6 = VII.236   (p. 115)   J = 4Q L OL M ≠ G

G contains δρυμον where all other traditions have πεδιον.
The analysis of this reading parallels that of the preceding
reading. In the light of J's agreement with 4Q L OL for the
two readings, and in the light of J's habitual disagreement
with M in all the other readings of this chapter so far, there
is no need to posit any specifically M influence here; J is
effectively dependent on L.

B. The Disagreement of J with 4QSam[a]

1. J ≠ 4Q M G

Just as 4Q occasionally shows its individual independence
from other forms of the tradition, so does J show his independence, even while repeating biblical material.

2 S 2:15, etc. = VII.9, etc. (pp. 42-45)   J ≠ 4Q G ≠ M

In the sequence of Ishbaal narratives, J shares the 4Q G
pluses by naming the subject at 2 S 4:1,2. But of all the traditions, only J names his characters with consistent accuracy
(though P comes close). In these readings J should be viewed
as an historian aspiring to be faithful primarily to the story
and not to a Vorlage.

While achieving fidelity to his story, he nonetheless lets
us know his dependence on a text of Samuel (not C) in Greek
(not Hb) by naming his characters Ιεβοσθος (אישבשת M; Ιεβοσθε
G; אשבעל C[M]; Ιοβααλ C[G]) and Μεμφιβοσθος (מפיבשת M; Μεμφιβοσθε
G; מריב בעל C[M]; Μεριβααλ and Μεμφιβααλ C[G]).

1 S 6:1 = VI.18   J ≠ 4Q M G

4Q   [בעה חודשים ‏ש (or ‏ארבעה(?)]

M T P   שבעה חדשים

G   επτα/μηνας (trp L)

J   μηνας τεσσαρας

Since no biblical ms has a variant on "seven," 4Q should
methodologically be reconstructed with שבעה. But when we ask
whence Josephus derived his "four months," we should not forget
the five readings in which J = 4Q alone and his frequent agreement with 4Q on numerals (see p. 177).

2 S 3:30 = VII.36   J ≠ 4Q M G

[בגב[עון 4Q; בגבעון M T P; εν Γαβαων G; προς Χεβρωνι J.
This is a simple *lapsus calami* in J: he does place the battle
εν Γαβαων in VII.11 (cf. Loeb, p. 377, note c).

2. J = G ≠ 4Q M

1 S 1:12 = V.345   (p. 141)   J = G ≠ 4Q M

Ηλει ο ιερευς G; Ηλεις ο αρχιερευς J. A plus in G.

1 S 1:21,24 = V.346   (p. 48)   J = G ≠ 4Q M

J's παρησαν agrees with G against 4Q and against M, and
his addition of δεκατας repeats *literatim* a tangential gloss
found only in G.

1 S 5:10 = VI.4   (p. 123)   J = G ≠ 4Q M

In 4Q M the ark moves from Ashdod through Gath to Ekron,
while in G it moves from Ashdod through Gath to Ascalon. J
ignores Gath but agrees with G in naming Ascalon.

1 S 5:11 = VI.2   (p. 123)   J = G ≠ 4Q ≠ M

J uses G's exact word συγχυσει, while not reflecting
either יהוה of 4Q or מות of M.

1 S 8:18^{fin} = VI.42   (p. 141)   J = G ≠ 4Q M

J reproduces a long plus from G.

1 S 10:27 = VI.67   (p. 69)   J = G ≠ 4Q M

J agrees with G exactly in having δωρα as the last word of
1 S 10, against the singular of 4Q M.

1 S 15:29 = VI.153   (p. 142)   J = OG ≠ 4Q M G[h,L]

J reproduces another long expansion found only in OG, including εμμενει OG, εμμενειν J.

Another reading from this same verse should be integrated with this one: J's στρεφειν echoes the G (4Q) reading αποστρεψει against M. Even though the formula is J = 4Q G ≠ M, we can see from the combination of these two readings that for the complete verse, J = G ≠ 4Q ≠ M.

2 S 5:13 = 1 C 14:3 = VII.70   J = G OL ≠ 4Q M G[h] ≠ C

4Q	עוד פיל[ג]שׁים ̇ו[נשׁים]
M T P	עוד פלגשׁים ונשׁים
G OL[b]	ετι γυναικας και παλλακας
Acx	ετι (+επτα cx) παλλακας και γυναικας
C[M]	עוד נשׁים
C[G]	ετι γυναικας
J	αλλας γυναικας ... και παλλακας

Cf. Well., Notes. ונשׁים should be restored with M G. Most lines in this column of 4Q are averaging 51-55 characters, with extremes at 46 and 58. Each of the three lines preceding this one has 53. If ונשׁים and the rest of this line are restored after M G, the count is 54; if restored without ונשׁים, 48.

Well. raises the possibility, endorsed by Cross, that originally only פלגשׁים stood in the S text, as now only נשׁים stands in C. But the entire S tradition (including 4Q?) has both, and I would propose that the Chronicler, meeting a text identical with M and 4Q, deleted David's concubines to insure the legitimacy of the sons' pedigree. See his final remark after the parallel list of these names: כל בני דויד מלבד בני פילגשׁים (1 C 3:9).

Well. is correct that the M order has a stronger claim to originality than the G order. G might transpose for protocol; why would 4Q M transpose? J is similarly open to suspicion of having reversed the order; but it remains true that J = G in content, order, and vocabulary, against all other traditions.

2 S 6:13 = 1 C 15:25 = VII.85   (p. 235)   J = G OL ≠ M ≠ 4Q C

J's επτα χορων is dependent on the G OL variant επτα χοροι, with no other text having anything resembling χοροι.

2 S 8:1 = 1 C 18:1 = VII.98   J = G ≠ 4Q M G^h ≠ C

4Q	מתג האמה
M	מתג האמה
T	תקון אמתא
P	רמח גמא
G	την αφωρισμενην (αφαλνισμ- dlp)
OL^V	dilectionem
α'(ajz)	τον χαλινον (+του z) υδραγωγιου (του πηχεος j)
σ'	την εξουσιαν του φορου τοπος εστιν
i^mg	την [των αλλοφυλων] ενο.ι.
c^M	גת ובנתיה
c^G	την Γεθ και τας κωμας (θυγατερας e₂) αυτης
J	πολλην της χωρας αποτεμομενος και προσοριοας τη των Εβραιων

Cf. Well., Driver, Notes, NAB (footnote to the narrative).

4Q reads with M, giving no new knowledge beyond Well., Driver. Thus, we shall not attempt a solution to the textual problems here. Rather, we shall point out that amid all the confusion here J indicates once again that he is dependent upon the OG text of S. 4Q M T P C^MG σ' all presumably speak of a definite place (α' is a translation of M); J does not. G OL^V list only very generic terms: "David took the appropriated land from the Philistines" G; "the delight of the Philistines" OL^V. J gives a two-part paraphrase of αφωρισμενην, saying that David cut off for himself (απο---μενος) much of the Philistines' land and added it to the boundaries (-οριζ-) of the Hebrews. J displays this same practice with αποδιδρασκοντες (1 S 25:10) on p. 186 below. G's αφοριζειν may reflect מגרש (as it does 37x in Josh), but no matter--J says what only G has said, and his paraphrase is precisely of G's απο-ὀριζειν. J = G ≠ 4Q M G^h ≠ C.

3. J = Gk ≠ Hb

In the following readings J ≠ 4Q in varying degrees, but the main import appears to be his dependence on a text in the Greek language.

In chapter VIII a detailed analysis of Josephus' text through 2 S 6 isolates eight J readings attributable specifically to Greek language factors of that OG/pL chapter. In addition to these, four more readings show J dependent on

content found only in texts which happen to be in the Greek
language, while J = G *literatim*.

To these we may here add the following:

1 S 25:3 = VI.296   (p. 79)   J = Gk ≠ Hb; (4Q = G ≠ M)
Beginning with a reading in which G = 4Q ≠ M, Josephus
erroneously interprets G's κυνικος as κυνικης ασκησεως!

2 S 10:6 = 1 C 19:6 = VII.121 (p. 155) J = Gk ≠ Hb
J's erroneous treatment of Συρος as "king of the Mesopotamians" is transparently attributable to his use of a Greek
text without checking it against a Hebrew text. And only L of
Samuel has the masculine Συρον here.

Three further readings show in varying degrees J dependence on a Gk Vorlage.

1 S 10:3,4 = VI.55   (pp. 52, 125)   J = Gk ≠ Hb
G   τρεις ανδρας αναβαινοντες προς τον θεον εις Βαιθηλ...
     τρια αιγιδια... τρια αγγεια αρτων... ασκον οινου...
     ⁴... και δωσουσιν σοι δυο απαρχας αρτων και λημψη
L   τρεις ανδρας αναβαινοντες προς τον θεον εις Βαιθηλ...
     τρεις εριφους... ασκον οινου... τρια αγγεια αρτων...
     ⁴... και δωσουσιν σοι   απαρχας αρτων και λημψη
J   τρεις ανθρωπους εν τη οδω προσκυνησαι τω θεω εις Βεθηλα...
     τρεις αρτους... εριφον... ασκον οινου...
     και δωσουσι σοι αρτους δυο, συ δε ληψη

Note that J echoes L's εριφους, the singular possibly being due to J's assessment of the likelihood of a man carrying
three kids from one town to another. ασκος is used for נבל
only here and in Jer 13:12. Above, on p. 170, we saw J repeat
φακον from G (1 S 26:11) in the only passage for which LXX
translates צפחת by φακος.

1 S 10:14 = VI.58   J = Gk ≠ Hb
4Q   [שאול] ויאמר דוד
M   ויאמר דוד שאול
G   και ειπεν ο οικειος αυτου
L   και λεγει αυτω ο οικειος (πατραδελφος b) αυτου
α'   ο πατραδελφος
J   του συγγενους αυτου Αβηναρου ... των αλλων οικειων

For שאול, 4Q = M ≠ G J. For οικειος, J is again dependent
on G, because οικειος does not have the same range of meaning
as דוד and is used for דוד only with regard to this specific
person (10:14ff and 14:50), though Amos 6:10 has this correspondence once in the plural. οικειος is more frequently used
(7x) to translate שאר.

1 S 28:25 = VI.339   (p. 79)   J = Gk ≠ Hb (4Q = G ≠ M)
     In a reading for which 4Q = G ≠ M and in a parallel read-
ing J follows the G vocabulary closely, though as usual he re-
serves his right to his own style of Hellenistic syntax.

4. J = L ≠ 4Q G

1 S 2:22 = V.339   (pp. 57f., 133)   J = L M ≠ 4Q G
     There are two noticeable expansions in this verse. 4Q
adds the age of Eli, an expansion peculiar to 4QSam[a] here
(though see 1 S 4:15). And M appends a note about Eli's sons
with the women at the shrine. OG has neither expansion, though
the M expansion found its way into G mss early enough to influence J. J = G L M ≠ 4Q in lacking the first expansion, and J =
L M ≠ 4Q G in having the second.

2 S 3:2 = VII.21   J = L ≠ 4Q M OG OL
     בנים 4Q M T P; υιοι BAN+ OL[m]; υιοι εξ LMcx++; παιδες ...
εξ J.
     Once more, J uses an early gloss found only in Gk texts.

2 S 3:7 = VII.23   (p. 65)   J = L M α′ ≠ 4Q OG
     ושמה M; om 4Q OG; ονομα LN+ ⊭ J. In this and the past two
examples, J has incorporated expansions found in L (M) but
lacking in 4Q OG.

5. J = L ≠ G (4Q ambiguous)

     Prior sections have catalogued examples of Josephan de-
pendence on G as opposed to 4Q M, on Greek as opposed to Hebrew,
and on L specifically within the G tradition. Because of the
cumulative significance of these findings, attention should be
directed to three further readings from 4Q, even though 4Q
itself cannot help our decision.

1 S 25:10 = VI.298   J = L ≠ G

    4Q   ?] המחפר[שים
    M   המתחפרצים
    G   αναχωρουντες
    L ϑ'   οι αποδιδρασκοντες
    J   οι δραπεται ... καταλιποντες

The significance of J's dependence on L mounts when this
reading is compared with 2 S 8:1 on p. 183 above. There also J
reflects a Gk compound by reproducing the root in one word and
the morpheme in another.

2 S 3:27 = VII.34   J = L ≠ G

    4Q   ויש֯[ב אבנ]ר֯
    M T P   וישב   אבנר
    G   και επεστρεψεν τον Αβεννηρ (+Ιωαβ post επ' cx)
    La₂ ᴢ   και απεστρεψεν   Αβεννηρ
    J   Αβεννηρος ... υπεστρεψεν

The Hb can be either Qal or Hiphil, but the lack of את and
the inclusion of יואב as subject of the next verb indicate Qal.
Similarly, επεστρεψεν can be transitive or intransitive. G
interprets וישב as Hiphil and transitive (BAMN all have τον);
only boa₂c₂e₂ ᴣ^W(vid) ᴢ and J interpret the Hb as Qal and
therefore use Abner as subject. Consequently, J = L ≠ G.

2 S 11:7^{fin} = VII.132   J = L OL ≠ (4Q) M G

    4Q   המלחמ[ה ה֯ ר]יאמ֯[ר
    M T P   המלחמה : ויאמר
    G   του πολεμου.   και ειπεν
    L 71 ᴣ   ο πολεμος και ειπεν υγιαινει και ειπεν
    z   του πολεμου και ειπεν εις ειρηνην και ειπεν
    a₂   του πολ. και ειπεν Ουριας παντες εις ειρηνην και ειπεν
    OL^b belli et dixit Urias Omnes rectae sunt. Et dixit
    OL^h po..lo et respon..... Omnia .....te s... .. dixit
    J   λεγοντος δε παντα κατα νουν αυτοις

Cf. Notes. J has Uriah respond to David's question. This
response could have been supplied independently by J, but in M
G the king's question goes brusquely unanswered, and J does
seem to be a genuine reflection of the L plus. With Cross, I
suspect a common haplography: ולשלום המלחמה (ויאמר לשלום) ויאמר

דויד -- the line is indeed ripe for haplographic omission,
since לשלום already occurs 3x in the last 6 words of the question!

4Q's spacing probably requires the shorter text, and the
final letter before ויאמר favors ה of המלחמה. A tenuous possibility exists, however, that, since 4Q's final letter can
also be ם of ם[ויאמר לשלו, 4Q had ויאמר לשלום (with L OL J),
perhaps having lost another phrase by haplography. OL[h], in
fact, exhibits that very phenomenon:

OL[h]   et po[pu]lo et ⟨bello et⟩ respon[dit ei] Omnia [rec]te s[unt].

L   ει υγιαινει ο λαος και ει υγιαινει ο πολεμος και ειπεν υγιαινει.

Whatever the decision on 4Q, again in this reading, J = L
OL ≠ G.

6. J = M ≠ 4Q

We have seen numerous readings in which J = 4Q ≠ M. Conversely, we saw, in section 4 above, three readings in which J
= M ≠ 4Q: the double reading in 1 S 2:22 and the plus in 2 S
3:7. In addition to those three, there are two others:

1 S 11:9-10 = VI.76   (p. 133)   J = M G L ≠ 4Q

4Q has a plus of about one line which no other ms appears
to reflect.

2 S 12:15 = VII.154   (p. 138)   J = M G L ≠ 4Q

Here 4Q omits one word by simple haplography. J, with all
other traditions, includes the reading.

These last two readings appear to be peculiarities of ms
4QSam[a]. Since there is no specifically Hb influence involved,
since J = G L as well as M, and since J agrees with L in addition to M in the readings just mentioned from section 4, while
agreeing with L against M 4Q in the remaining reading (2 S 3:2)
from that section, there is no reason to suspect that J is dependent upon M (or any Hb ms) for these readings.

In fact, for all the portions of the Samuel text for which
4QSam[a] is extant, no reading has been found which indicates
either that Josephus derived his narrative or detail from M
specifically or from a manuscript specifically in Hebrew. In
other words, the formulae J = M ≠ 4Q G L and J = Hb ≠ Gk never

occur where 4Q is extant.

7. J = C ≠ 4Q M G

In section A.2 just above we saw seven readings in which J = C ≠ M, but in all of them J = 4Q G C ≠ M. In section A.4 above we saw five more readings in which J = C ≠ M, but in all of them J = 4Q C ≠ M G. We should press further to find if there is a significant number of readings in which J = C ≠ 4Q M G. We find five:

2 S 3:3 = 1 C 3:1 = VII.21   (p. 81)   J = C^M ≠ 4Q G C^G ≠ M

Niese and Marcus both choose Δανιηλος (the reading of J mss ROME and Lat) as J's name for the second son of David. Other J mss have: Δαλουηλος P, Δαλουιηλος S. 4Q seems to read דלויה, G and the majority of C^G mss have Δαλουια, Bgc$_2$ of C have Δαμνιηλ (Δαν- g). Only M T P have Chileab.

I should opt for Δαλου(ι)ηλος as the original J reading for four reasons. (1) It is the *lectio difficilior*, and here this principle is wisely followed. For (2) Franz Blatt observed in *The Latin Josephus* (p. 25) that "Biblical names were given the form they had in the Vulgate" [at 1 C 3:1 "Daniel"!], meaning that the forms of names in J-Lat are witnesses to the Vulgate but not reliable witnesses to the original J text. Furthermore, (3) Niese's preference here for mss RO is misdirected (cf. Thackeray's similar critique in note 29 to the Introduction above), for these mss err on two adjacent names as well, while PS faithfully preserve the OG:

(a) Αβιγαιας G^{SC} J^{PSME} Lat; Αβισσαιου R; Αβισσαιας O.

(b) Αβιταλης [see p. 82] G^{SC} J^{PSE}; om ROM; Abithar Lat. Finally, (4) the general pattern established in the remainder of this volume suggests that J followed readings of the 4Q tradition in a Greek form, and that is precisely what we find here as well (strengthened by J's following the Greek error of ΑΒΙΓΑΙΑ for ΑΒΙΓΑΙΛ!). In sum, J does not agree with C; he is much closer to 4Q G C^{AN++} Syh^C.

2 S 5:3 = 1 C 11:3 = VII.53   J = C ≠ 4Q M G OL

4Q	[om]
M T P G OL^b	om
C^{MG}	+κατα τον λογον Κυριου δια χειρος Σαμουηλ

J   υπο του θεου δια Σαμουηλου χειροτονηθειη

J transfers this plus in C from 11:3 to 11:2 and adds
other details as well (David's sons, conquering Philistines)
not in C. Thus, though J continues to use a Samuel text, it
appears that he incorporates into that S narrative details
found only in C.

2 S 5:8 = 1 C 11:6 = VII.63-64   J = C ≠ 4Q M G OL
4Q   om
M T P G OL   om
C^MG   και εσται ... εις στρατηγον. και ανεβη επ αυτη
                εν πρωτοις Ιωαβ υιος Σαρουια
J   επι την ακραν αναβαντι ... στρατηγιαν ....
                ο Σαρουιας παις Ιωαβος   εφθη ... αναβας

          In C this vignette of Joab is in place, for the history of
David is just beginning, and this explains how Joab became com-
mander of David's army. The list of David's warriors then follows. In S, however, Joab has already been acting as leader of
David's men (cf. 2 S 2:12-32; 3:22-39). J, who has already
named Joab as David's commander-in-chief in VII.11, 31, is not
troubled by including here (together with the details about the
blind and ˉthe lame in S, not found in C) the C notice about
Joab's gaining the position of commander-in-chief. Since this
episode does not occur in any S tradition, including 4Q, it
again appears that J is openly supplementing his S narrative
with pertinent additions from his C text. Comparison of J with
C^G for both this and the preceding reading suggests that his
borrowing was from a C text in Greek (see also p. 244).

2 S 6:1 = 1 C 1:1-3 = VII.78-79 (p. 214) J = C ≠ (4Q) M G OL
          The introduction to J's narration of 2 S 6 appears on many
counts to have been derived from C and not S. The long introductory section of 1 S 11:1, preserved by J and 4Q alone,
should be kept in mind as we consider the 2 S 6 introduction,
but 4Q spacing indicates that that particular ms had no more
than M G have for 2 S 6:1. See pp. 213-215 for discussion of
this material, including J's dependence on a Greek text of C.

2 S 6:6 = 1 C 13:9 = VII.81   (p. 195)   J = C ≠ 4Q G ≠ M G^h

Only the short top stroke of a *nun* versus a *kaph* separates
the 4Q reading (נוֹדֵן) from the C J reading (כִּידֵן).

Thus, of the five readings in this section initially categorized as J = C ≠ 4Q M G, one proper name defies the category
and the other can offer no support; but the two pluses in 1 C
11:3, 6 (// 2 S 5:3, 8) and the long introduction to 1 C 13 (//
2 S 6) are strong examples in which J depends on Chronicles and
not on Samuel for his details. The two pluses in 1 C 11 make
one suspect that J is dependent on a Greek text of Chronicles,
and three (or possibly four) readings in 1 C 13 prove that suspicion true.

C. Conclusion

The evidence in part A of this chapter demonstrates a
solid and significant affiliation of Josephus with the 4QSam[a]
tradition through the medium of a Greek Vorlage. In 5 readings
(A.1) J and 4Q alone preserve archaic Samuel readings now lost
to all other ms traditions, and, in three of these, J betrays
dependence on a specifically Greek Vorlage. This means that
just as some genuine S readings have perished from the M tradition, so have some genuine S readings perished from the G tradition, at times deliberately excised from G due to their non-
correspondence to the altered Massoretic *veritas*.

G explicitly joins the 4Q J alliance against M in 34 additional readings (A.2), of which 10 are striking, 21 show Greek
influence on J, and 6 show precisely L influence on J. Eight
further readings (A.3 and 5) strengthen the case for 4Q L influence on J, where M and G diverge.

In another direction (A.4) C joins the 4Q J alliance
against M G in 5 readings. 4Q or J dependence on C is untenable here, because 4Q J in these readings simply continue the
characteristic patterns exhibited throughout 1-2 Samuel where C
influence is impossible. Rather, the C agreement is due to C's
original dependence on an ancient ancestor of 4Q. Consequently,
the trustworthiness of C as a witness to the ancient Palestinian text of Samuel rises, since it may preserve genuine S
readings where 4Q is lacking and M is corrupt.

Part B examines the disagreements in the 4Q J relationship.

J shows an independence (B.1) attributable to his primary role as historian, to indeterminable factors, and to occasional slips.

The most frequent manner in which J departs from 4Q in favor of another biblical Vorlage is in his 11 agreements with G against 4Q M (B.2).

The specifically Greek influence on J is demonstrated in 17 additional readings, all but 2 of which are striking (B.3). And the specifically L influence is evident in 6 further readings (B.4 and 5).

J agrees with M against 4Q in 5 readings (B.6), but in all 5 J effectively depends on L. In fact, we can say that, for all the portions of the Samuel text for which 4QSam^a is extant, J shows no dependence on M specifically or on a Vorlage in the Hebrew language.

J agrees with C against 4Q M G in 3 solid pluses (B.7): the two other readings involving proper names are excessively weak. Insofar as J is dependent on C for the 3 pluses, he appears to be dependent on a Gk form of C. But, in light of the readings in which J = 4Q C ≠ M G and J = 4Q G C ≠ M, and especially in light of the dramatic 4Q J plus at 1 S 11:1, it is not at all impossible that other exemplars of the same Samuel tradition as 4Q contained these three apparent exceptions.

J uses a slightly revised form of the OG (see B.4 and A.5), but that revised form is the early stratum, pL. J shows no connection with the specifically *kaige* stratum of the *kaige* recension (see p. 36 and its note 90).

Thus, we can conclude that J used a text of Samuel strikingly close to 4QSam^a, but that that text was in the Greek language, closely connected with OG/pL and clearly distant from both M and the *kaige* and hexaplaric recensions. Furthermore, although J appears to have supplemented his narrative with details from C on rare occasions, such insertions are rare, and they stem from a source in Greek.

Chapter VII

QUANTITATIVE ANALYSIS OF 2 SAMUEL 6

By grouping readings qualitatively according to patterns
of agreement, the previous chapters attempted to demonstrate
(1) that 4QSam^a exhibits a Palestinian texttype and (2) that
Josephus manifests dependence on the Palestinian text family,
mirroring unique reflections of the 4QSam^a text, through the
medium of a Greek Vorlage.

Quantitative agreement is less significant than qualitative, but it is nevertheless important. In this chapter,
therefore, we shall inquire quantitatively into the text of 4Q
and J, presenting the continuous text of 4Q for an entire chapter and that of J for the same chapter, in order to enable the
reader to obtain a less dissected and more wholistic feel for
the texts of 4Q and J, and to see typical patterns.

The most desirable material for analysis was judged to be
that which best fulfilled the following requirements. The
chapter should have a large amount of text preserved in 4Q. It
should have parallel material in Chronicles. It should be
represented by the Old Greek. And finally, it should provide
sufficient variants to make the analysis worthwhile and to
yield results.

The only chapters of Samuel for which both an extensive
Chronicles parallel exists and the Old Greek is available are 1
S 31 and 2 S 5--10. 2 S 6 was chosen, since it has the largest
amount of text preserved for 4Q. This chapter bountifully fulfilled the condition of sufficient variants, although it is not
abnormally rich in variants (as is, e.g., 1 S 2), and thus is
not atypical.

The present chapter falls naturally into two parts. The
first part will compare the Hebrew texts of 4Q, S^M, and C.
Since 4Q is, after all, a text of Samuel, heavy agreement with
S against C is to be expected. Where 4Q agrees with C against
S, the logical question of 4Q's possible dependence on C will
be raised. Our general question will be whether quantitative
analysis will confirm or confound the results of the preceding

chapters' qualitative analysis.

The second part will compare the text of Josephus for 2 S 6 (= VII.78-89) with $S^{M\ G\ L\ 4Q}$ and $C^{M\ G\ L}$, again to ascertain whether J is dependent on a Palestinian texttype. A third step in this direction will be postponed until chapter VIII below, where the Greek texts will be scrutinized for the purpose of determining whether J's source was a Palestinian text *in Greek*.

A. The Text of 4QSam^a

Below are listed the Hebrew texts of S^M, 4Q, and C^M for those parts of 2 S 6 in which 4Q is both extant and at variance with either S^M or C^M. Pertinent remarks or important readings from G or J are given in the right column.

	S^M	4Q	C^M	Notes
		2 S 6:2 = 1 C 13:6		
1	אתו	אתו	---	
2	מבעלי	בעלה	בעלתה	G conflate, but lacks gloss
3	---	היא	אל	
4	---	קרי[ת] ה	קרית	πολιν Δαυειδ C^G
5	---	[יערים]	יערים	Καριαθιαριμ C^L
6	---	[אשר]	אשר	
7	יהודה	ליהוֹדה (sic ms)	ליהודה	
8	להעלות	להעלו[ת]	להעלות	
		. . .		
9	האלהים	הא[ל]ל[וה]ים	האלהים	
10	---	את	יהוה	
11	אשר	אשר	ירשב	
12	נקרא	נ[קרא]	הכרובים	
13	שם שם	[שם]	אשר	4Q spacing precludes שם 2° and צבאות.
14	יהוה	[יהוה]	נקרא	
15	צבאות	[---]	שם	
16	ישב	[יר]שב	---	
17	הכרבים	הכרוב[ים]	---	
		. . .		
		2 S 6:3 = 1 C 13:7		
18	האלהים	[יהו]הֹ	האלהים	Κυριου OG; θεου L C^G
19	אל	על	על	εφ' G
20	עגלה	עג[לה]	עגלה	

	S^M	4Q	C^M	Notes
		. . .		
21	מבית	מבית	מבית	
22	אבינדב	א[בינדב]	אבינדב	Αμειναδαβ G^{S,C}
		. . .		
23	נהגים	נֹהֹגֹׁיֹֹם	נהגים	
24	את	אֹ[ת]	---	
25	העגלה	הֹעגלה	בעגלה	μετα των βοων J
		2 S 6:4		
26	הדשה--בגבעה	---	---	G^{S,C} lack M's 6-word dittography.
27	עם--הארון	עֹ[ם]--[ה][אֹרֹוֹן]	---	C lacks this 7-word clause.
		. . .		
		2 S 6:5 = 1 C 13:8		
28	וכל	[וכול]	וכל	και παντες οι υιοι L; και οι υιοι OG; και πας C^G
29	בית	בֹּנֹי	---	
30	ישראל	ישׂׂראֹׁל	ישראל	
		. . .		
31	עצי	[עץ]	עז	G conflate
32	ברושים	[ו]בֹמֹזֹׁרֹֹת	ובשירים	
		. . .		
		2 S 6:6 = 1 C 13:9		
33	נכון	נודן	כידן	4Q נידן or
		. . .		
34	---	[את] יֹדו	את ידו	עחד χειρα αυτου G^{S,C}
35	אל	אל	לאחז	επι G; προς L
36	ארון	ארון	את הארון	
37	האלהים	ה[א][ל]והים]	---	
		. . .		
		2 S 6:7 = 1 C 13:10		
38	ויהו	[ו]יכהו	ויכהו	
39	שם	שם	---	εκει G^{S,C}
40	האלהים	האלוהי[ם]	---	
41	על השל	[על אשר]	על אשר	41-45 om OG; επι τη προπετεια G^h L; C^G = 4Q C^M
42	---	[שלח]	שלח	
43	---	[ידו]	ידו	
44	---	אֹל	על	
45	---	[ה]אֹרֹון	הארון	
		. . .		

	S^M	4Q	C^M	Notes
46	עם ארון	ל[פני]	לפני	G Conflate
47	האלהים	[הא]ל[ו]ה[ים]	אלהים	

• • •

2 S 6:9 = 1 C 13:12

48	ויאמר	לאמור	לאמר	G = 4Q C

• • •

49	ארון	[הארון]	ארון	$G^S = M^S$; 4Q unsure; η κιβωτος
50	יהוה	[---]	האדהים	του θεου
51	---	[ויבוא]	---	και ηλθεν
52	---	ארון	---	η κιβωτος
53	---	יהוה	---	του κυριου (θεου oe$_2$) L

• • •

2 S 6:13 = 1 C 15:26

54	ששה	[---]	---	επτα hab επτα χορων J;
55	צעדים	[---]	---	χοροι $C^G = C^M$; 4Q?
56	ויזבח	[?]	ויזבחו	και θυμα
57	---	שב[עה]	שבעה	---
58	שור	פרים	פרים	μοσχος
59	---	ושבע[ה]	ושבעה	---
60	ומריא	[אילים]	אילים	και αρνα G

• • •

2 S 6:14 = 1 C 15:27

61	---	וכל--המשררים ---		10-word plus C; om S^M 4Q
62	---	[---]	ועל	
63	דוד	[ודו]יד	דויד	
64	חגור	חגור	---	
65	אפוד	אפוד	אפוד	
66	בד	בד	בד	

2 S 6:15 = 1 C 15:28

67	ודוד	ודו[יד]	וכל	

• • •

68	ובקול	[ובקו]ל	ובקול	
69	שופר	שופר	שופר	
70	---	...ובחצצרות ---		$C^{M,G}$ insert a list of instruments

2 S 6:16 = 1 C 15:29

71	והיה	ויהי	ויהי	$G^{S,C}$ = 4Q $C^M \neq S^M$

	S^M	4Q	C^M	Notes
		. . .		
		2 S 6:17 = 1 C 16:1		
72	דוד	יד[דו]	דויד	
73	ויעל	ויעל	ויקריבו	
74	דוד	דויד	---	
75	עלות	עו[לות]	עלות	

Comparative Quality of the Hebrew Texts.[1]

4Q is the best of the three Hb texts for this chapter, with eight superior readings (##2, 13-15, 19, 26, 31-32, 34, 46, 71) and no errors (except the self-corrected *lapsus calami* in #7). C is a close second, with six of the same superior readings (##19, 26, 31-32, 34, 46, 71, plus possibly #2), and only one error (the confused transposition of ##10-15; #2 is also possibly an error). Neither text has suffered haplography or dittography, although expansions are numerous, especially in 4Q (##1, 3-6, 27, 29, 37, 39-40, 41-45, 57-60 in 4Q; 3-6, 41-45, 57-60, 61, 70 in C).

The Massoretic Text of Samuel, however, retains its reputation as a poorly preserved text. Containing only two superior readings (##3-6 and 57-60), it displays one haplography (#34 -- *contra* GKC 117g), two dittographies (#13 -- again *contra* GKC 125c -- and #26), fewer expansions than 4Q but more than C (##1, 15, 27, 29, 37, 39-40, 41-45), and four errors (##2, 31-32, 71, and 41), the last of which is an error within an expansion!

Hebraizing Revision in the Greek Text of 2 S 6.

Thackeray and Barthélemy separate 2 S 1-11:1 sharply from the second half of 2 S, assigning 2 S 6 to the "older translator" or the "Old Greek." While their division retains much of its justification, there is, nonetheless, evidence in this chapter of revision, at least some of which is by the hand of the "later translator" or the "*kaige* recension."

We can begin with three doublets in G for which the text of 4Q is extant:

---

1. Readings ##49-53, 56, due to their ambiguity, will not be included in the statistics.

(1) Cf. ##2-7 above = 2 S 6:2:

    4Q (C) (sic)ליהֹוה [אשר יערים ת]קרֹיא היא בעלה

    M   יהודה מבעלי

    G   απο των αρχοντων Ιουδα εν αναβασει

(2) Cf. ##31-32 = 2 S 6:5:

    4Q C   ֹ[בכול עז ו]בֹ̇שֹ̇י̇רֹֹ̇ים

    M   בכל עצי ברושים

    G   εν οργανοις ηρμοσμενοις εν ισχυι και εν ωδαις

(3) Cf. ##46-47 = 2 S 6:7:

    4Q C   [ה]̇א[ו]לֹ[ים]ֹ לֹ[פני האֹ

    M   עם ארון האלהים

    G   παρα την κιβωτον του κυριου ενωπιον του θεου

The general practice of the revisor of G is to prefix to
the preserved OG translation his approximation toward M. Beginning with the third and clearest example: the latter member
ενωπιον του θεου = האלהים לפני 4Q C; the former member = M
(κυριου for האלהים).[2]

In the second example, the latter member εν ισχυι και εν
ωδαις clearly reflects 4Q C (omitting כל). The former member
(also omitting כל) is enigmatic (cf. 6:14 where εν οργανοις
ηρμοσμενοις = עז בכל [?]; cf. also the confusion attested in
H-R 159a and 1008b), but G is apparently attempting to reflect
a plural construct chain (= M), not a conjoined pair (= 4Q C).[3]

In the first example, the latter member εν αναβασει
[Ιουδα] would reflect what was probably the original Hb:
יהודה (ה)בעלה* (for αναβασις = עלה, cf. Judg 11:13,16; 19:30; 1
K 18:36, etc.). Both common sense and our sparse textual evidence indicate that the determinative יהודה is a near-essential
part of the text. The name בעל is too commonplace to be used
without the determinative (just as "Springfield" requires a
state name following; cf. Josh 19:8; 11:17, 12:7, 13:5; Judg
3:3, 20:33; 2 K 4:42; 1 C 5:23; Song 8:11). Textually, in Josh

---

    2. For the OL[S] reading *juxta arcam Dei*, cf. below, p. 219.

    3. Vercellone has an OL reading *in organis armizatis*; cf.
the corruption *percutiebat in organis et armigatis* OL[S] at 6:14.
Armizatis, of course, is not Latin but a morphological Latini-
zation of ηρμοσμενοις [< αρμοζω].

18:14, before the pre-exilic gloss יערים קרית היא was added,
the wording ran יהודה בני עיר בעל קרית אל. And similarly, in
our present passage no text of Samuel (save 𝒢^C which substi-
tutes כל?) or of Chronicles omits יהודה. Only in Josh 15:9,10,
11 does בעלה occur without the necessary determinative יהודה,
but that passage is the boundary list specifically for the
tribe of Judah!

Thus, G's misunderstood εν αναβασει is not a complete reflection of its Vorlage, but *Ιουδα at least (and possibly the
whole gloss *αυτη εστιν Καριαθιαρειμ η εστι του Ιουδα) has been
excised; the original Greek which composed the latter member of
the doublet read εν αναβασει Ιουδα (or εν αναβασει αυτη εστιν
Καριαθιαρειμ η εστι του Ιουδα).

The former member of the first doublet, απο των αρχοντων
Ιουδα, is an exact (if misguided) translation of M's erroneous
consonantal text.

To sum up, the latter member of doublets #3 and #2 patently
agrees with 4Q C, and the latter member of #1 most likely
agrees with the unglossed 4Q C text. On the other hand, the
former member closely agrees with M in examples 1 and 3,
whereas in example 2 nothing can be confidently said about the
former member of M or G beyond the suspicion that G is attempting to translate a syntactic construction closer to that of M
than to that of 4Q C.

A fourth doublet in G occurs within a 4Q lacuna at 6:6
(cf. ##35-37), but G and C help us reconstruct 4Q:

4Q	וישלח עזא [את] יֹדו אל ארון ה[א]ל[ו]הים/ לאחזו כי [
M	וישלח עזה אל ארון האלהים ויאחז בו כי
C^{M,G}	וישלח עזא את ידו לאחז את הארון כי
G^S	και εξετεινεν Οζα την χειρα αυτου επι (προς L) την

κιβωτον του θεου κατασχειν αυτην και εκρατησεν αυτην,
οτι

First, it should be noted that 4Q = G C ≠ M for ידו את
(haplog. M), and also that M misspells the name of עזא: 4Q =
C ≠ M. These points, plus the three doublets just considered,
support our proceeding along the hypothesis that 4Q = G C ≠ M
in this reading as well.

Here, however, the doublet pattern has been reversed. The
latter member of the doublet και εκρατησεν αυτην = M, whereas

the former member κατασχειν αυτην (= לאחזו) resembles C (without following the word order of C).

The extant leather of 4Q (אל ארן) permits us to see that for word order 4Q = S^{M,G} ≠ C. Spacing is tight for 4Q, making לאחזו preferable to ויאחז בו, though that point cannot be pressed too far. But how can it be proven that κατασχειν αυτην (= C) is the OG, that it agrees with 4Q, and that και εκρατησεν αυτην (= M) is a later revision?

Κατεχειν and κρατειν are both used by OG, KR, and α' (!) for אחז (as well as for חזק), so no rigid distinction can be made on the grounds of simple occurrence. But where there is substitution of one for the other, the tendency is for KR to substitute κρατειν for κατεχειν and for other verbs, as in these examples: 2 S 20:9, Jg 16:21, 20:6, Dn 10:8, 11:2,6 (6 certain cases); 1 S 15:27, 2 K 11:12, Ps 56(55):1 (3 possible cases). Two certain examples to the contrary were found (Jg 7:8, Dn 11:43) and one possible example to the contrary (2 K 12:13[12]). Thus, the tendency is three to one for KR to substitute κρατειν for κατεχειν, etc.

Since και εκρατησεν αυτην is definitely the M member of this doublet, and since it is probably the hebraizing revision, its removal may yield the OG (G^{MN} in fact omit!). The resulting G (especially G^{L}) text, and it alone, agrees with 4Q! Only the לאחזו = κατασχειν αυτην correspondence is uncertain; but its probability is high due to the frequent general pattern of 4Q = G C ≠ M and due to the lack of basis for G's infinitive if a 4Q type of Vorlage did not contain it. It may be added, furthermore, that J has κατασχειν *literatim* here (VII.81).

The probable reconstruction of 4Q, then, is as listed above, and it remains only to explain why the doublet pattern of M-approximation prefixed to OG (= 4Q C) is reversed here.

The arrangement within the first doublet above provides a slightly better fit on the basis of content. Within the second and within the third it does not matter -- on the basis of content -- which member precedes. Thus, the later, revisionist element of the doublet tends to precede as long as the content so permits.

In this fourth doublet, the ordinary pattern would be awkward (εξετεινεν ... την χειρα ... και εκρατησεν αυτην κατασχειν

αυτην, οτι), whereas, if the M-approximation is placed after
the OG (εξετεινεν ... την χειρα ... κατασχειν αυτην και εκρατησεν αυτην, οτι), the doublet is hardly noticeable, sounding
like a translation of normal Hebrew repetitiousness.

So far, it has been shown that (when content permits) that
element of the doublets which approximates the M text tends to
precede spatially that element which agrees with 4Q C, but can
the allegation be founded that the approximations toward M are
chronologically subsequent in such a way as to label them later
hebraizing (KR?) revision of the OG toward the Massoretic text?

First, the general (but not absolute) principle has long
since been established that, for a pair of Greek variants, one
closely approximating M, the other more free, the hebraization
tends to be subsequent correction of earlier, freer rendition.
Second, the deletion of Ιουδα in favor of the erroneous απο των
αρχοντων Ιουδα indicates that εν αναβασει [Ιουδα] was the super-
seded translation. Third, the substitution of κρατειν for
κατεχειν in the fourth doublet was seen with fair probability
to be the work of a later KR revisor. Finally, we can see in
6:2 (= 1 C 13:6; cf. ##14-15 above) a clear example of the KR
hand:

4Q	[-- ויהוה]
M	יהוה צבאות
C^M	יהוה
G	κυριου των δυναμεων
L	κυριου σαβαωθ
$C^{G,L}$	κυριου

Calculations of space for 4Q are so close here that it is almost certain that 4Q lacks צבאות. G is thus an approximation
dependent upon the M plus; more important, however, is the fact
that των δυναμεων for צבאות is a key characteristic of Barthélemy's *kaige* recension (*DA*, pp. 82-83; note also Shenkel's KR
characteristic:: αρχων της δυναμεως = שר הצבא, *Chronology* p.
114). Unfortunately, we cannot confirm L as either pL or L_2,
since σαβαωθ could be a liturgical plus, an early transliteration of a proto-M reading, or a late variant of των δυναμεων.

The same reading occurs in 6:18 (= 1 C 16:2) where the
pattern is identical, except that there 4Q is completely lacking. Because of the clear case in 6:2, this identical reading

may also be classified KR.

We thus have six instances in 2 S 6 of hebraizing revision of OG toward M.

Agreements among the Texts

Having compared the texts of 4Q, S^M, and C^M, and having seen both that 4Q offers the best of the Hebrew texts and that the G text has been somewhat revised toward M, we are now in a position to judge the agreements among the various texts more critically.

The text of 4Q agrees with M against C in the following 11 readings: 1, 10-17 (order), 24-25, 27, 35-37, 39-40, 61, 62-64, 67, 70, 73-74.

4Q = C ≠ M, however, in these 13 readings: (2), 3-7, 13, 15 (om צבאות), 19, 26, 31-32, 34, 41-45, 46-47, 48, 57-60, 71.

Displaying its independence, 4Q ≠ M ≠ C in eight readings: (2), 3, 10, 13-15, 18, 29, 33, 44.

In the second part of this chapter the agreements of the G text will be seen more fully, but to help illuminate the text-affiliation we will include here the support of the OG. A pattern of 4Q = M G ≠ C is what is to be expected; that is, that S texts will agree among themselves, and that C texts will differ from them. Upon the frequency of the pattern 4Q = G C ≠ M will depend the persuasiveness and value of the hypothesis that 4Q G C are witnesses to an old Palestinian text of S, as opposed to the Massoretic texttype. Readings fitting the pattern 4Q = C ≠ M G will have to be analyzed to determine whether 4Q depends on C, or vice-versa, or whether G has undergone hebraizing revision.

4Q = M G ≠ C. In all of the 11 readings where 4Q = M ≠ C above, and only in those, G supports 4Q M.

4Q = G C ≠ M. There were 13 readings above in which 4Q = C ≠ M; in 9 of those, G supports 4Q C against M: 2, 13, 19, 26, 31-32, 34, 46-47, 48, 71. The other four are in the following classification.

4Q = C ≠ M G. Seven examples of this pattern were found: 2, 3-7, 14-15, 31-32, 41-45, 46-47, 57-60. But three of these readings (##2, 31-32, 46-47) occur in the preceding classification because they signal the G doublets just discussed. They

(together with ##14-15 and 41-45) involve hebraizing revision
of G, therefore are not OG, and therefore are to be excluded
from this pattern. The other four readings (##3-7, 14-15, 41-
45, 57-60) will be analyzed below for possible dependence of 4Q
or C upon the other.

Dependence of C on a 4Q Texttype

When studying the significance of these quantitative results, one notices that 4Q often agrees with M^S (11 times) but
that 4Q exhibits even more remarkable agreement with C (13
times). The question then arises, whether 4Q is not an exemplar
of the M^S family, simply dependent upon correction toward C for
its superior readings, pluses, etc. The normal direction, of
course, is for Chronicles to be regularly dependent on Samuel
in composition, in Hebrew text, and even somewhat within the
Greek translations. But in isolated instances, such as the
single ms 4QSam^a, it is fully possible that a S ms may have
been corrected on the basis of C readings.

In order to demonstrate dependence of 4Q on C or vice-
versa, one would normally look for cases in which $4Q = C \neq M$
basically, but where either 4Q or C shows development from the
other's reading, such as a further expansion or clarification
or an error.

It is tempting also to look at the pluses in 4Q which are
lacking in C and argue that C is independent of 4Q, otherwise C
would have included the pluses. The argument, however, works
both ways and in either case is false. The divergent pluses in
each simply post-date the separation of the two texts, viz.,
the original composition of C for which Samuel was the basis.
What the disagreement on pluses does tend to prove is that the
final C text is not closely dependent on 4Q itself or on a near
ancestor of it, and similarly that 4Q is not dependent on C or
on an ancestor of C which was anywhere near contemporary with
4Q. Rather, they both go back to a somewhat distant common
archetype. Our question is whether we can find readings which
will point to dependence at close range.

As we search the thirteen readings (above, p. 202) in
which $4Q = C \neq M$, we find four (##2, 3, 7, 10-17) in which
there is a possible development by 4Q or C from the text of the

other. Immediately, we may dismiss #7 which is a simple error
(lectio facilior) corrected by our scribe himself; there can be
no question that his Vorlage read anything but יהודה and that
he himself plainly recognized it--a moment too late.

It is possible that בעלה (#2) already includes the ה-
locative, on the supposition that בעל יהודה* is the name of the
town (Driver). The following data favor this supposition: (1)
מבעלי יהודה M (dittography of yod?) perhaps presupposes בעל;
בעלה (2); Josh 18:14; (3) קרית בעל היא קרית יערים עיר בני יהודה
Josh 15:9 = εις Βααλ (B)AGNΘ rell OL 𝔊 𝔄, εις Βααλαϑ gnt(dp);
and (4) מבעלה M G[(vid)]dgnpt Josh 15:10 may be an erroneous
back-formation, cf. απο Βααλ BANΘ rell OL 𝔊.

If בעל* is the name, C would be an error which would presuppose the tradition of the ancestor of 4Q. If בעלה, however,
is the name, C's now correct locative, adding directional
clarification, would still depend on that 4Q tradition.

The possible uncertainty of #2 may be helped by #3. אל is
a directional clarification, adding greater precision than 4Q;
it is difficult, on the contrary, to imagine replacing אל with
היא. Thus, #3 and probably #2 point toward C dependence on the
4Q tradition.

A fairly clear case of C dependence on the 4Q text tradition is ##10-17. C is a corruption which obviously presupposes
the 4Q M (thus, S) tradition; the lack of שם 2° and צבאות point
directly toward the 4Q tradition in distinction from the M tradition.

Of the four possible clues to dependence, then, one (#7)
is disqualified from testimony either way, whereas two (##3,
10-17) and perhaps a third (#2) are fairly reliable indications
of C dependence on the 4QSam[a] tradition. Since 4Q contains no
errors, it obviously does not follow C in any errors; but note
that C's one certain error (10-15) depends on a 4Q text tradition. Not one clue even hints at 4Q dependence on C.

As we look at the G evidence, this conclusion is further
reinforced. Again dealing with the thirteen readings in which
4Q = C ≠ M, G supports 4Q as a true S text (not reversely dependent on C) in nine of those readings. Only in 3-7, 15, 41-
45, 57-60 is 4Q not supported by G[S]. Already this is a valuable show of strength against M for the affiliates of the Old

Palestinian Samuel text, 4Q G C; but the value is even greater
than it at first appears.

In 3-7 we have seen that *Ιουδα has been excised from the
OG text; there remains the small possibility that the rest of
the expansion was excised along with Ιουδα in the hebraizing
revision. The alternative, that the expansion was never in OG,
would better accord with the characteristic lack of expansions
in the Egyptian text. Whether OG had the expansion (and thus
confirms the reading as genuinely S) or not, חת- and אל point
to C as the later form of the expansion, thus derived from the
old Palestinian Samuel expansion not found in (the Egyptian or)
the Massoretic texttype.

The dependence of C on the 4Q tradition has already been
shown for 10-17, and in addition it is highly probable that,
for ##14-15 within it, the OG (κυριου alone) also supported 4Q.

4Q could show dependence on C in ##41-45, especially if no
other S ms had the plus. But M^S is obviously an error, floun-
dering precisely on the basis of the plus. Thus, M^S originally
contained the clause as did 4Q, which means that it was an
early S expansion, early enough to influence the composition of
C. The OG apparently lacked the plus, going back to an early,
characteristically concise, Egyptian Hebrew text. Since M had
lost most of the expansion, G^h "corrected," translating the M
remnant of it. The small possibility exists, of course, that
the expansion was in OG (together with the Massoretic and Qumran traditions of Samuel) but that it was excised by the later
G revisor (as *Ιουδα and perhaps the rest of ##3-6) when he inserted επι τη προπετεια. Although the OG, then, does not support 4Q, more than adequate support is obtained through the
error in M.

But notice the pattern here. OG apparently lacked the
plus, M had lost most of it, and G^h translated the mutilated
form of M. Thus:

      hab 4Q C^{MG} J;

      om (M) OG;

      G^h poorly attempts to restore.

The pattern is almost identical with that in 3-7:

      hab 4Q C^{MG} J;

      om M OG;

G^h poorly attempts to restore.
Were it not that M preserves the truncated עַל הֻשֹׁל in #41,
traces of the originally S expansion would have vanished from
all S mss (save 4Q J), and the two patterns would be identical.
This provides strong basis for confidence that 3-7 also was an
old Palestinian Samuel expansion, and not a C expansion which
4Q appropriated!

The final example, ##57-60, must remain ambiguous. It is
impossible to arrange the variants in this verse in such a way
as to do justice to their complexity, and it is impossible to
reconstruct 4Q with confidence for the first half of the verse.
Only the following can be noted.

In 6:13a J = G ≠ M ≠ C (de 4Q). In 6:13b 4Q = C ≠ M ≠ G;
G = M probably for ##58 and 60, but G ≠ M for #56. The only
agreement for the entire verse (beyond $C^M = C^G$) is between J
and G^S. J mentions only three items: (i) the Ark-bearers,
which every text has; (ii) the Levites, which is shown in the
next section (p. 214) to be a free addition of J, not derived
from a Vorlage; and (iii) the seven choirs, which is attested
in G^S OL^{SV} alone. J is clearly dependent on G here, but from
where did G obtain its reading? The line-up of G OL J for επτα
χοροι, the lack of G variants, and the presence of שבעה in 4Q C
indicate a possible שבעה חבלים* in the Egyptian Hb text of
Samuel, if not in the very lacuna in 4Q itself. But that is
conjecture, and the reading remains ambiguous: there is insufficient grounds for positing either that C is dependent on 4Q
or that 4Q is dependent on C.

Summary.

To summarize, then, focusing first on the G evidence: G =
M ≠ 4Q only for two words (##58 and 60) where 4Q expands;
otherwise G supports 4Q when 4Q sides with M against C (all 11
times) as well as when 4Q sides with C against M (9 out of 13
times). Three of the exceptions to the latter are due to the
fact that 4Q C share expansions characteristic of the Palestinian text of S (a conclusion based on separate evidence)
which the characteristically more concise Egyptian text of
Samuel lacked. The fourth (##14-15) is not an exception.
After the demonstrated KR plus is removed from G, the restored

OG does in fact support 4Q C, bringing to a total of 10 out of
13 the number of agreements in which the Palestinian Samuel
witnesses 4Q G C agree against the Massoretic text.

Focusing on the larger issue of 4Q and C dependence, in
thirteen readings it was possible that 4Q might depend on C.
But in ten of the thirteen, the OG/pL of S testifies that the
reading is a genuine S reading on which C was originally dependent (as is normal). For the remaining three, (a) ##41-45
is apparently lacking in the OG but was certainly in the old
Hebrew tradition of S. (b) The reading ##3-7 is more amoeban,
but insofar as there are any clues, they point toward Samuel
originality: i) the overall pattern is nearly identical with
that of ##41-45 which definitely shows S originality; (ii) the
OG apparently lacked ##3-6, but the reading is contiguous with
a near certain G^h excision from OG; and (iii) הייא probably and
בעלה possibly indicate 4Q originality. (c) Finally, ##57-60 is
ambiguous, with the evidence pointing no more strongly in favor
of 4Q dependence on C than it does in favor of C dependence on
an old S reading. Thus, there is, among the thirteen possibilities, not one clear bit of evidence and scant possible evidence for the unlikely supposition that 4Q is dependent on C.

On the other hand, while ##57-60 remains ambiguous, ten
clear examples and two highly probable examples (##3-7 and 15)
demonstrate C dependence on an old S text of which 4Q is a
direct descendant.

But strong as this argument is, even stronger proof of
4Q's independence from C is patent in the consistency of 4Q's
patterns of variation from M^S in those parts (the major part of
the text!) for which C does not reproduce S material.

B. The Text of Josephus

In the second part of this chapter we shall compare the
text of Josephus with the text of 2 S 6 which we have just
analyzed. The details of Josephus' text (VII.78-89) will be
listed in order, and the possibility of Josephus' deriving the
detail from the texts of Samuel (M G L 4Q) and Chronicles (M G
L) will be noted thus:

    =   derivable
    (=)   probably derivable

/   not derivable
(/)   probably not derivable
[ ]   probable 4Q reconstruction
     A blank for 4Q indicates a lacuna, for which no judgment should be made.

J	M	G	L	4Q	M	G	L	Notes
VII.78		2 S 6:1			1 C 13:1			
1 battle precedes	=	=	=		/	/	/	J = 2 S 5:25 ≠ 1 C 12:40
2 David consulted	/	/	/		=	=	=	
3 with elders,	/	/	/		/	/	=	
4 leaders, and chiliarchs	/	/	/		(=)	=	=	
5 decided to	/	/	/		=	=	=	
6 summon	(=)	=	=		=	=	=	*ריאסף M^S for ויסף
7 countrymen from whole land	(=)	(=)	(=)		=	=	=	
8 (lack of total)	(/)	(/)	(/)		(=)	(=)	(=)	J tends to echo numbers if in Vorlage
9 in prime of life	=	=	=		/	/	/	
10 then priests	/	/	/		=	=	=	
11 and	/	/	/		=	/	=	Levitical priests C^G cf. p. 230 #17
12 Levites	/	/	/		=	=	=	
13 go to	/	/	/		=	=	=	
14 Kariathiarima	/	/	/	=	=	(=)	=	cf. #16
15 to carry Ark	=	=	=	=	=	=	=	
16 from there (= Kariath.)	/	/	/	[=]	=	(/)	=	C^G confused
17 to Jerusalem	(=)	(=)	(=)		=	=	=	J = C 13:3 προς ημας
18 keep & worship it there	/	/	/		(=)	(=)	(=)	##18,20 understood from 19
VII.79		2 S 6:1			1 C 13:3			
19 for if in Saul's reign	/	/	/		=	=	=	
20 would not have suffered	/	/	/		(=)	(=)	(=)	
21 people assembled	=	=	=		=	=	=	
22 king came to Ark	=	=	=		=	=	=	
23 priests	/	/	/	[/]	/	/	/	
24 carried it	=	=	=	=	=	=	=	

J	M	G	L	4Q	M	G	L	Notes
VII.79		2 S 6:1			1 C 13:3			
25 out of Amina-dab's house	=	=	=	=	=	=	=	εις G^BA ≠ OG; cf. 1 S 7:1; LMN++ = OG
26 put it on new wagon	=	=	=	=	=	=	=	
27 committed it	/	/	/	/	/	/	/	
28 to brothers	(/)	=	=	[(/)]	(=)	=	=	Ahio Hb T; αδελφοι Gk
29 and sons	=	=	=	[=]	/	/	/	
30 to draw it	=	=	=	=	=	=	=	
31 with oxen	(/)	(/)	(/)	(/)	(/)	/	/	μετα των βοων J
VII.80		2 S 6:5			1 C 13:8			
32 king led	=	=	=	[=]	=	=	=	
33 and all	=	/	=	[=]	=	=	=	
34 the people	=	=	=	=	=	=	=	
35 hymning	/	=	=	=	=	=	=	ברושים M, no word for sing
36 and singing	/	=	=	=	=	=	=	
37 all native melody	(=)	(=)	(=)	(=)	(=)	(=)	(=)	J summary
38 strings	=	=	=	=	=	=	=	
39 dancing	=	=	=	=	=	=	=	
40 psalms	/	=	=	=	=	=	=	cf. #35
41 plus trumpets	/	(=)	(=)			=	=	=	4Q lacuna; could = S or C
42 and cymbals	=	=	=	[=]	=	=	=	
43 Ark to Jerus.	(/)	(/)	(/)	(/)	(/)	(/)	(/)	J narration
VII.81		2 S 6:6			1 C 13:9			
44 came to thresh-ing floor	=	=	=	=	=	=	=	
45 of Cheidon	/	/	/	/	=	/	=	4Q נידן\גודן C; כידן
46 Oza died	=	=	=	=	=	=	=	
47 by wrath of God	=	=	=	=	=	=	=	
48 oxen tilted Ark	=	=	=	=	=	=	=	
49 he stretched out hand	/	=	=	=	=	=	=	
50 to check it	=	=	=	[=]	=	=	=	
51 not priest touching it	/	/	/	[/]	/	/	/	Rabbinic; cf. Loeb, p. 403, note c.
52 God made him die	=	=	=	=	=	=	=	

	J	M	G	L	4Q	M	G	L	Notes
	VII.82		2 S 6:8				1 C 13:11		
53	Both king	=	=	=	=	=	=	=	
54	and people	/	/	/	[/]	/	/	/	
55	"displeased"	/	=	=	/	/	=	=	angry Hb; disheartened G; J follows euphemistic G
56	at Oza's death	=	=	=	=	=	=	=	
57	called "Oza's Breach"	(=)	=	=	(=)	(=)	=	=	J = G translation
58	David, fearing	=	=	=	=	=	=	=	
59	he too might suffer	=	=	=		=	=	=	
60	if brought Ark into city,	=	=	=		=	=	=	
61	since Oza died	=	=	=		=	=	=	
62	because he out-stretched hand,	/	/	/	=	=	=	=	only J 4Q C^{MG} repeat #49
	VII.83		2 S 6:9				1 C 13:13		
63	did not bring Ark	=	=	=		=	=	=	
64	to himself in city	=	=	=		=	=	=	
65	diverted to Obadaros,	=	=	=		=	=	=	
66	a Levite;	/	/	/		/	/	/	Gittite S C
67	there 3 months	=	=	=		=	=	=	
68	good to Obad.	=	=	=		=	=	=	
	VII.84		2 S 6:12				1 C 14:1		om ##69-72 C
69	king heard	=	=	=		/	/	/	
70	Obad. prospered,	=	=	=		/	/	/	
71	feared no harm	/	/	(=)		/	/	/	= L OL plus
72	brought Ark	=	=	=		/	/	/	
	VII.85		2 S 6:13				1 C 15:25		14:1--15:24 = C insertions
73	priests carried	/	/	/		(/)	(/)	(/)	Levites C; cf. #66
74	seven	/	=	=	=	=	=	=	6 paces M
75	choirs led	/	=	=		/	/	/	7 bulls C; 4Q?
76	which king marshalled	/	/	/	[/]	/	/	/	
77	king playing & plucking lyre	/	(=)	=		/	(=)	(=)	J = L; leaping & whirling M^S; dancing & sporting C

	J	M	G	L	4Q	M	G	L	Notes
	VII.85		2 S 6:13				1 C 15:25		
78	Michal mocked	=	=	=		=	=	=	
	VII.86		2 S 6:17				1 C 16:1		
79	Ark into tent	=	=	=	[=]	=	=	=	
80	which David set up	=	=	=	[=]	=	=	=	
81	burnt offerings	=	=	=	=	=	=	=	
82	and peace offerings	=	=	=	[=]	=	/	=	σωτηριου c^G
83	feasted the people	=	=	=		=	=	=	4Q *deest* for rest of 2 S 6
84	men, women	=	=	=		=	=	=	
85	and children	(/)	(/)	(/)		(/)	(/)	(/)	"all" SC
	VII.86		2 S 6:19				1 C 16:3		
86	gave out breads &	=	=	=		=	=	=	J = S^{GL} (C^L) *literatim*
87	part of sacrifice	=	=	=		=	=	=	
88	dismissed people	(=)	(=)	(=)		(=)	(=)	(=)	= 1 C 16:43; 16:4-42 is C insertion
89	& went home	=	=	=		=	=	=	
	VII.87		2 S 6:20						C omits remainder
90	Michal came to D.	=	=	=					
91	"blessed" David	/	=	=					J repeats G euphemism; om M
92	but reproached	=	=	=					
93	for dancing	/	=	=					ορχουμενος J; ορχουμενων G^L OL M! הרקים; הרקד(י)ם*; (=) T = M סריקיא
94	disorderly	(=)	(=)	(=)					
95	nude	=	=	=					
96	before maids	=	=	=					the maids of your slaves S$^{M, G}$
97	*and* slaves	/	/	/					
	VII.88		2 S 6:21						C omits
98	he not ashamed	(=)	(=)	(=)					
99	to please God,	=	=	=					
100	God honored him	=	=	=					
101	above Saul & all	=	=	=					
102	he would play	/	=	=					
103	and dance often	=	=	=					

J	M	G	L	
VII.88		2 S 6:21		
104 caring not if	(=)	(=)	(=)	
105 disgraceful to *her*	/	=	=	to him M; to her G OL
106 and to maids	/	/	/	
VII.89		2 S 6:23		
107 Michal bore David no children	=	=	=	
108 five by later marriage	/	/	/	J harmonizes with 2 S 21:8
VII.90		2 S 7:1		17:1 in 1 C
109 David wants temple	=	=	=	

J's primary dependence is upon a text of S, not of C. His order as well as various readings testify to this.

The order of VII.78-89 gives strong evidence of dependence on S for beginning, middle, and end. (a) VII.78 (= 2 S 6:1 = 1 C 13:1, cf. #1 above) immediately follows the rout of the Philistines narrated at the close of 2 S 5, which rout occurs in C at 1 C 14![4] (b) VII.78-89 is a unified narrative of the ark's transport from Kiriath-jearim to Jerusalem; it is likewise a unified narrative in S; but C interrupts (see ##73, 88) this narrative several times with lengthy (e.g., all of 1 C 14) extraneous materials and scatters the story-line through 1 C 13; 15:1,3,15-16,25-29; 16:1-3,43. (c) VII.87-89, the denouement for J and S, is lacking in C,[5] and the story is followed directly in J (VII.90) and 2 S (7:1) by David's desire to build a temple (#109), whereas C (16:4-42) follows with cultic material and a psalm, narrating David's desire for a temple only in 17:1.

---

4. 1 C 14:17 closes, furthermore, with a report about the spread of David's fame, which J in agreement with S lacks. For the order, cf. also Vann., p. 144.

5. 1 C 15:29 relates that Michal saw and despised David but does not narrate the altercation which S (followed by J) narrates in detail.

In addition to the argument from order, there are five
readings in which J = S ≠ C. J could derive the following features only from S (C lacks):

    9   the prime of life
    29   and sons
    69-72   The king heard of Obadaros' prosperity, and,
            fearing no harm, brought the Ark to himself.
    75   seven choirs (only from GL)
    90-108 (discussed immediately above).

Despite J's primary dependence on a text of S, the opening
part of J's account agrees with that of C, not of S. J relates
David's consultation with the elders, leaders, and chiliarchs,
the recruiting from the whole country, the priests and Levites,
Kiriath-jearim, and the inattention to the Ark during Saul's
reign (the major part of ##2-20)--none of which is in S^MGL.

Apart from this introduction, however, there is not a
single detail in J for which he is solely dependent on C; i.e.,
there is no detail in J found also in some C mss but lacking in
all S mss. The three apparent exceptions (##45, 62, 73) to
this are specious.

In #45 the name of the threshing floor is confused in all
texts. J's "Cheidon" appears to be derived from כידן C. But
4QSam^a has נידן\נודן, and in Hasmonaean palaeography both *waw*
and *yod* are ligatured to preceding *kaph* and *nun*, while the only
difference between *kaph* and *nun* is the presence of a short
horizontal top stroke for *kaph*: ב\ﬥ cf. *BANE*, pp. 166-167.

The detail in #62 also occurs in 4Q, and we noted in the
preceding section that the corrupt remnant of this expansion in
S^M testifies to the fact that it was originally a S reading,
not a C detail.

In #73 J has των μεν ιερεων βασταζοντων αυτην (= the Ark).
M has נשאי ארון, G αιροντες την κιβωτον, C^M הלוים נשאי ארון,
and C^G τους Λευειτας αιροντας την κιβωτον.

In this chapter, J mentions priests and/or Levites four
times (##10-12, 23, 51, 66) in addition to #73. In ##10-12 J
says "priests and Levites," exactly as his source (here C^ML)
says. In #23, using the same vocabulary as in #73, he says ην
βασταξαντες ... οι ιερεις, while neither "priests" nor
"Levites" occurs in any ms. In #51, he draws on no biblical

source (but rather, Rabbinic interpretation) for his notice
that Oza was not a ιερευς. And finally, in #66, no biblical ms
for this passage tells him that Obadaros was a Levite (though
cf. the lists in 1 C 15:18,21,24); they all have "Gittite" instead.

Thus, in three of the other four occurrences of priests
and/or Levites, J has freely added the detail, in contrast to
his source. In the one case (##10-12) where his source does
mention priests and/or Levites, J copies this exactly. In #73,
then, all three facts--(1) that three out of four times J adds
priests/Levites in contrast to his source, (2) that when he
does borrow from his source, he does so exactly, and (3) that
here he is using the identical vocabulary of #23 where his
source lacked priests and/or Levites--indicate that J is probably adding "priests" freely, not deriving it from "Levites"
of C.

The lack of the pattern J = C ≠ S after the introductory
section indicates that our comments should proceed in two
stages, discussing ##2-20 first and then the remainder of the
chapter.

The patterns of agreement for ##2-20 are as follows:

$J = C \neq S$	2, 3, 4, 5, 10, 11, 12, 13, 19 (cf. 7, 8, 17, 18, 20)
$J = S \neq C$	9
$J = 4Q\ C \neq S^{MGL}$	14 (cf. 16)
$J = C^M \neq C^{GL}$	never
$J = C^{GL} \neq C^M$	(cf. 4)
$J = C^G \neq C^L$	never
$J = C^L \neq C^{MG}$	3
$J = C^{ML} \neq C^G$	11 (cf. 14, 16: = 4Q also)

The nine certain and five probable readings in which J =
C ≠ S clearly demonstrate that J has drawn these details from a
narrative like that found in 1 C 13:1-6 (not 2 S 6:1-2).

Within the C testimony, J is never dependent on the Hebrew
alone nor on C^G alone, but on the contrary is manifestly dependent on C^L uniquely in #3, is lexically dependent[6] on $C^{L\,(G)}$

---

6. This proleptic conclusion will be discussed in the
next chapter (pp. 230, 242-243, 245) and shown to be even more

in #4, and relates details from C^{ML} not found in C^G (##11,16).
From this small amount of C testimony, the tenuous conclusion
would be that J supplements his S narrative with this material
drawn from C^L. Two small bits of data, however, still signal
for incorporation into that conclusion. Reading #9 shows that,
even within this "supplement from C^L," J draws a detail from
his short S source.

The second bit of data, viz., J = 4Q C ≠ S^{MGL} in ##14 and
16, especially with the preceding sixteen lines in 4Q lost,
glistens with an iceberg's visibility.

In the dramatic plus (cf. pp. 166-170) at the beginning of
chapter 11 in 1 S (a chapter without parallel in C), J = 4Q
alone, where S^{MGL} have lost the original narrative, quite
likely by M haplography and then subsequent excision of GL
material on the basis of M. The identical pattern (except that
C now parallels S) again at the beginning of this chapter for-
bids a skeptical suppression of the possibility that the old
Palestinian Samuel text contained the material in ##2-20.

The last sixteen lines of the prior column in 4Q, which
contained the beginning of 2 S 6, are exasperatingly missing.
Space calculations, however, indicate that 4Q finished 2 S 5
and began 2 S 6 in approximately the same amount of space that
S^{MGL} did. And since there is no reason to believe that the end
of 2 S 5 differed in the S texts, we cannot suppose that 4QSam^a
contained an introductory section for 2 S 6 which contained the
material in J and C for ##2-20. This seriously diminishes, of
course, the probability that the old Palestinian text of 2 S 6
contained the longer version, though that possibility lingers
in gossamer form. We are working, nonetheless, with 4QSam^a,
and our conclusions must accord with its certain or probable
witness, and thus we conclude that for ##2-20 J supplemented
his narrative with material from C (and probably C^L specifically), though within that supplement he used one detail found
only in S (#9) and one detail which 4QSam shared (#14, cf. #16).

Because of the large number of possible combinations of
textual patterns for the remainder of the chapter (##21-109),
we shall discuss J's agreement with each of the possible

_____

compelling than presented here.

Vorlagen individually. We shall begin with 4Q.

4QSam^a

4Q is extant for only 31 of J's 108 details, reconstruction being possible for another 14 details, totalling 45. For
five of the 31 extant readings, however, only with probability
can it be judged that J could or could not have derived his detail from 4Q. Thus, there are only 26 items in which 4Q and J
can clearly agree or disagree, and there are only 19 additional
items in which 4Q and J can with probability be judged to agree
or disagree.

In 88½% of the clear readings (23 out of 26) J = 4Q, while
only in three details (##27, 45, 55) does J clearly disagree
with 4Q. Of the 19 probable readings, J = 4Q in 12 (63%),
while J ≠ 4Q in seven (37%). These, however, are raw statistics.

Of the three clear disagreements between J and 4Q, (a) J
did not acquire #27 from any biblical manuscript, and therefore
it is nullified; (b) #45 is the problematic Cheidon, where 4Q
is, after all, only one short stroke (נ/כ) away from J C; and
(c) J disagrees with the 4Q Hebrew text for #55 in favor of
agreement with the Greek text (see below)!

Thus, J = 4Q clearly in 23 out of 25 possible instances
(92%), disagreeing only by a stroke in one reading and disagreeing in the other because J used his 4Q texttype in Greek.

Of the seven details which J probably did not derive from
4Q (##23, 28, 31, 43, 51, 54, 76), all but #28 are not derived
from any biblical ms, and thus are to be ignored. And in #28
(see below) it is again precisely because J used a Greek Vorlage that he disagrees with 4Q--or, rather, agrees with its
Greek counterpart, G L.

M^S

Josephus, then, shares an amazing alliance with 4Q. When
we match M against this alliance, it becomes certain that M was
not J's Vorlage.

While J is diverging from 4Q in the three clear J ≠ 4Q
disagreements (##27, 45, 55), M gains no ground: (a) #27 is
similarly nullified for M; (b) M, with נכון in #45, is

noticeably farther than 4Q from J C; and (c) M shares with 4Q
the starker Hb reading in #55 which G and its dependents, J and
OL, have mollified.

It is yet more startling that, in those 23 clear agreements
between J and 4Q, M^S fails to agree with J 4Q seven times (##14,
35, 36, 40, 49, 62, 74). Since #40 is for J merely a repetition of 35 and 36, we can get a fairer view of M by discounting
that disagreement. Nonetheless, J = 4Q ≠ M in 27% (6 out of
22) of the J 4Q correspondences. Number 14 depends on a 4Q
plus; ##35-36 are due to an erroneous variant in M; #49 is due
to an M haplography and #62 to an M corruption of the expansion
in 4Q; and #74 is possibly due to an expansion in 4Q where M
preserves perhaps the superior reading.

Thus, J follows the 4Q texttype in its inferior as well as
superior readings, in its expanded as well as non-apocopated
readings. He never agrees with M^S against 4Q, but agrees with
4Q in 92% of its extant readings, though M fails to keep pace
in 27% of those 4Q J readings. Of the two clear and one probable cases of disagreement between 4Q and J, 4Q is once merely
a single stroke away from agreement (while M is noticeably further away), and twice 4Q bows with M to J's choice of a Greek
Vorlage. M was not Josephus' Vorlage.

G L

Whereas J never agrees with M against G L, conversely J =
G L ≠ M thirteen times (##28, 35, 36, 49, 55, 71, 74, 75, 77,
91, 93, 102, 105; cf. 6, 40, 41, 57).

M simply lacks #91 and errs in ##35, 36, 49. Where M departs from G L on variants (##74-75, 77, 93, 105), J follows
G L.[7] In #71 J depends on a plus found only in L OL.

With the possible exception of J's puzzling μετα των βοων,

---

7. This is probably the pattern for #41 as well; where J
has σαλπιγγος, M has a list of instruments but no trumpets, and
G has a similar list but includes αυλοι, which means "any wind-
instrument," even (with Ευναλιου, Anth.P. 6.151) "trumpet."
C^{MG} have ובחצצרות / σαλπιγξιν here. But 2 S 6:15 (= 1 C 15:28)
includes שופר / σαλπιγγος. And J's lists of instruments, as
will be seen in the next chapter, borrow from each other.

none of his readings suppose a Hebrew rather than a Greek Vorlage, though eight of the above readings point with varying
degrees of insistence toward a Greek not a Hebrew Vorlage (##
28, 55, 74, 75, 77, 91, 93, 102).

(#28) In the consonantal Hebrew text of S C (de 4Q) אחיו
seems ambiguous, capable of being either the proper name Ahio
or the singular or plural form "his brother(s)," the context
also permitting either interpretation. But S^M in 6:4b (om C^M)
removes the possibility of ambiguity: ואחיו הלך לפני הארון.
As it stands, M reads "and Ahio (or: his brother) walked before the Ark." G, however, with και οι αδελφοι αυτου επορευοντο,
had opted for "his brothers," and it is no coincidence that J
wrote αδελφοις.

(#55) The Hebrew texts (4Q, M, and C^M) all have ויחר at
6:7 and 6:8. For the latter, OG, with the slight but clever
substitution of και ηθυμησεν (6:8) for και εθυμωθη (6:7),
achieves a theologically less offensive translation. C^G,
against C^M!, echoes OG exactly; neither has a variant for
either verb (save the hebraizing revision οργιλον of σ' at 6:8),
and *Contristatusque* survives in OL^S. For a similar softening
in G of man's anger toward God in M, cf. Jon 4:9. J's εδυσ-
φορησαν again betrays his use of a Greek, not Hebrew, Vorlage.

(##74-75) J's επτα χορων is dependent on the G L OL variant επτα χοροι, with no other text having anything resembling
χοροι (4Q de; hab שבעה פרים).

(#91) Only G L have this reading. Note that G L present
another euphemism,[8] followed seriously by J (VII.87).

(#93) In the pre-Hasmonaean stage of palaeography and
orthography, the variants הרקדם and הרקים arose (cf. מרקד 1 C
15:29). α' and σ' are faithful to M, but all other G mss, plus
OL, read ορχουμενων. J reads ορχουμενος.

(##102, 77) The verbs for #102 are ושחקתי; και παιξομαι
και ορχησομαι G omn; *et ludam, saltabo* OL^S. *Ludere*, παιζειν,

---

8. For our purposes, it matters not whether M lacked or
excised an original "cursed"; but cf., interestingly, 1 S 25:22,
where a tendentious scribe has removed another possible curse
from David, this time by adding איבי (lacking in OG, inserted
into G^h): כה יעשה אלהים לדוד * כה יעשה אלהים לאיבי דוד became
כה יעשה אלהים לאיבי דוד.

and שׁחק all mean "to play" in the sense of "to sport." The
Latin and Greek verbs also mean "to play a musical instrument,"
a meaning not shared by the Hebrew verb. J here reads παιζειν
τε και πολλακις χορευσαι (VII.88 Niese; it does not matter
whether we follow his or Marcus' edition), and fortunately he
leaves no doubt how he understands παιζειν. For, four sen-
tences earlier (VII.85 = #77), he has αυτου δ' εν κινυρα παι-
ζοντος και κροτουντος, meaning not "to play, to sport," but
expressly "to play a musical instrument." But #77 adds not
just lexical precision; it adds precision concerning Vorlage.
For M has מפזז ומכרכר (leaping and whirling); de 4Q; מרקד ומשׂחק
(dancing and sporting) c^M; ορχουμενον και ανακρουομενον (dancing and plucking strings) G; παιζοντα και ορχουμενον και ανακρουομενον L; ορχουμενον και παιζοντα c^G. J's εν κινυρα παι-
ζοντος και κροτουντος cannot be derived from M or c^M; επτα χορων
(##74-75) immediately preceding in J eliminates c^MG; G is possible, but only in L are both J words found!

The Testimony of the Old Latin

It is not suggested that OL was J's Vorlage, but the traditional view that OL usually reflects OG and/or pL warrants
our inclusion of its testimony here. The traditional view is
fully vindicated for 2 S 6. Pertinent fragments will be noted
according to the numbering system of J's details above.

(#8) *70,000* OL^V = G; ≠ 30,000 M. As observed above, J,
following C, omits.

(#49) *pro ignorantia: et mortuus est juxta arcam Dei* OL^S.
This OL fragment quoted from Jerome by Sabatier follows the M
G^h (≠ J 4Q OG c^MG) reading in #49 and continues in that pattern
with its next clause: *juxta arcam Dei* = the former member of
the G doublet παρα την κιβωτον του κυριου (= M G₂), the latter
member, ενωπιον του θεου (= 4Q OG c^MG), being omitted. If this
is truly OL, then it derives from an OG text which had already
undergone some revision toward M, or it itself corrects toward
M (note *Dei* = M ≠ G). Whichever is the case, it is the only
OL fragment which clearly does not reflect OG and therefore
should not and does not agree with J.

(#55) *contristatusque* OL^S. As observed above, OL, together with c^G and J, follows the euphemistic G against all Hb

texts.

(#71) *et dixit Dauid Revocabo benedictionem in domum meam*
OL^V; *dixitique Dauid Ibo et reducam arcam cum benedictione in
domum meam* OL^S; + και ειπεν $\overline{δαδ}$ επιστρεψω (+ την κιβωτον του $\overline{θυ}$
και b´) την ευλογιαν εις τον οικον μου bgozc$_2$e$_2$. Only L OL
have this plus; J incorporates it negatively: θαρσησας ως
ουδενος κακου πειρασομενος την κιβωτον προς αυτον μετακομιζει.

(##74-75) *septem chori* OL^V; *et erant cum Dauid septem
chori, et victima vituli* OL^S = OG J only.

(#93) *unus ex saltoribus* OL^{SV} = OG J ≠ M.

(#102) *et ludam, saltabo* OL^S = OG J ≠ M.

(#105) *nugax in conspectu tuo* OL^{SV} = OG J ≠ M.

Thus, once (#8) OL = G ≠ J, where J is following C against
all known S mss. And once (#49) OL(?) is already reflecting
the developed G$_2$ text, as opposed to the OG, and so J disagrees
with (the not yet existing) OL, siding rather with OG 4Q C^{MG}.

But in seven other cases J = OL G ≠ M (##55, 71, 74, 75,
93, 102, 105), and for one of these J = OL L ≠ G (#71).

C. Conclusion

The extant text of 4QSam^a through 2 S 6 not only agrees
with C slightly more often than it does with M, it shows a
superior Hebrew text. The 4Q C agreement is not, however, to
be attributed to 4Q dependence on C but to C's original dependence on the old Palestinian Samuel text of which 4QSam^a is a
descendant.

The witness of G, and frequently OL, in support of 4Q
both for 4Q's agreements with M (thus genuine S readings) and
for its agreements with C (thus Palestinian S readings) again
coincides with the 4Q G pattern for the remainder of 1-2 Samuel
where C lacks a parallel.

The text of J through 2 S 6 shares an amazingly close
alliance with 4Q, scoring 92% straight agreement, 96% if allow-
ance is made for the fact that J's Vorlage was in a Greek form,
and 100% if the minute difference is ignored in a proper name
infected with rampant corruption in all traditions. J is, on
the other hand, clearly distant from M.

He shows close agreement with the OG/pL text. Eight readings betray a specifically Greek Vorlage, while none indicates a

Hebrew Vorlage (except for the non-persuasive μετα των βοων possibility which will be discussed in chapter VIII, part D).

Thus, the witnesses 4Q G L OL C J will often, especially where M is suspect, provide or point to the original text of Samuel.

"Aalglatt," begins Mez, "slippery as an eel, J slips away over the difficulties of its Vorlage, just as Josephus himself did over the tumbled ruins of his people."[1]

Mez nonetheless made a valiant attempt to demonstrate that that Vorlage was a Greek bible of a proto-Lucianic nature. And though his attempt did not fully succeed, leaving openings for the attacks of Rahlfs, Smith, and others,[2] his efforts did attain a qualified success. Similarly, without raising hopes to exaggerated altitudes, the present study intends to demonstrate anew that the bible which lay before Josephus as he compiled the Samuel portion of his *Jewish Antiquities* was a Greek bible of an Old Greek/proto-Lucianic nature.

One can never rule out the possibility, of course, that Josephus had two or more bibles (Greek, Hebrew, Aramaic) and that as a historian he used all at his disposal to check, correct, and amplify his narrative. The present hypothesis, however, is that, whether or not he used other aids, Josephus continuously and predominantly used a Greek bible, as opposed to a Hebrew (or Aramaic) bible, as his main source for 1-2 Samuel.

There are, admittedly, Josephan readings which cannot be accounted for, but this is true of every biblical manuscript and of every extended series of quotations from the bible. In addition to the explanations of the human margin of error due to Josephus and of the vicissitudes of the bi-millennial transmission of his text, otherwise unaccountable readings can be explained in part as marginal annotations made by Josephus himself in his Greek bible intermittently during the decade and

---

1. "Aalglatt, wie Josephus durch die stürzenden Trümmer seines Volkes, schlüpft Jos. über die Schwierigkeiten seiner Vorlage hinweg." Adam Mez, *Die Bibel des Josephus*, p. 2.

2. For Rahlfs' critique, cf. pp. 24-27 and 251f. Henry Preserved Smith's analysis in *The Books of Samuel* (ICC; Edinburgh, 1899), pp. 402-407, is of little help.

more which he spent composing the *Antiquities*. What scholar's
much-used source book is not replete with corrections, additions, recordings of private judgments, etc., made throughout
the years he has labored over his material?

With these possibilities in mind, we shall commence by
considering a few basic facts showing that it was fully possible for Josephus to have made use of a Greek bible, and then
we shall present yet more evidence indicating that he did in
fact make heavy use of a Greek bible. Finally, we shall review
the evidence interpreted as indicating a Semitic Vorlage.

A. The Possibilities

That it was possible for Josephus, whose native language
was Aramaic or Hebrew, to use the Greek language is obvious
from his many volumes composed in Greek. Though he confesses
his employment of assistants (*Ap*. I.50), he nonetheless boasts
of his labors and achievements in mastering the Greek language
(*Ant*. XX.262-265), and there is in fact no reason to doubt that
he had acquired some proficiency in Greek.[3]

The Greek Old Testament was available in Italy in the late
first century of our era, witnessed by Clement of Rome (flor.
96).[4] Justin, in Rome a half century after Josephus, not only
used a Greek bible but even used the precise Old Greek/proto-
Lucianic type of bible that we are assigning to Josephus[5] or a
developed (KR) form of it.[6] Besides, Josephus himself may well

---

3.   See the discussion of Josephus' knowledge of Greek in
J. Sevenster, *Do You Know Greek? How Much Greek Could the First
Jewish Christians Have Known?* (NTS XIX; Leiden, 1968), pp. 61-
76; cf. also Thackeray, *Josephus*, pp. 100-124.

4.   Jellicoe, *The Septuagint and Modern Study* (Oxford,
1968), p. 87.

5.   Cf. Wilhelm Bousset, *Die Evangeliencitate Justins des
Märtyrers* (Göttingen, 1891), p. 20; Mez, p. 84, and Metzger, p.
33.

6.   Joost Smit Sibinga, *The Old Testament Text of Justin
Martyr, I: The Pentateuch* (Leiden, 1963), pp. 149-150. Sibinga,
who so far has published results only for the Pentateuch, does
express the necessary caveat of distinguishing between

have brought a copy of the Greek bible from his native Palestine (*Vita*, 416-418), knowing that he was bound for the Hellenophile imperial capital.

He would not have been prohibited from using the scriptures in the Greek language. From what we can judge, he was not overly concerned in the debate over the Hebrew vs. Greek text. At the beginning of the *Antiquities* (I.9-12) he muses over the question of translating the scriptures into Greek, thereby divulging their content, and with scant hesitation decides to follow the Aristaean Eleazar in so doing. His paraphrastic treatment of the biblical text, moreover, shows his distant polarity from the Aqiba-Aquila school.[7] But if he had scruples over the question, the Babylonian Talmud documents the necessary permission: "The Books [of scripture] ... may be written in any language..., [although] Rabban Simeon b. Gamaliel says: The Books, too, they have only permitted to be written in Greek."[8] It should be remembered, in addition, that

conclusions for one segment of the Septuagint and those for another.

7. Cf. Thackeray, Loeb vol. IV, p. viii.

8. T. B. *Megillah*, 1.8, quoted from H. Danby, *The Mishnah* (London, 1954), p. 202. To have pertinent bearing on J, the dating of the "Greek permission" should be sought. As is not uncommon with the Talmud, the dating is problematic. First, two men bore the name Rabban Simeon ben Gamaliel, one living in the first century (10-80 C.E.) and the other in the middle of the second (140-165; cf. Danby's Appendix III, pp. 799-800). Danby evidently attributes the quotation being discussed to the latter (cf. his General Index, p. 838). But the second problem is the content itself: Simeon is reporting that some group in the past gave the permission for Gk translations. Who was the group, and when? At least it can be said that "the Mishnah was compiled in its present form at the end of the second century" (Danby, p. xiv), that the latest date for Simeon's statement is 165 C.E. (p. 800), and that his statement refers to *older* legislation. Thus, it is fully possible that the permission for the Greek scriptures was in effect as J wrote c. 90, whether or not the broader permission for "any language" was in effect.

Philo, a much more religious Jew than Josephus, used the scriptures in Greek nearly a century earlier.[9]

Finally, though Josephus was from a priestly family (Vita,
1; Ap. I.54) and thus presumably able to use the Hebrew scriptures, and though he boasts that "my compatriots admit that in
our Jewish learning I far excel them" (Ant. XX.262), still he
was a man over whom practicality held considerable sway, as his
position in the Jewish war against Rome demonstrates. And, if
one wishes to produce in a foreign tongue a large opus based in
great detail on a source extant in two languages, one of which
is already the target language, there is no question about the
practical, the logical, the natural course of action. Josephus
wanted to offer the biblical story to the Greek-speaking world;
his starting-point was naturally the ready-to-hand Greek bible,
not the Hebrew. Only two remarks of Josephus tempt us to think
otherwise.

First, in Ant. I.5 he declares that he is offering the
Greek-speaking world an account of "our entire ancient history
and political constitution, translated from the Hebrew records"
(εκ των Εβραικων μεθηρμηνευμενην γραμματων). At times this has
been interpreted by scholars[10] as a claim that Josephus himself
did the translation. But I must confess I find the passive
μεθηρμηνευμενην mistily non-committal concerning the identity
of the translator. Like other ancient authors Josephus is un-
besmirched by modesty and unhesitatingly brags about the extent
of his accomplishments.[11] Because he does not credit himself

---

9. For detailed analysis, cf. Peter Katz, Philo's Bible
(Cambridge, 1950).

10. Thackeray, Loeb vol. IV, p. xii.

11. "And now I take heart from the consummation of my
proposed work to assert that no one else, either Jew or gentile,
would have been equal to the task, however willing to undertake
it, of issuing so accurate a treatise as this for the Greek
world. For my compatriots admit that in our Jewish learning I
far excel them. I have also laboured strenuously to partake of
the realm of Greek prose and poetry, after having gained a
knowledge of Greek grammar...." (Ant. XX.262-263, Feldman's
translation in the Loeb series). Further, as Thackeray

with this facet of his accomplishment, it is not likely that
Josephus used a Hebrew bible and did the translation himself.
It is much more likely that he used a Greek bible, which was,
as he says, translated from the Hebrew records. It can be
further noted that even Thackeray who believed that Josephus
claimed to have done the translation himself believed it for
the Octateuch alone.[12] He asserts that for the books of Samuel,
which alone are under consideration in the present study, "the
Josephan Biblical text is *uniformly* of this Lucianic type."[13]

Secondly, in *Ap.* I.54 Josephus refers to the *Antiquities*,
which εκ των ιερων γραμματων μεθηρμηνευκα. Here the verb is
active and not ambiguously passive. But what does that verb
mean? Two contexts in the same work illumine its meaning. The
first context is precisely the context of these very words.
Josephus is defending himself as a historian (not as a lin-
guist, as in *Ant.* XX.262-263) against his calumniators and says
that indeed he is properly qualified both to write *The Jewish
War* because he was an eye-witness and participant in its events,
and to write αρχαιολογιαν, ωσπερ εφην, εκ των ιερων γραμματων μεθηρμηνευκα, γεγονως ιερευς εκ γενους και μετεσχηκως
της φιλοσοφιας της εν εκεινοις τοις γραμμασι. His meaning,
thus, is that he is qualified to μεθερμηνευειν the sacred writings because he is a priest and because he is an initiate in
the philosophy therein contained; as a priest and initiate he
is qualified to interpret the contents of the sacred writing--
not to translate them from Hebrew into Greek!

The second illuminating context is the context to which
the ωσπερ εφην of the last quotation refers. In *Ap.* I.1 Josephus begins by stating that he has already demonstrated the
antiquity of his race in the *Antiquities*, which εκ των παρ ημιν

(*Josephus*, p. 104) points out, the *Jewish War*, "an excellent
specimen of Atticistic Greek," passed uniquely as Josephus' own
work for about a quarter of a century until he finally admitted
in *Ap.* I.50 that he had used collaborators. This tardy admis-
sion, thinks Thackeray, was possibly "extorted from him by ex-
postulation" by the neglected assistants.

12. Thackeray, Loeb vol. IV, p. xii.

13. Thackeray, *Josephus*, p. 85; italics his.

ιερων βιβλιων δια της Ελληνικης φωνης συνεγραψαμην. Whiston, an accomplice in the confusion, renders this clause: "are translated by me into the Greek tongue." But συγγραφειν means "*conscribere*, compose, compile"; it does not mean "translate."

Thus, Josephus says (1) that he has compiled a history of the Jews in Greek, translated from the Hebrew writings, and (2) that he is qualified to interpret them because he is a priest and initiate. He never clearly says that he himself did the translation from the Hebrew language into the Greek language. If he did, although it may be credible for the Octateuch, as Thackeray believed, one would have to challenge him, as below, for the books of Samuel.

B. The J and G Texts for 2 S 6

It is fully possible, then, that Josephus could have used a Greek bible, and it would have been the logical and practical thing to do. Now it remains to demonstrate that he did in fact make use of a Greek bible.

Building upon our detailed study of 4QSam^a and parallel texts for 2 S 6, we can analyze the Greek text of J for that chapter in order to see whether the clues it gives indicate dependence upon a bible in Hebrew or a bible in Greek.

The complete text of *Ant*. VII.78-89 is presented below in order. The column at the left, marked "Biblical," contains all those words and only those which directly reflect a reading from any Hb or Gk ms of S or C. The indented column, marked "Non-Biblical," contains the J words which do not have a direct basis in such biblical mss.

In the central column, marked "pL Text," are words selected from the L text of S or (from ##1-30 especially) from the L text of C. These are often, but not necessarily, in the biblical order; rather, they are arranged to correspond to J's order, for facility of comparison. Usually they are identical with the B text (which is mainly OG here), and pertinent variants are listed either in this same column or in the "Notes" column. Also, since J at times makes use of words out of their context (sometimes for other purposes), these words will be included in the central column but will be placed in parentheses.

I have selected the siglum "pL" to denote the form of the

Greek text which of the presently preserved Greek readings
seems to have been both genuinely pre-Josephan and likely to
have been used by him. I am not using the siglum to denote a
"proto-Lucianic recension" *sensu stricto*, in contradistinction
to the OG. I am thinking of the type of "septuaginta" text
which Jerome said was called "koine" at the time of Origen but
which was after Lucian's time called "Lucianic" (cf. p. 17).
"OG/pL" may be just as accurate a siglum; but it seemed preferable to use the accurate but less cumbersome siglum "pL" after
defining it, (1) because several of the L readings as opposed
to G readings seem to have influenced J, (2) because there
seems to be no consistently strong distinction between OG and
pL, and (3) simply to avoid the frequent use of the more cumbersome siglum "OG/pL."

In the columns to the right, pertinent notes are offered
as well as the source (the verse from 2 S 6 or 1 C 13--16) from
which the biblical word is taken. In the left margin the individual J expressions are numbered for identification, and to
the left of the central column is a coding system which will be
explained at the beginning of the commentary which follows the
text.

	J Text		*pL Text*			*Source*	
	Biblical	*Non-Biblical*			*Notes*	*2 S*	*1 C*
	VII.78						
(a)		Τοιαυτης δ' αποβασης και					
		ταυτης της μαχης εδοξε					
1	Δαυιδη		1	Δαυειδ		13:1	
2	συμβουλευσαμενω		3	εβουλευσατο		"	
3	μετα		3	μετα		"	
4	των γεροντων		4	των πρεσβυτερων c^L only		"	
5	και ηγεμονων		3	και μετα παντος ηγουμενου		"	
6	και χιλιαρχων		3	και χιλιαρχων		"	
7	μεταπεμψασθαι		2	αποστειλωμεν		13:2	
8	των ομοφυλων		1	προς τους αδελφους ημων		"	
9	εξ		2	εν	[εξ Ισραηλ 2 S 6:1]	"	
10	απασης		2	παση		"	
11	της χωρας		2	γη		"	
12	προς αυτον		2	"προς ημας"		"	
13	τους εν		1	παντα		6:1	
14	ακμη της ηλικιας		1	νεανιαν	S only	"	
15	επειτα		3	και		"	
16	τους ιερεις		3	οι ιερεις		"	
17	και		3	και	c^{ML} only; om c^G	"	
18	Δηουιτας		3	οι Λευειται		"	
(b)		[και]			"και suspectum"		
					--Niese		
		πορευθεντας		επορευθη		6:2	
19	εις		3	εις		13:6	
20	Καριαθιαριμα		3	Καριαθιαρειμ πολιν Δαυειδ	4Q c^{ML} only; c^G	"	
21	μετακομισαι		2	επιστρεψωμεν μετενεγκωμεν	c^L c^G	13:3	
22	την του θεου		2	την κιβωτον		13:6	
23	κιβωτον		2	του θεου		"	
24	εξ αυτης		1	εκειθεν		"	
25	εις Ιεροσολυμα		1	"προς ημας"	= at Jerusalem	13:3	
(c)		και θρησκευειν εν αυτη λοιπον εχοντας					
		αυτην θυσιαις και ταις αλλαις τιμαις,					
		αις χαιρει το θειον·					

J Text VII.79		pL Text		Source	
Biblical	Non-Biblical		Notes	2 S	1 C
VII.79					
26 ει γαρ		1 οτι		13:3	
27 ετι Σαουλου		1 αφ' ημερων		"	
28 βασιλευοντος		1 Σαουλ		"	
29 τουτ' επραξαν,		2 ουκ εζητησαμεν αυτην		"	
30 ουκ		2			
(d)	αν δεινον				
	ουδεν				
	επαθον.				
	συνελθοντος	συνηγαγεν		6:1	
	ουν				
31 του λαου παντος,		2 πας ο λαος		6:2	
(e)	καθως				
	εβουλευσαντο,	εβουλευσατο	J refers back to:	13:1	
	παραγινεται	(παραγινονται)	cf. 6:16 also	(6:6)	
	ο βασιλευς				
	επι την κιβωτον,				
32 ην βασταξαντες		2 και ηρεν αυτην		6:3	
33 εκ της		3 εξ	εις BA error cf. 1 S 7:1	"	
34 Αμιναδαβου		4 οικου	Abi- M^SC	"	
35 οικιας		3 Αμειναδαβ		"	
(f)	οι ιερεις	(οι ιερεις)		(13:2)	
36 και επιθεντες		2 και επεβιβασεν	S	"	
		και επεθηκαν	σ' (S); C		13:7
37 εφ' αμαξαν		3 εφ' αμαξαν	επι C	"	"
38 καινην		3 καινην		"	"
39 ελκειν		1 ηγον	G^SC	"	
		ειλκον	be₂^mg only		"
40 αδελφοις τε		4 αδελφοι	Ahio Hb, T	"	"
41 και παισιν		1 υιοι	S only		
(g)	επετρεψαν				
	μετα των βοων.		J misinterprets?		
VII.80					
	προηγε δ'				

	J Text VII.80		*pL Text*		*Source*	
	Biblical	*Non-Biblical*		*Notes*	*2 S*	*1 C*
42	ο βασιλευς		1 και Δαυειδ		6:5	
43	και		1 και		"	
44	παν		2 παντες	= L 4Q M; om OG	"	
(h)		συν αυτω				
45	το πληθος		2 οι υιοι Ισραηλ		"	
(i)		υμνουντες				
46	τον θεον		2 ενωπιον Κυριου		"	
47	και αδοντες		2 εν ωδαις	≠ M	"	
(j)		παν ειδος μελους επιχωριον				
		συν τε ηχω ποικιλω				
48	κρουσματων τε		2 ανακρουομενον	##48-54, 118- 120, 160-163, 172-173 influ-	6:16	
49	και ορχησεων		2 και ορχουμενον	ence each other " (as do 6:5, 14-16, 21)		
50	και ψαλμων		1 ωδαις ψαλλοντες	S e₂ᵐᵍ only	6:5	13:8
(k)		ετι δε				
51	σαλπιγγος		2 σαλπιγγος		6:15	
52	και κυμβαλων		2 και εν κυμβαλοις		6:5	
53	καταγοντες		2 ανηγαγον		6:15	
54	την κιβωτον		1 την κιβωτον		"	
(l)		εις Ιεροσολυμα.				
	VII.81					
		ως δ'				
55	αχρι		1 εως		6:6	13:9
56	της Χειδωνος		2 της αλω[νος]	cf. discussion pp. 209, 213	"	"
57	αλωνος,		2 Χαιλων	om cᴳ		"
(m)		τοπου	(τοπος)	cf. 74	(6:8)	
		τινος ουτω				
		καλουμενου,	(εκληθη)	cf. 77	(")	
58	προηλθον,		1 παραγινονται ηλθον	S C	6:6	"
59	τελευτα		1 απεθανεν	cf. 69	6:7	

	J Text VII.81		*pL Text*		*Source*	
	Biblical	*Non-Biblical*		*Notes*	*2 S*	*1 C*
60	οζας		1 οζα		6:7	
61	κατ' οργην		2 οργη	LMN++; om BA+	"	
62	του θεου˙		2 ο θεος		"	
63	των βοων γαρ		1 οτι ... ο μοσχος		6:6	
64	επινευσαντων		1 περιεσπασεν		"	
65	την κιβωτον		1 την κιβωτον		"	
66	εκτειναντα		3 εξετεινεν	om M	"	
67	την χειρα		3 την χειρα		"	
68	και κατασχειν		3 κατασχειν		"	
(n)		εθελησαντα,				
		οτι μη ων ιερευς				
		ηψατο ταυτης,				
69	αποθανειν εποιησε.		2 απεθανεν		6:7	
	VII.82					
70	και ο μεν βασιλευς		1 και Δαυειδ		6:8	
(o)		και ο λαος				
71	εδυσφορησαν		4 ηθυμησεν	≠ M	"	
72	επι τω θανατω		3 υπερ ου διεκοψεν		"	
73	του Οζα,		3 εν τω Οζα		"	
74	ο δε τοπος		3 και ο τοπος		"	
(p)		εν ω ετελευτησεν				
75	Οζα		3 Διακοπη		"	
76	διακοπη		4 Οζα		"	
77	καλειται.		3 εκληθη		"	
78	δεισας δ'		2 και εφοβηθη		6:9	
79	ο Δαυιδης		1 Δαυειδ		"	
80	και λογισαμενος,		2 λεγων		"	
(q)		μη ταυτο παθη				
		τω Οζα				
		δεξαμενος		"Πως εισελευσεται		"	
81	την κιβωτον		1 η κιβωτος		"	
82	παρ' αυτον		1 προς με;"		"	
83	εν τη πολει,		1 εις την πολιν		6:10	
(r)		εκεινου				

	J Text VII.82 *Biblical* *Non-Biblical*		*pL Text*	*Notes*	*Source* 2 S	1 C
84	διοτι	3	δια το			13:10
(s)		μονον				
85	εξετεινε	3	εκτειναι	second time (cf. ##66–	6:6	"
86	την χειρα	3	την χειρα	67):J 4Ω C only	"	"
87	προς αυτην	3	προς την κιβωτον		"	"
(t)		ουτως	και		6:7	13:10
		αποθανοντος,	απεθανεν		"	"

VII.83

88	ουκ	3	και ουκ		6:10	
(u)		εισδεχεται μεν	εκκλιναι		"	
89	αυτην	3	αυτην		"	
90	προς αυτον	3	προς αυτον		"	
91	εις την πολιν,	3	εις την πολιν		"	
92	αλλ᾽ εκνευσας	1	και εξεκλινεν	L C^G; απεκ- G	"	
93	εις	2	εις		"	
(v)		τι χωριον				
		ανδρος δικαιου,				
94	Ωβαδαρου	1	Αβεδδαδαν (?)		"	
(w)		ονομα				
		Ληουιτου				
		το γενος				
95	παρ᾽ αυτω	1	εν οικω Αβεδδαδαν		6:11	
96	την κιβωτον	1	η κιβωτος		"	
(x)		τιθησιν.	(τιθεασιν)	cf. #130	(6:17)	
97	εμεινε δ᾽	2	και εκαθισεν		6:11	
98	επι τρεις	2	τρεις		"	
(y)		ολους	(ολον)		"	
99	μηνας	2	μηνας		"	
100	αυτοθι	1	εν οικω Αβεδ.	εκει Acx only, but followed by γλωσσοκομον (= α᾽!)	"	
101	και τον οικον	2	και τον οικον		"	
102	του Ωβαδαρου	1	Αβεδδαδαν		"	

	J Text VII.83		pL Text		Source	
	Biblical	*Non-Biblical*		*Notes*	*2 S*	*1 C*
(z)		ηυξησε τε	ευλογησεν		6:11	
103	και πολλων		1 και παντα		"	
104	αυτω		2 τα αυτου		"	
(aa)		μετεδωκεν				
		αγαθων.				

VII.84

		ακουσας δε				
105	ο βασιλευς		1 τω βασιλει		6:12	
(bb)		οτι ταυτα				
		συμβεβηκεν				
106	Ωβαδαρω		1 Αβεδδαδαν		"	
(cc)		και εκ πενιας και ταπεινοτητος αθροως				
		ευδαιμων και ζηλωτος γεγονε παρα πασι				
		τοις ορωσι και πυνθανομενοις				
107	την οικιαν		2 τον οικον		"	
108	αυτου,		2 αυτου		"	
(dd)		θαρσησας ως		J's litotes		
109	ουδενος κακου		4 την ευλογιαν	negatively mirrors the	"	
				positive		
(ee)		πειρασομενος		addition		
				found only		
110	την κιβωτον		1 την κιβωτον	in L OL.	"	
111	προς αυτον		1 "εις τον οικον μου"		"	
112	μετακομιζει,		<u>2</u> ανηγαγεν		"	

VII.85

(ff)		των μεν				
		ιερεων				
113	βασταζοντων		<u>2</u> αιροντες	σ' βασταζοντες	6:13	
114	αυτην,		1 την κιβωτον		"	
115	επτα δε		3 επτα	≠ M	"	
116	χορων		4 χοροι	G L OL only	"	
(gg)		ους διεκοσμησεν				
		ο βασιλευς				
		προαγοντων,	ανηγαγον		6:15	
117	αυτου δ'		3 και αυτος	L only	6:14	

	J Text VII.85		pL Text		Source	
	Biblical	Non-Biblical		Notes	2 S	1 C
118	εν κινυρα		3 εν κινυραις	cf. #48; κροτεω (#120) = play stringed instrument	6:5	
119	παιζοντος και		4 παιζοντα και	L only (hab παιζ- at 6:5	6:16	
120	κροτουντος,		3 ανακρουομενον	G L; but only L has the pair together) ≠ M	"	
(hh)		ωστε				
121	και		1 και		"	
(ii)		την γυναικα				
122	Μιχαλην		1 Μελχολ		"	
123	Σαουλου δε		2 θυγατηρ		"	
124	θυγατερα		3 Σαουλ		"	
(jj)		του πρωτου				
		βασιλεως	(βασιλεα)		(")	
125	ιδουσαν		3 ειδεν		"	
126	αυτον		3 αυτον		"	
(kk)		τουτο ποιουντα				
127	χλευασαι.		2 εξουδενωσεν.		"	
	VII.86					
128	εισκομισαντες δε		3 εισφερουσιν	φερ- ΒΑ+	6:17	
129	την κιβωτον		3 την κιβωτον		"	
130	τιθεασιν		4 τιθεασιν	L only	"	
131	υπο		2 εν μεσω		"	
132	την σκηνην		3 της σκηνης		"	
133	ην Δαυιδης		3 ης Δαυειδ		"	
134	επηξεν αυτη		3 επηξεν αυτη		"	
135	και θυσιας τελειας		2 και ολοκαυτωματα		"	
136	και ειρηνικας		3 και ειρηνικας		"	
137	ανηνεγκε,		3 ανηνεγκεν		"	
138	και τον οχλον		1 και τω λαω		6:19	
(ll)		ειστιασε				
139	παντα		3 παντι		"	
140	και γυναιξι		3 απο ανδρος		"	
141	και ανδρασι		3 και εως γυναικος		"	
(mm)		και νηπιοις				

	J Text VII.86		pL Text		Source	
	Biblical	Non-Biblical		Notes	2 S	1 C
142	διαδους		2 εμερισεν διεμερισεν	L G c^G	6:19 "	16:3
143	κολλυριδα αρτου		4 κολλυριδα αρτου	G L c^L only	"	"
144	και εσχαριτην		4 και εσχαριτην	G L only	"	
145	και λαγανον		4 και λαγανον	G L, b (of C) only	"	"
146	τηγανιστον		4 απο τηγανου	G L c^L only	"	"
147	και μεριδα		3 εμερισεν		"	
(nn)		θυματος.	και θυμα	≠ M	6:13	
148	και τον μεν λαον		3 και πας ο λαος		6:19	
(oo)		ουτως κατευωχησας απεπεμψεν,				
149	αυτος δ'		1 και Δαυειδ		6:20	
150	εις τον οικον		3 τον οικον		"	
151	[τον] αυτου		3 αυτου		"	
152	παραγινεται.		1 απεστρεψεν (παραγινονται)	cf. (e)	" (6:6)	
	VII.87					
153	Παραστασα		2 εις απαντησιν	##153-180 om C	6:20	
154	δε αυτω		1 Δαυειδ		"	
155	Μιχαλη η		1 Μελχολ		"	
(pp)		γυνη				
156	Σαουλου δε		1 η θυγατηρ		"	
157	θυγατηρ		2 Σαουλ		"	
(qq)		τα τε αλλα				
158	αυτω κατηυχετο		4 ευλογησεν αυτον	G L only	"	
(rr)		και παρα του θεου γενεσθαι ητει πανθ' οσα παρασχειν αυτω δυνατον ευμενοι τυγχανοντι, και δη κατεμεμψατο, ως		J takes literally the euphemism in G L only		
159	ακοσμησειεν		1 δεδοξασται		"	
160	ορχουμενος ο		4 ορχουμενων	G L OL only	"	
(ss)		τηλικουτος				
161	βασιλευς		1 ο βασιλευς		"	

J Text VII.87		pL Text	Source
Biblical	*Non-Biblical*		*Notes*	*2 S*	*1 C*

162	και γυμνουμενος	1	αποκαλυφθεις		6:20
163	υπο της ορχησεως	2	ορχουμενων	cf. #160	"
164	και [εν δουλοις	2	των δουλων	om και S; J? cf. p. 211	"
165	και εν] θεραπαινισιν.	1	εν οφθαλμοις παιδισκων		"

VII.88

(tt) ο δ᾽ ουκ αιδεισθαι ταυτα ποιησας
      εις το τω θεω κεχαρισμενον

166	εφασκεν,	1	και ειπεν		6:21
167	ος αυτον	2	"ος με		"
168	και του πατρος αυτης	2	υπερ τον πατερα σου		"
169	και	2	και υπερ		"

(uu) των αλλων

170	απαντων	2	παντα		"
171	προετιμησε,	2	εξελεξατο		"
172	παιζειν τε και	4	και παιξομαι	≠ M	"

(vv) πολλακις

173	χορευσαι	2	και ορχησομαι		"

(ww) μηδενα

174	του δοξαι	2	με δοξασθηναι		6:22
175	ταις θεραπαινισιν	1	των παιδισκων		"
176	αισχρον	1	αχρειος εν		"
177	και αυτη	4	οφθαλμοις σου"	G L OL only	"

(xx) το γινομενον
      ποιησαμενος λογον.

VII.89

178	η Μιχαλη	1	και τη Μελχολ		6:23

(yy) αυτη Δαυιδη
      μεν συνοικουσα

179	παιδας	2	παιδιον		"
180	ουκ εποιησατο,	1	ουκ εγενετο	End 2 S 6.	"

(zz) γαμηθεισα δε υστερον   A harmonization
      ω παρεδωκεν αυτην ο πατηρ   by J with 2 S
                                   21:8. (Despite
                                   his comment, J

J Text		pL Text		Source	
Biblical	Non-Biblical		Notes	2 S	1 C

Σαουλος, τοτε δε αποσπασας αυτος ειχε, πεντε παιδας ετεκε. και περι μεν τουτων κατα χωραν δηλωσομεν.

does not treat of Michal later.)

C. Commentary

The truth of the present hypothesis, that J used a Greek not a Hebrew Vorlage, is disclosed basically intuitively, and the data have been arranged with this in mind. It is neither possible nor particularly helpful for our purposes, further-more, to classify exhaustively and precisely all the differ-ences between J and OG/pL. Explanation of the data, nonethe-less, and justification for the hypothesis are called for, and so the data will be grouped according to those categories which upon analysis prove themselves to be functionally important.

In Josephus' narration of 2 S 6, there are 52 departures of varying length and importance from his biblical source, irrespective of language, texttype, etc. These non-biblical details (marked with letters a-zz) are, accordingly, set aside from discussion, although it is interesting to notice that, even within these departures from biblical content, there is some evidence of possible borrowing from G phraseology (cf. e, m, t, x, gg, nn; though echoing G closely, b, f, h, o, y, ff are too general to be considered evidence).

There remain 180 expressions for which J is dependent on a biblical Vorlage. And as we look over his text, we may pose as Josephus' instructor in Greek, having given him the assignment of retelling the narrative of 2 S 6 in stylish Hellenistic Greek. He is to use only the Hebrew of 4QSam[a] or the Massoretic text; he may not use a Septuagintal text. Since his fictional audience for this assignment is a Hellenistic public, accus-tomed to the methods and styles of Thucydides and Dionysius of Halicarnassus, of Polybius and Nicolaus of Damascus, he is not

to use Hebraisms, specifically Jewish terms (without explanation), or the inconcinnities of biblical Greek. He has lexical
and syntactic freedom, as well as the historian's customary
freedom for shifting from direct to indirect discourse and the
like, and he is, finally, to produce a polished narrative in an
elegant style.

As we check over that assignment, we are satisfied that J
has produced a polished recasting of the biblical chapter, but
as we initially glance at the pL text, we notice the following
108 similarities to J's 180 expressions:

    ##1, 2, 3, 5, 6, 10, 12, 16, 17, 18, 19, 20, 22, 23, 30,
    31, 33, 34, 35, 37, 38, 40, 43, 44, 47, 48, 49, 51, 52,
    54, 57, 60, 61, 62, 65, 66, 67, 68, 69, 73, 74, 75, 76,
    77, 79, 80, 81, 83, 84, 85, 86, 87, 88, 89, 90, 91, 93,
    96, 98, 99, 101, 104, 105, 107, 108, 110, 115, 116, 117,
    118, 119, 120, 121, 123, 124, 125, 126, 129, 130, 132,
    133, 134, 136, 137, 139, 140, 141, 143, 144, 145, 146,
    147, 148, 150, 151, 156, 157, 160, 161, 163, 164, 167,
    168, 169, 170, 172, 174, 179.

Since J and pL are sharing the same story and the same
language, a certain amount of lexical congruence is to be expected, but a prima facie rate of 60% is so high that it demands a closer scrutiny to determine whether J can in fact be
independent.

As we begin our differentiation, we should keep in mind
the general dependence of J on C for ##1-30 and on S for ##153-
180, discussed in the previous chapter, though it assumes less
significance here, where our concern is with the language of
J's Vorlage, whether from S or from C.

In the presentation of the text above, there is a coding
system prefixed to the pL column. The numbers, appearing to
the left of the pL column, refer to the J expressions to their
left (not to pL) and indicate an "adjusted assessment" of each
J expression, denoting the degree of probability for the hypothesis that J was dependent on a Greek Vorlage. The number 1
denotes no real indication of J dependence either on a Greek
Vorlage as opposed to a Hebrew Vorlage, or vice-versa.

The number 2 denotes that the J expression could come from
either a Hebrew or a Greek Vorlage, but probability points to a

Greek Vorlage, due to the resemblance of the Greek texts. The
importance of this category will depend not on individual expressions, but on the frequency of examples. Included also in
this group, but underlined, are expressions with closer agreement than is here apparent; these will be discussed below.

The number 3 denotes strong indication of a Greek Vorlage,
either because of agreement in peculiar words or because of
close agreement in extended phrases or clauses, where assertion
of independence becomes highly implausible.

The number 4 denotes a detail or expression which could
not have been derived from a Hebrew Vorlage but necessarily
points to a specifically Greek Vorlage. These will be discussed below.

Though a certain amount of subjective judgment is necessarily at work here, the following seems a fair assessment of
the degrees of probability for determining J's Vorlage.

(1) Of the 180 expressions, J could have produced these
56 from any Vorlage; there is no reason to assert dependence
either on a Hebrew or on a Greek Vorlage:

##1, 8, 13, 14, 24, 25, 26, 27, 28, 39, 41, 42, 43, 50,
54, 55, 58, 59, 60, 63, 64, 65, 70, 79, 81, 82, 83, 92,
94, 95, 96, 100, 102, 103, 105, 106, 110, 111, 114, 121,
122, 138, 149, 152, 154, 155, 156, 159, 161, 162, 165,
166, 175, 176, 178, 180.

(2) The following 56 readings point with some probability toward a Greek Vorlage:

##7, 9, 10, 11, 12, 21, 22, 23, 29, 30, 31, 32, 36, 44,
45, 46, 47, 48, 49, 51, 52, 53, 56, 57, 61, 62, 69, 78,
80, 93, 97, 98, 99, 101, 104, 107, 108, 112, 113, 123,
127, 131, 135, 142(+147), 153, 157, 163, 164, 167, 168,
169, 170, 171, 173, 174, 179.

(3) There is strong indication of a Greek Vorlage for the
following 51 readings:

##2, 3, 5, 6, 15, 16, 17, 18, 19, 20, 33, 35, 37, 38, 66,
67, 68, 72, 73, 74, 75, 77, 84, 85, 86, 87, 88, 89, 90,
91, 115, 117, 118, 120, 124, 125, 126, 128, 129, 132, 133,
134, 136, 137, 139, 140, 141, 147, 148, 150, 151.

(4) These 17 readings are of high importance, since they
are lacking in some traditions and thus point specifically

toward a certain Vorlage:

    ##4, 34, 40, 71, 76, 109, 116, 119, 130, 143, 144, 145,
    146, 158, 160, 172, 177.

Discussion of the Classifications and Their Significance.

    (1) Proper names as such lie outside the scope of this
study, and their uncomplicated occurrence is accordingly
ignored. This blends perfectly with our purpose here, for the
simple occurrence of proper names such as Δαυιδης or their sub-
stitutes, βασιλευς, αυτον, and the like, would appear much the
same in J whether he was using a Hb or a Gk bible.

    Two other types of "1" readings bear a small amount of
significance. Readings in which J simply diverges from pL tend
to weaken the hypothesis for a Greek Vorlage; but conversely,
the fact that J is consciously polishing and rearranging tends
to discount the Hebrew significance of the divergences just
mentioned. Thus, though some "1" readings have some small significance, that significance is beyond our control. Fifty-six
of J's 180 expressions (or 31.1%) fall under this nebulous
first category.

    (2) Most of the expressions in the second category show
exact agreement for common words, slight changes, or obvious
shifts such as that from direct to indirect discourse; others
call for some discussion.

    (a) J should be expected (with varying degrees of
necessity) to change Hebraisms and peculiarities of biblical
Greek such as these:

    ##11, 29, 46, 97, 127, 131, 135, 153, 171.
Cf. others, e.g., ##158, 177, and 72-73 (in between 71 and 75-
76) where independent evidence shows that J depends on a Greek
Vorlage.

    (b) Though with J's protean nature and without a
concordance for his works it is impractical to attempt an ex-
haustive study of his expressions, the following examples will
provide sufficient sample of his types of shifts. In the story
of the capture of the Ark (V.352-355 = 1 S 4:1-7), J uses nine
of the expressions from our present passage:

    ##4, 7, 21 (cf. 112, 128), 22-23, 24, 45, 78[bis], (dd).
V. 352 employs πληθος (cf. #45) for ο λαος (1 S 4:3). V.353

includes δεισαντες (cf. #78) as an added interpretation by J,
followed shortly after (V.355) by δεδιοτες = εφοβηθησαν (4:7).
πεμπειν and γερουσια (V.353) replace αποστελλειν (4:4) and
πρεσβυτεροι (4:3). While την κιβωτον του θεου...κομιζειν (V.
353; cf. ##22-23, 21//112//128) renders λαβωμεν την κιβωτον του
θεου...και αιρουσιν εκειθεν (4:3-4), εκειθεν (cf. #24) in G is
ignored by J. Finally, in addition to δεδιοτες in V.355, J
adds the psychological, abstract θαρσος (cf. dd) which characteristically is not expressed in 4:5-7. Thus, in a fragment of
another Ark passage, J makes 9 shifts similar to those he makes
in our present passage. This indicates that the expressions
involved are not "disagreements" but "characteristic substi-
tutes" or agreements in J, γερουσια (#4) especially aiding to
diminish the "chance" possibility (cf. below under "4").

(c) A similar example (for V.17 = Josh 3:3) involves:
##21//112//128 and 32//113, plus 15-18 (rated "3").

M   [הארון] = אתו נשאים הלוים והכהנים

G   και τους ιερεις ημων και
       τους Λευειτας αιροντας αυτην

J   οι ιερεις την κιβωτον εχοντες, επειτα
       οι Λευιται την σκηνην...κομιζοντες

Note that J has επειτα for και (cf. #15); priests *and* Levites
(= L G ≠ M, cf. ##16-18 where J = L^C M ≠ G); both εχοντες and
then κομιζοντες for αιροντες [κιβωτον] (cf. ##21, 112, 128, and
32, 113); and the free addition την σκηνην with κομιζοντες,
emphasizing the distinction between priests and Levites.

(d) Confirming the foregoing, we can note that
αιρειν is used frequently for נשא in G, whereas βασταζειν
occurs only 2x in S K C--once erroneously for βλαστανειν in
Alexandrinus at 2 S 23:5, and once in 2 K 18:14 for נשא in the
context of Hezekiah's bearing tribute--but never in connection
with the Ark. In contrast, J never uses αιρειν in reference to
the Ark (cf. *Lexicon to Josephus*, p. 13), but instead uses
βασταζειν 3x (2x in our chapter', ##32 and 113, and once in
VIII.101; cf. *Lexicon*, p. 103b), as does Symmachus in 6:13
(#113).

(e) Finally, J cannot echo γη in #11, because it
does not mean "country, *patria*" in acceptable Greek prose; he

must alter it to χωρα or another equivalent. And for #7, J has
syntactically rearranged his source, "sending after those of
his compatriots from the whole country who were in the prime of
life." His source (whether Hb or Gk) "dispatches to our brothers remaining in the whole land"; thus, this shift is a narrative creation of J, independent of and without regard to his
source, Hb or Gk. But once he has made the shift, αποστελλειν
is not freely available to J for reproduction, for his normal
word is πεμπειν, with αποστελλειν usually being restricted to
the sense of "dispatch authoritatively, commission" (*Lexicon*,
p. 67a). The latter fits the (Hb or Gk) biblical sense, but it
does not fit J's rearranged sense. These expressions, then,
should not be considered as disagreements with pL (admitting a
Hb Vorlage as equally possible), but rather as characteristic
substitutions of J. See the discussion of γεροντων (#4) below,
which is a similar "characteristic substitution" where it is
clear that J can only be dependent on a Greek text.

Thus in addition to 40 prima facie agreements on this
"probable" level, parallel examples show that 16 further expressions should be interpreted as probable characteristic sub-
stitutes by J for the G words in our chapter, bringing the
total to 56. The resultant 31.1% agreement at this level bal-
ances the 31.1% in the first category of expressions which fail
to indicate either a Hb or a Gk Vorlage.

(3) The 51 readings at this third level are focused in
their proper critical perspective when seen as constituting the
following extended passages:

##2-6, 15-20, 32-40, 66-77, 84-91, 113-151(!)
This amounts to 28.3% (for "3" readings, 43.9% if the complete
passages are counted) of the biblically derived material. Even
if there were not category "4" below, this quantity of extended
agreement, despite the fact that J is deliberately changing
from his Vorlage for better vocabulary and style, renders untenable the assertion that he is independent of pL.

(4) This category leaves no room for doubting the general
direction our evidence has been taking.

(a) In the C section (##1-30), #4 strongly indicates
L of Chronicles as J's Vorlage. ##17 and 20 might admit C^M as
the Vorlage, especially since J has γεροντων in #4 where L has

πρεσβυτερων. But the close, continuous similarity to the Greek
text in ##1-6(7) argues against a C^M Vorlage, while ##4, 17,
and 20 rule out C^G.

The decision for C^L is clinched by noting that J elsewhere
(V.353 = 1 S 4:3; V.332,335 = Ruth 4:2,4) uses the more pres-
tigious γερουσια for πρεσβυτεροι, and hierarchically parallels
the Spartan γερουσια with a Jewish γερουσια in the salutation
of Jonathan's latter to the Spartans (XIII.166). γεροντες is
thus not a J disagreement from pL because he used a Hb Vorlage,
but it is a characteristic substitute of J for πρεσβυτεροι dependent precisely on the Greek text of pL^C.

Three more points must be noted about L of Chronicles as
J's Vorlage. First, C^G never agrees with J against C^L. Secondly, C^L agrees with J against S^{MGL} in ##85-86; is a partial
witness (again in contrast to C^{MG}) for ##143-146; agrees with J
in #36 (with C^G) and (without C^G) in 39, 50, 58; and is probably responsible for J's reading in #56. Thirdly, in three of
the readings for which we would thus far conclude that C^L is
J's Vorlage (##20, 85, 86; cf. 56) 4Q also contains those readings. This again suggests what could be proved only if 4Q were
sufficiently extant: that it was not C^L itself which was the
real Vorlage of J, but that J's Vorlage was that Greek text of
Samuel which (together with C^M) was one of the sources of C^{GL}.

(b) In the chapter as a whole, there are seventeen
readings for which J depends on a specifically Greek Vorlage.
In nine of these he is dependent on content which is found only
in texts which happen to be in the Greek language (or their
descendants); i.e., they do not occur as such in M^{SC} or 4Q:

##4, 34, 40, 71, 109, 115-116, 158, 160, 177.
The last four occur only in S^{GL}, #4 only in C^L, #109 only in
S^L, and ##34, 40, and 71 are common to the Gk texts of S C in
contrast to the Hb texts of 4Q S C.

Though this is a list of readings based on the content of
the Gk text, note that lexically J = pL exactly in four of them
(##34, 40, 115-116, 160). ##4 and 71 have undergone voluntary
lexical polishing and #158 necessary lexical polishing, since
ευλογειν does not mean "bless" to J's audience. ##109 and 177
have undergone literary polishing: #109 is an example of
litotes and syntactic polishing, and #177 is a shift to

indirect discourse.

       (c) In addition to those nine readings for which J
depends on content found only in Greek texts, J owes eight
readings precisely to the Greek language contained in 2 S 6, as
opposed to the Hebrew language (i.e., it is impossible or ex-
tremely unlikely that J produced these readings from a Vorlage
in Hebrew):

    ##75-76, 119, 130, 143, 144, 145, 146, 172.

(##75-76)	4Q	[פר]ץ עזא
	M	פרץ עזה
	C^M	פרץ עזא
	G^{SC}	Διακοπη Οζα
	J	Οζα Διακοπη

J has transposed the order of Διακοπη Οζα but he has done so
independently of Hb or Gk Vorlage.

    M gives the aetiological explanation and then the (mis-
spelled) place-name פרץ עזה. G follows, translating, rather
than transliterating,[14] both the explanation and the place-name.
J paraphrases the explanation (επι τω θανατω του Οζα #72-73)
to avoid the Hebraism; nonetheless, despite having lost the
poignancy of the aetiology thereby, he remarkably turns up with
the identical translation of G!

    The exact same process takes place in I.337 (= Gen 33:17):
M has the etymological explanation of Succoth then the place-
name. G translates (rather than transliterating) the place-
name εις Σκηνας, and logically translates the explanation as
well: εποιησεν σκηνας. J's εις τας ετι νυν Σκηνας λεγομενας
follows the G translation, while performing an enthememetic
leap over the explanation.

    In the larger clause ##74-77, J even retains the syntax,
the vocabulary, and the case of G, whereas, in his free borrowing from this parenthesis for the non-biblical clause (m), he

---

    14. It would seem that the logical way of presentation
would be transliteration (because the original is the name of
the place) accompanied by translation (because the writer
wishes the reader to know the meaning of the name in his own
language). Such is the case, for example, in Mk 15:22//Mt
27:33, in contrast to Jn 19:17.

had altered it to the more Hellenically stylish genitive absolute.

To remove any lingering possibility of chance, we need only observe that διακοπη is infrequent in G (12x, always for פרץ) and very rare in Greek literature, occurring only once each in Hippocrates and Plutarch.

Thus (discounting J's transposition as a departure from both Hb and Gk texts), we note that he has the identical--not transliteration--but translation of G, with the only two other possibilities removed of arriving independently at that translation: (1) recounting the aetiology precisely in terms of his translation, and (2) use of a frequent Greek word for that translation. And his dependence on G is confirmed by another example of the same, otherwise inexplicable process.

(##119 and 172) These readings, discussed in chapter VII, p. 219, depend upon an interpretation possible only from a Vorlage in the Greek language.

(#130) This reading by itself is a weak example, but it accumulates force when combined with other L vs. G readings, such as ##109, 44, 117, 119, 128.

(##143-146) This set of readings is another powerful indicator that J used a Greek Vorlage.

M	G	J
חלת	κολλυριδα	κολλυριδα
לחם	αρτου	αρτου
אחת		
ואשפר	και εσχαριτην	και εσχαριτην
אחד		
ואשישה	και λαγανον απο τηγανου	και λαγανον τηγανιστον
אחת		

J civilizes the barbarism απο τηγανου with the more graceful adjective; otherwise he copies G literally. Coincidence is ruled out. κολλυρις never occurs in Greek literature, occurs only 5x in LXX, and of those 5 occurrences is never used to translate חלה elsewhere. εσχαριτης occurs only here in LXX and only twice in Greek literature, once each in those two oft-read fourth century B.C. comic writers Antidotus (Πρωτ. 2) and Crobylus ('Απαγκ. 2). And λαγανος occurs only 2 (or possibly 3) times in Greek literature, and only 8x in LXX, but never to

translate אשׁישׁה except here. In short, J could never have
derived ##143-146 from M, from general LXX usage, or from general classical usage. He is totally and exactly dependent on
OG, to which he gives a slight polish.

D. Evaluation of Contrary Evidence

In the face of this positive evidence, there seem to be
only three possible objections against our conclusion: (1)
since J and OG/pL are telling the same story in the same language, a large amount of congruence is to be expected; (2) the
evidence collected above appears more weighty than it really
is, due to the language similarity, while it is very difficult
to heap up examples where J would depend upon a Hebrew Vorlage;
and (3) the evidence presented warrants conclusions only for 2
S 6, not for 1-2 Samuel.

The first two objections are based on true premises. When
one examines the first objection, however, even though he be
eager to establish that J did use a Hebrew Vorlage after all,
it is difficult to imagine being comfortable with a conclusion
that J is independent of pL when even on a superficial level
there is 60% agreement between J and pL. When a closer scrutiny results in a line-up of 31.1% ambiguous evidence, 68.9%
evidence pointing in varying degrees of probability (including
9.4% certainty!) toward pL influence, and not one reading
pointing toward Hebrew influence, the objection must be aban-
doned.

But this last point occasions the second objection: the
reason that no readings which indicate Hb influence were found
is that it is very difficult to find unambiguous examples of
Hebrew influence on J. Now this is indeed true; but, granted
the difficulty, there is not even one trace of evidence of
Hebrew influence, except for (g). If it is argued that μετα
των βοων is an error in J, misinterpreting and therefore pre-
supposing a Hebrew בעגלות*, the following points should also be
made:

(1) That hypothesis presupposes both an error on J's
part and an error in the Hb text for which there is no docu-
mentation.

(2) G has εν τω βουνω otherwise unreflected in J at

the place where J's misinterpretation appears. An assumption
of dependence on G would still require the error on J's part,
but would not require positing a non-documented error in G.

(3) This would be the only example of Hebrew influence, as opposed to 17 clear examples of influence that could
come only from the Greek.

(4) Single examples prove little, as #100 demonstrates. Acx alone have εκει where J has αυτοθι, Grell having
εις οικον or εν οικω Αβεδδαδαν. The very next word in Acx,
however, is γλωσσοκομον--Aquila's word for the Ark. Claiming
Hb influence for μετα των βοων would be as persuasive as claiming Aquilan influence for αυτοθι.

Again, even if there were several clear examples of Hb
influence, how would one explain the 9 readings dependent on
content that are found only in Greek mss? And how explain the
8 readings that presuppose the Greek language itself?

Finally, even if there were clear examples of Hb influence,
it would have to be shown that J was directly dependent on the
Hebrew, not indirectly. Consider 2 K 12:6(5):

M	את בדק הבית
BLAN++	το (του A) Βεδεκ του οικου
⟨74⟩	το Βεδδεκ
h^mg 𝔄^mg	τα δεοντα
σ'	τα δεοντα
α'	την επισκευην
OL^V	berech de domo

No extant Greek ms has Berek; the OL error stems clearly from
a mistake of Hb, not Gk, letters; but OL^V was certainly not
made directly from a Hb Vorlage. OL^V has derived its reading
indirectly from the Hb Vorlage through the medium of an erroneous Gk Vorlage.

Thus, there is one ambiguous example that points toward Hb
influence; but there are at least two weak links between it and
alleged Hb influence, it stands alone, and it stands ambiguously alone in the face of overwhelming evidence to the contrary.

But there remains the third objection: even if J used a
Gk Vorlage for 2 S 6, that does not warrant conclusions concerning all of 1-2 Samuel. This objection is valid only in

relation to the continuous, detailed analysis employed in this
chapter. Chapters II-V and especially VI present evidence of G
influence on J throughout 1-2 Samuel. Even in some of the instances in which J = 4Q alone, J was seen to demonstrate dependence on a Greek medium. On the other hand, no instances
were found in which J either appeared to be influenced by a
distinctly Hb Vorlage or agreed with M against G L.

In the interests of objectivity, however, we may consider
the evidence of others who do posit a Hebrew (or Aramaic) influence on J's narrative of the books of Samuel: Mez and
Rahlfs, Thackeray and Marcus.

Mez' first series of readings comprises proper names specifically, and so we shall study his second series, which he
and others assess as "more exact." Rahlfs' *Lucians Rezension
der Königsbücher* devotes a section (pp. 83-92) to the "Ver-
hältnis des Josephus zu L in den Samuelisbüchern." And the
Loeb notes of Thackeray and Marcus attempt throughout the
Samuel narrative to list clues for Hebrew, Aramaic, or Greek
influence on Josephus. These sources have been checked for all
readings where 4Q is extant.

Mez, of course, comes to the conclusion that J used a
proto-Lucianic text. But he does include evidence to the contrary, and it is this which we shall attempt to isolate. He
lists 51 readings for the books of Samuel, and 4Q is extant
for 11 of them. Of those eleven, 8 have been presented above
as showing a pattern of J = 4Q G/L ≠ M.[15] These show no trace
of specifically Hebrew influence but rather often show distinct
similarity to the Greek. One reading (#XXX = 1 S 2:22 = V.339,
see pp. 57-58 and 185 above) is lacking in 4Q OG but does occur
in L as well as in M; but on p. 187 we saw that J probably

---

15. 1 S 10:27 = VI.68,   p. 176 (Mez, #XL)
     1 S 11:8 = VI.78,   p. 177 (#XLII)
     1 S 14:47 = VI.129, p. 177 (#XLVII)
     1 S 17:4 = VI.171, p. 177 (#L)
     2 S 8:4   = VII.99, p. 176 (#LX)
     2 S 8:7   = VII.105, p. 174 (#LXII)
     2 S 18:11 = VII.240, p. 177 (#LXVII)
     2 S 24:17 = VII.327, p. 174 (#LXXVII)

agrees with L in readings such as this, because the pattern J =
L ≠ M occurs often, but the pattern J = M ≠ 4Q G L never occurs.
At any rate, there is no indication in this reading of specifically Hebrew or M influence on J. In a second reading (#LXIII
= 2 S 10:18 = VII.128), 4Q has only [ע]שׁבֹ extant, and all texts
agree with this element; thus it is not discussed elsewhere in
this study.

The final reading from Mez (#XXXIV = 1 S 6:1 = VI.18) is
the unique example in which Mez mentions specifically Hebrew
influence. Where J has "four months," all other texts have
"seven months," and Mez quotes Thenius' view that the J reading
reflects a mistaken ד for the Hb numeral ז. Mez' personal
view, however (see his p. 57), is that such an explanation for
this type of variant merits "kräftiges Misstrauen." Mez' mis-
trust finds strong support in the following: ד and ז are not
easily confused in Hasmonaean or Herodian Hebrew scripts; it is
equally possible that Δ and Z were confused at the Greek stage
(cf. Liddell-Scott, s.v. "Z"); and--much more to the point--4Q
contains only בעה[ ] (cf. p. 181) which could be ארבעה as
easily as שׁבעה. In fact, p. 177 lists four other readings involving numerals for which J = 4Q G ≠ M, with none to the contrary. In brief, for the single example where Mez posits the
possibility of Hebrew influence on J, the J variant may equally
well be from Gk, but it is more likely to be from a texttype
such as 4Q whose normal pattern for variant numerals is 4Q = G
J ≠ M, thus cancelling a specifically Hb vs. Gk factor.

Rahlfs discusses only 5 readings for which 4Q fragments
are extant. One reading (Συρος plus χιλια ταλαντα in 2 S 10:6
= VII.121) has already been displayed (pp. 25-27) as a sparkling
example of 4Q's refutation of Rahlfs. Now that we are discussing the specifically Hb vs. Gk problem, we may add that even
Rahlfs himself did not use this example to prove that J was dependent upon a Hb Vorlage. He failed to draw the distinction,
but we have seen (p. 155) that the Συρος error in J is possible
only from a Vorlage in Greek.

Similarly, in Rahlfs' criticism of Mez' "luftigen Hypo-
thesenbau" concerning the "Jezreel" reading (1 S 28:1 = VII.325,
cf. pp. 171-172 above) Rahlfs does not find fault with Mez'
textual details (which do prove to be off the mark) but rejects

his theory (which in principle is correct). For this reading
as well, J errs due to a pre-existent error in a specifically
Greek Vorlage.

For the three remaining readings[16] Rahlfs' criticism of
Mez is not at all that J is dependent upon a Vorlage in Hb but
rather that the readings are the more widespread G readings and
not specifically L. Thus, of the possible contrary evidence
from Rahlfs, in three cases he agrees that J displays G L readings, and in the remaining two cases, the 4Q material demonstrates that J is dependent upon a texttype similar to 4Q but
in a specifically Greek form.

Thackeray and Marcus have many footnotes in the Loeb edition which attempt to indicate the language source for specific
J readings. We shall examine those for which the 4Q text is
extant. The need for insistence upon close inspection of possible Vorlagen can be seen from one of Thackeray's early comments on 1 S 3:10 = V.349:

4Q   de

M T P   ריאמר שמואל דבר (מריא+ P) כי שמע עבדך

G   και ειπεν Σαμουηλ Λαλει (+n̄ē Lcx+ א̸)
         οτι ακουει ο δουλος σου

J   ακουσας ηξιου λαλειν επι τοις χρωμενοις· ου γαρ
         υστερησειν αυτον εφ οις αν θελησειε διακονιας.

Ellipses make the text of J somewhat difficult here, but
two things are clear: λαλειν ... γαρ reflects דבר כי (M), or
more likely, λαλειν οτι (G); and επι τοις χρωμενοις is a free
addition by J reflecting no known biblical Vorlage.

Thackeray nevertheless comments (Loeb, p. 156, note b):
"Greek 'speak upon (*i.e.* 'concerning') His oracles,' again suggesting a Semitic original; the Hebrew use of *dibber* *ʿal* is
exactly parallel." Thackeray correctly equates דבר על with
λαλειν επι, but the question becomes: "a Semitic original
what?" επι τοις χρωμενοις is not a reflection of a written
Vorlage, and so this certainly does not suggest a Semitic original *Vorlage*. What it may suggest (at most) is a Semitic original *native language* of the author who--as is commonplace--

---

16. 1 S 17:4; 2 S 18:11; and 2 S 24:17. Cf. note 15,
immediately above.

speaks the words of a new language in the phonology and syntax of his native language.

Despite Thackeray's misleading comment here, a perusal of the Loeb notes concerning Vorlagen, at least three-fourths of which favor a G Vorlage, would convince one that J used G. We are here concerned, however, with reviewing the contrary evidence.

There are 34 readings in the Loeb notes which involve a question of Vorlage and for which 4Q is extant. Twenty-six of these[17] agree with the hypothesis developed in the present study. Five further notes, when considered fully, also support that hypothesis.

1 S 28:1 = VI.325, Loeb, p. 330, note a: εις Ρεγαν. We have seen (pp. 171-172) that 4Q now affords the original source for the J reading, which J inherited in an already corrupted Gk form. The two subsequent verses offer two more striking examples of J dependence on the Greek: 1 S 28:2 [לראשי]ש 4Q M, αρχισωματοφυλακα G, φυλακα του σωματος J; and 1 S 28:3 האבות M [4Q], τους ενγαστριμυθους G J; cf. Loeb, p. 331, notes b and d.

2 S 2:8 = VII.10, Loeb, p. 363, note c: [מחנ[ים 4Q M, εκ της παρεμβολης εις Μαναεμ (om εις Μ' LANcx X̄) G, Μαναλιν ... Παρεμβολας J. The doublet in G is obviously an inner-Gk doublet (a translation plus a transliteration), and J echoes the Gk doublet.

2 S 8:7 = VII.104, Loeb, p. 415, note c: (χρυσας ...) και τας πανοπλιας J. "Not mentioned in Scripture," says Marcus. But και παντα τα οπλα τα χρυσα is a plus found in L only, while σ',[18] who not infrequently reflects J words and style, has πανοπλιας.

2 S 10:6 = VII.121, Loeb, p. 425, note c: χιλια

---

17. Cf. Loeb, vol. V, page 167 note b, 168a, 193d, 195e, 200a, 205e, 243b, 253b, 315b, 317f, 331b, 362b, 391d (+393b), 400c, 401g, 403d, 405c, 410b, 412a, 415e, 425d, 427c, 442b, 449c, 453d, 488b.

18. Against B-M and de Montfaucon, Field's persuasive analysis (I, 558a) concludes: "πανοπλιας ... sed interpres est Symmachus, non Aquila."

ταλαντα J: "the sum is not mentioned in 2 Sam." But we have
seen 4Q's אלף ככר כסף.

2 S 24:17 = VII.328, Loeb, p. 536 note a: ο ποιμην
J. "The word 'shepherd' is found in the Targum and some LXX
mss in 2 Sam.," though neither in M^S nor in C^M correctly. Marcus' note here is misleading. It is true that ביד רעיא is
"found" in the Targum, but only later in the verse. Not "some"
but *all* G mss, except the later, haplographic B* which was restored by B^{ab}, have ο ποιμην exactly as J and in the exact
position as J.

Thus, only three readings remain which may show Hb influence on J.

1 S 27:12 = VI.324, Loeb, p. 329 note i: הב[אש] 4Q M,
אתגראה T, ησχυνται G, εμισησε J. "So the Targum of 1 Sam.
xxvii. 12; Heb. 'is in bad odour among his people,' ... LXX 'is
put to shame among his people.'" The Targum does not, in fact,
have "hate" as opposed to "become odious" (4Q M) or "be dis-
graced" (G). Jastrow lists only "to attack; to become impas-
sionate, be hot with sexual passion" for גרי (Ithp.), and Jean-
Hoftijzer lists only *"actionner."* εμισησε is simply a typical
paraphrase by J which could derive from M or G or T.

2 S 3:3 = VII.21, Loeb, p. 369 note c: Δανιηλος. J
appears to be closest to the Hb of C (and farthest from M^S).
But Marcus (following Niese's choice) selects the *lectio facilior* (see p. 188), without even mentioning the *lectio difficilior*
(quae praeferanda sit) Δαλου(ι)ηλος in mss P S which comes
closer to 4Q G^S!

2 S 6:6 = VII.81, Loeb, p. 402 note a: Χειδωνος.
Again the J mss show a spread of variants similar to those of
C^G, while 4Q's נידן\נודן differs from כידן of C^M by only the
short, top stroke of כ vs. נ.

Out of the 34 readings from the Loeb notes, therefore, 31
support our hypothesis once 4Q is taken into consideration, and
only 3 conflict with it. The first (329i) is overstated and
its evidence not persuasive. The second and third involve
proper names, both of which display a problematic textual history. The second (369c) is a *lectio facilior* distracting us
from the correct reading, and the third (402a) differs from 4Q
by only a small part of one letter.

E. Conclusion

The evidence presented in chapters VI and VII is sufficient in itself to ground the conclusion that Josephus used a
Greek bible as his Vorlage for the Samuel portion of the *Antiquities.*

But for two reasons an in-depth study of the language of
Josephus' Vorlage seemed worthwhile. First, an inductive conclusion based on a series of individual readings is not a
totally satisfactory method for determining the source of a
historian's monumental history. This was the method of Mez, of
Rahlfs especially, and of the present study up through chapter
VI. But an a priori inquiry into the possibilities and likelihood of Josephus' deliberately choosing a Hebrew or a Greek
bible as his source for the Samuel narrative, plus a sustained
examination of a lengthy and continuous passage, promised to
give a broader and deeper basis for confidence in the results
of an inductive investigation.

Secondly, it is usually accepted uncritically that Rahlfs
has disproved Mez. It is to Brock's credit that he has brought
fresh critical examination to the problem. Since he concludes
(see p. 35 above) that Rahlfs' criticism of Mez is valid in
general and that Josephus used the Hebrew as well as the LXX, a
reexamination of the problem after analyzing the testimony of
4Q should advance our control of the problem.

Part A, then, makes clear that it was fully possible for
Josephus to use a Greek bible and that this would have been his
logical and practical choice. Parts B and C show that 31.1% of
the J material for 2 S 6 is too ambiguous to point either
toward a Hebrew or a Greek Vorlage, but that another 31.1%
mildly indicates a Gk Vorlage, 28.3% strongly indicates a Gk
Vorlage, and the final 9.4% unequivocally confirms a Vorlage in
the Greek language. No evidence at all was uncovered which
could be interpreted as clearly or even probably pointing to a
Vorlage in Hebrew.

Part D, examining the single datum in J which might suggest a Hebrew Vorlage, showed that there is a double weakness
in that suggestion, apart from its unique witness in the face
of overwhelming contrary evidence. Then the arguments of Mez
and Rahlfs, Thackeray and Marcus were reviewed. All except

Rahlfs had agreed that the main source of J was a Greek bible,
but, in the light shed by 4Q, a reexamination of their arguments for a Hebrew (or Aramaic) Vorlage left not a single persuasive indication, even from Rahlfs, of a Hebrew Vorlage--
primary or supplementary--for the parts of 1-2 Samuel for which
4Q is extant.

CONCLUSION

The major Samuel scroll from Qumran, though less than 10% extant, does not disappoint us in our hopes that it illumine the textual situation in the late Second Temple period. It speaks eloquently to the Massoretic, the early Septuagintal, the Chronicler's, and the Josephan textual traditions for 1-2 Samuel.

4QSam^a is an examplar of a Samuel text tradition at home in Hasmonaean Judah. The fragmentary scroll and its textual tradition are significantly different from, and frequently superior to, the Massoretic tradition that became our *textus receptus*. That textual tradition, or more pointedly, a Samuel text exceedingly close to 4QSam^a, provided the basis in early post-exilic Judah for the Chronicler's recasting of his people's history. Furthermore, it was, in a less expansionist form, much closer than the Massoretic tradition to the Hebrew basis of the pristine Egyptian (Old Greek) translation produced in the late third or early second century. In its more expansionist form it provided the basis for occasional additions and corrections in the early stratum of the Lucianic Greek recension.

The proto-Lucianic problem will most likely continue to be debated. Its opponents will point to the paucity of evidence even in its own stronghold (the agreements with the 4QSam fragments), and its proponents will point to the additions and revisions in L, divergent from both M and OG, the unique basis of which is the 4Q tradition.

What can be confidently asserted about the Lucianic text is, first, that Lagarde, Cross, and Brock are correct (against Kahle and against Barthélemy) in considering L a recension of the single Old Greek translation; secondly, that Mez, Cross, Brock, and Tov are correct in asserting a complex stratification of the L tradition, including at least an Old Greek basis, systematic polishing of the Greek, and recensional activity dependent upon the hexaplaric material; thirdly, that Thackeray correctly distinguished βγ from α ββ, and Barthélemy correctly

proved that βγ is a recension based on OG; and fourthly, that
Mez, Thackeray, and Cross are correct (against Rahlfs and
against Howard) that Josephus used a Greek bible of the proto-
Lucianic tradition for his Samuel narrative. In short, the
theory of recensional development, tested as a working hypothesis for this study, is in its general lines amply confirmed.

Concerning the subtler distinctions between the Old Greek
and the early stratum of the Lucianic recension, several points
must be noted. The present study claims to have demonstrated
that seven examples from the α ββ section show 4QSam[a], M, and
OG each differing, while L agrees exactly with 4Q. Now the L
tradition is obviously linked very intimately with OG, OG does
not stand in need of revision in those seven instances, yet L
revises nonetheless with 4QSam[a] as the unique (extant) basis
for revision.

Meanwhile, Brock has established the recensional nature of
the fully developed L text, focusing it around the Antiochene
martyr's date and area. Jerome has informed us that Origen--
already before Lucian--knew a *koine* or widespread text tradition subsequently to be labelled "Lucianic." A number of studies, including those of Fischer, Cross, and the present writer,
have proved an early date for some of the Lucianic recensional
characteristics. And Barthélemy, Johnson, Cross, Brock, and
the present writer all find the total accumulation of Samuel
material in Greek to be ultimately dependent upon a single
Greek Version plus generally predictable and explainable revisions and corruptions of that single Version.

Thus, one must definitely reckon with a proto-Lucianic
text tradition, based on OG, but even in its early stratum (before the turn of the era) revised. It did not simply suffer
corruption, as Barthélemy alleges, but it was revised, with
corrections and additions provided to make it conform to the
4QSam text tradition in contemporary Palestine.

Since we do not have the precise exemplar from that tradition, but only a close affiliate in 4QSam[a], since that affiliate is less than 10% extant, and since it itself is close to
the original Hebrew Vorlage of OG, clear, solid evidence for
proto-Lucianic revisional activity does not come in quantity.
More precisely, the *possibility* for evidence is severely

limited quantitatively. But some evidence is there. And, though it cannot be proved that the revisional activity is the work of one man or school, it is plausible, since all the revisions can be termed "corrections toward 4QSam."

Thus, a proto-Lucianic text tradition must be dealt with. It should, perhaps, be cautiously termed a series of proto-Lucianic revisions, rather than being boldly termed the proto-Lucianic recension. The phenomenon is fragile. But though an antique haze enfolds it, the proto-Lucianic reality is there.

Finally, Josephus clearly employed a bible of the 4QSam tradition as his basis for the Samuel portion of the *Jewish Antiquities*, and he clearly used a Greek form of it. For the sections of Samuel for which 4QSam[a] is extant, he shows not a single detail which is clearly or even probably dependent on a bible of the Massoretic tradition or on a biblical text in the Hebrew language. His bible was in Greek, it was a slightly revised form of OG, and it was intimately affiliated with the 4QSam[a] tradition. In brief, Josephus used a bible which exactly fits our description of the proto-Lucianic Greek text.

Josephus thus joins the group 4Q G L OL C J which often, especially where the Massoretic text is troubled, provides or points toward an ancient, *preferanda* form of the text of Samuel.

BIBLIOGRAPHY

I. Texts

The Bible in Aramaic. Vol. II: *The Former Prophets according to Targum Jonathan.* Ed. Alexander Sperber. Leiden, 1959.

Biblia Hebraica. Ed. R. Kittel *et al.*, 12th ed. Stuttgart, 1961.

Bibliorum Sacrorum Latinae Versiones Antiquae, seu Vetus Italica. 3 vols. Ed. Pierre Sabatier. Rheims, 1739-49. Paris, 1751.

The Codex Alexandrinus in Reduced Photographic Facsimile: Old Testament, Part II: *1 Samuel--2 Chronicles.* London, 1930.

Flavii Iosephi Opera. 7 vols. Ed. Benedictus Niese. Berlin, 1887, 1885-95.

Josephus, *Jewish Antiquities.* 6 vols. Tr. H. St J. Thackeray, Ralph Marcus, *et al.* Cambridge, Mass., 1930-1965.

Josephus, *The Life. Against Apian.* Tr. H. St J. Thackeray. Cambridge, Mass., 1926.

Librorum Veteris Testamenti Canonicorum Pars Prior Graece. Ed. Paul Anton de Lagarde. Gottingen, 1883.

The Old Testament in Greek According to the Text of Codex Vaticanus, Supplemented from Other Uncial Manuscripts, with a Critical Apparatus Containing the Variants of the Chief Ancient Authorities for the Text of the Septuagint, Vol. I: *The Octateuch;* Vol. II: *The Later Historical Books;* Vol. III, Part I: *Esther, Judith, Tobit.* Ed. A. E. Brooke and N. McLean, with H. St J. Thackeray for Vols. II-III, 1. Cambridge, 1906-1940.

Septuaginta, Id est Vetus Testamentum graece iuxta LXX interpretes. 2 vols. Ed. Alfred Rahlfs. 7th ed. Stuttgart, 1962.

Septuaginta: Vetus Testamentum Graecum Auctoritate Academiae Scientiarum Gottingensis editum. Vol. I: *Genesis,* ed. J. W. Wevers. Vol. VIII, 1: *Esdrae liber I,* ed. R. Hanhart. Vol. VIII, 3: *Esther,* ed. R. Hanhart. Vol. IX, 1-3: *Maccabaeorum libri I-III,* ed. W. Kappler and R. Hanhart. Vol. X: *Psalmi cum Odis,* ed. A. Rahlfs. Vol. XII, 1: *Sapientia*

261

Salomonis. Vol. XII, 2: *Sapientia Iesu Filii Sirach.* Vol.
XIII: *Duodecim Prophetae.* Vol. XIV: *Isaias.* Vol. XV:
Ieremias, Baruch, Threni, Epistula Ieremiae. Vol. XVI, 1:
Ezechiel. Vol. XVI, 2: *Susanna, Daniel, Bel et Draco,* ed.
(vols. XII-XVI) J. Ziegler. Göttingen, 1931-1974.

Translatio Syra Peschitto Veteris Testamenti ex codice Ambrosi-
ano saeculo fere VI, photolithographice edita curante et
adnotante Sac. Ob. Antonia Maria Ceriani. Mediolani,
1873-1883.

Vannutelli, P. *Libri Synoptici Veteris Testamenti seu Librorum*
Regum et Chronicorum Loci Paralleli. Rome, 1931.

Variae Lectiones Vulgatae Latinae Bibliorum. 2 vols. Ed.
Carolus Vercellone, Rome, 1860 and 1864.

Vetus Testamentum iuxta LXX Interpretum versionem e Codice
omnium antiquissimo Graeco Vaticano 1209 phototypice
repraesentatum. 5 vols. Rome, 1889-1890, reissued in 4
vols., 1904-1907.

II. *Reference Works and Studies*

Albright, W. F. "New Light on Early Recensions of the Hebrew
Bible," *BASOR* 140 (1955), 27-33.

Barthélemy, Dominique, O. P. *Les Devanciers d'Aquila.* Supplements to *V.T.,* X. Leiden, 1963.

_____. "Redécouverte d'un chaînon manquant de l'histoire de
la Septante," *RB* 60 (1953), 18-29.

_____. "A Reexamination of the Textual Problems in 2 Sam 11:2
- 1 Kings 2:11 in the Light of Certain Criticisms of *Les*
Devanciers d'Aquila," *1972 Proceedings: IOSCS and Pseude-*
pigrapha. Ed. Robert A. Kraft. Missoula, 1972, pp. 16-89.

de Boer, P. A. H. *Research into the Text of 1 Samuel I-XVI.*
Amsterdam, 1938.

_____. "I Samuel 17. Notes on the Text and the Ancient Ver-
sions," *Oudtestamentische Studiën* 1 (1942) 79-103.

_____. "Research into the Text of I Samuel XVIII-XXXI," *Oud-*
testamentische Studiën 6 (1949) 1-100.

Boettger, Gustav. *Topographisch-historisches Lexikon zu den*
Schriften des Flavius Josephus. Amsterdam, 1966.

Brock, Sebastian P. "Lucian *redivivus*: Some Reflections on
Barthélemy's *Les Devanciers d'Aquila,*" *Studia Evangelica* 5

[= TU 103] (1968), 176-181.

_____. "The Recensions of the Septuagint Version of I Samuel."
D.Phil. dissertation, Oxford, 1966.

Burkitt, Francis Crawford. *The Old Latin and the Itala.*
Texts and Studies, IV, No. 3. Cambridge, 1896.

Cross, Frank Moore. *The Ancient Library of Qumran and Modern
Biblical Studies.* 2nd ed. New York, 1961.

_____. "The Contribution of the Qumran Discoveries to the
Study of the Biblical Text," *IEJ* 16 (1966) 81-95.

_____. "The Development of the Jewish Scripts," *The Bible and
the Ancient Near East.* Ed. G. Ernest Wright. Garden City,
1965, pp. 170-264.

_____. "The Evolution of a Theory of Local Texts," *1972 Pro-
ceedings: IOSCS and Pseudepigrapha.* Ed. Robert A. Kraft.
Missoula, 1972, pp. 108-126.

_____. "The History of the Biblical Text in the Light of Dis-
coveries in the Judaean Desert," *HTR* 57 (1964) 281-299.

_____. "A New Qumran Biblical Fragment Related to the Orig-
inal Hebrew Underlying the Septuagint," *BASOR* 132 (1953)
15-26.

_____. "The Oldest Manuscripts from Qumran," *JBL* 74 (1955)
147-172.

_____. "Studies in Ancient Yahwistic Poetry." Ph.D. disser-
tation, Johns Hopkins, 1950.

Danby, Herbert. *The Mishnah.* London, 1954.

Dieu, L. "Retouches lucianiques sur quelques texts de la
vieille version latine (I & II Sam.)," *RB*, n.s. 16 (1919)
372-403.

von Dobschütz, Ernst. *Das Decretum Gelasianum de libris recipiendis et non recipiendis* [= TU 38/4]. Leipzig, 1912.

Dörrie, Heinrich. "Zur Geschichte der Septuaginta im Jahrhundert Konstantins," *ZNW* 39 (1940) 57-110.

Driver, S. R. *Notes on the Hebrew Text and the Topography of
the Books of Samuel.* Oxford, 1890.

Eissfeldt, Otto. *The Old Testament: An Introduction.* Tr. from
the 3rd German edition by Peter R. Ackroyd. New York,
1965.

Englert, Donald M. C. *The Peshitto of Second Samuel.* JBL
Monograph Series, III. Philadelphia, 1949.

Feinberg, Lawrence. "A Papyrus Text of I Kingdoms (I Samuel)," *HTR* 62 (1969) 349-356.

Feldman, Louis H. *Scholarship on Philo and Josephus, 1937-1962.* New York, 1963.

Field, Frederick, ed. *Origenis Hexaplorum quae supersunt sive veterum interpretum Graecum in totum Vetus Testamentum fragmenta.* 2 vols. Oxford, 1875.

Fischer, Bonafatius. "Lukian-Lesarten in der Vetus Latina der vier Königsbücher," *Studia Anselmiana* 27-28 (Rome, 1951) 169-177.

Ginsberg, H. L. "The Dead Sea Manuscript Finds: New Light on Eretz Yisrael in the Greco-Roman Period," *Israel: Its Role in Civilization.* Ed. M. Davies. New York, 1956.

Greenberg, Moshe. "The Stabilization of the Text of the Hebrew Bible, Reviewed in the Light of the Biblical Materials from the Judean Desert," *JAOS* 76 (1956) 157-167.

Goshen-Gottstein, M. H. "Hebrew Biblical Manuscripts," *Biblica* 48 (1967) 243-290.

Hadas, Moses. *Aristeas to Philocrates.* New York, 1951.

Hanhart, Robert. "Fragen um die Entstehund der LXX," *VT* 12 (1962) 139-163.

Harrington, Daniel J. "Text and Biblical Text in Pseudo-Philo's 'Liber Antiquitatum Biblicarum.'" Ph.D. dissertation, Harvard University, 1969.

Hatch, Edwin, and H. A. Redpath. *A Concordance to the Septuagint and the Other Greek Versions of the Old Testament.* 3 vols. Oxford, 1897.

Hatch, Edwin. *Essays in Biblical Greek.* Oxford, 1889.

Holmes, Robert, and James Parsons, eds. *Vetus Testamentum graecum cum variis lectionibus.* 5 vols. in 4. Oxford, 1798-1827.

Howard, George. "Frank Cross and Recensional Criticism," *Vetus Testamentum* 21 (1971) 440-450.

_____. "*Kaige* Readings in Josephus," *Textus* 8 (1973) 45-54.

Janzen, J. Gerald. *Studies in the Text of Jeremiah.* Harvard Semitic Monographs, 6. Cambridge, Mass., 1973.

Jellicoe, Sidney. "The Hesychian Recension Reconsidered," *JBL* 82 (1963) 409-418.

_____. Review of D. Barthélemy, *Les Devanciers d'Aquila* in

JAOS 84 (1964) 178-182.

_____. *The Septuagint and Modern Study.* Oxford, 1968.

_____, ed. *Studies in the Septuagint: Origins, Recensions, and Interpretations.* New York, 1974.

Johnson, Bo. *Die hexaplarische Rezension des 1. Samuelbuches der Septuaginta.* Studia Theologica Lundensia, 22. Lund, 1963.

Josephus, Flavius. *The Latin Josephus: I. Introduction and Text: The Antiquities, Books I-V.* Ed. Franz Blatt. København, 1958.

Kahle, Paul E. *The Cairo Geniza.* 2nd ed. Oxford, 1959.

_____. "The Greek Bible Manuscripts Used by Origen," *JBL* 79 (1960) 111-118.

Katz, Peter. *Philo's Bible.* Cambridge, 1950.

Kennedy, H. A. A. "Latin Versions, The Old," *HDB* III, 58-62.

Kennicott, Benjamin. *Dissertatio Generalis in Vetus Testamentum Hebraicum cum Variis Lectionibus.* Brunovici, 1783.

_____. *A Dissertation in Two Parts: Part the First compares I Chron. XI with 2 Sam. V and XXIII; and Part the Second contains Observations on Seventy Hebrew MSS, With an Extract of Mistakes and Various Readings.* Oxford, 1753.

_____. *Remarks on Select Passages in the Old Testament, to which are added Eight Sermons.* Oxford, 1787.

_____. *Vetus Testamentum Hebraicum cum Variis Lectionibus.* Oxford, 1776-1780.

Klein, Ralph W. "New Evidence for an Old Recension of Reigns," *HTR* 60 (1967) 93-105.

_____. "Studies in the Greek Text of the Chronicler." Th.D. dissertation, Harvard University, 1966.

Klostermann, August. *Die Bücher Samuels und Könige.* Kurzegefasster Commentar. Nördlingen, 1887.

Klostermann, Erich. *Analecta zur Septuaginta, Hexapla, und Patristik.* Leipzig, 1895.

Koehler, Ludwig, and Walter Baumgartner, eds. *Lexicon in Veteris Testamenti Libros.* With a supplement. Grand Rapids/Leiden, 1958.

Kraft, Robert A. Review of Dominique Barthélemy, *Les Devanciers d'Aquila* in *Gnomon* 37 (1965) 474-483.

de Lagarde, Paul. *Ankündigung einer neuen Ausgabe der*

griechischen Übersetzung des alten Testaments. Göttingen,
1882.

_____. *Anmerkungen zur griechischen Übersetzung der Pro-
verbien.* Leipzig, 1863.

Lampe, G. W. H. *A Patristic Greek Lexicon.* Oxford, 1961.

Lemke, Werner E. "Studies in the Chronicler's History." Th.D.
dissertation, Harvard University, 1963.

_____. "The Synoptic Problem in the Chronicler's History,"
HTR 58 (1965) 349-363.

Liddell, H. G., and R. Scott. *A Greek-English Lexicon.* 9th
rev. ed. by H. S. Jones, *et al.* Oxford, 1961.

Mandelkern, Solomon. *Veteris Testamenti Concordantiae Hebra-
icae atque Chaldaicae.* 5th ed. Jerusalem, 1962.

Metzger, Bruce M. *Chapters in the History of New Testament
Textual Criticism.* Leiden, 1963.

Mez, Adam. *Die Bibel des Josephus untersucht für Buch V-VII
der Archäologie.* Basel, 1895.

Milik, J. T. *Ten Years of Discovery in the Wilderness of
Judaea.* Tr. J. Strugnell. Studies in Biblical Theology,
26. London, 1959.

Moore, George F. "The Antiochian Recension of the Septuagint,"
AJSL 29 (1912-13) 37-62.

Muraoka, T. "The Greek Texts of Samuel-Kings: Incomplete
Translations or Recensional Activity?" *1972 Proceedings:
IOSCS and Pseudepigrapha.* Ed. Robert A. Kraft. Missoula,
1972, pp. 90-107.

*New American Bible, Translated from the Original Languages with
Critical Use of All the Ancient Sources by Members of the
Catholic Biblical Association of America.* Vol. II, *Samuel
to Maccabees.* With Textual Notes. Paterson, New Jersey,
1969.

O'Connell, Kevin G., S.J. *The Theodotionic Revision of the
Book of Exodus.* Harvard Semitic Monographs, 3. Cambridge,
Mass., 1972.

Orlinsky, H. M. "The Columnar Order of the Hexapla," *JQR* n.s.
27 (1936-37) 137-149.

_____. "Origen's Tetrapla--a Scholarly Fiction?" *Proceedings
of the World Congress of Jewish Studies, I* (1952) 173-182.

_____. "The Septuagint as Holy Writ and the Philosophy of the

Translators," *HUCA* 46 (1975) 89-114.

_____. "The Septuagint--Its Use in Textual Criticism," *BA* 9 (1946) 21-34.

_____. "The Textual Criticism of the Old Testament," *The Bible and the Ancient Near East*. Ed. G. Ernest Wright. Garden City, 1965, pp. 140-169.

Pelletier, André. *Flavius Josephus: Adaptateur de la Lettre d'Aristée*. Paris, 1962.

_____. *Lettre d'Aristée à Philocrate*. Sources Chrétiennes. Paris, 1962.

Rahlfs, Alfred. *Lucians Rezension der Königsbücher*. Septuaginta Studien III. Göttingen, 1911.

_____. "Quis sit ὁ Σύρος," *Mitteilungen des Septuaginta-Unternehmens* I.vii. Göttingen, 1915, pp. 404-412.

_____. *Studien zu den Königsbüchern*. Septuaginta Studien I. Göttingen, 1904.

_____. "Über Theodotion-Lesarten im Neuen Testament und Aquila-Lesarten bei Justin," *ZNW* 20 (1921) 182-199.

Roberts, B. J. *The Old Testament Text and Versions*. Cardiff, 1951.

de Rossi, J. B. *Variae Lectiones Veteris Testamenti*. Reprint of the 1784-1798 Parmi ed. 4 vols. and suppl. in 2. Amsterdam, 1969-70.

Routh, M. *Reliquiae Sacrae*. Vol. IV. 2nd ed. Oxford, 1846.

Rowley, H. H. "The Proto-Septuagint Question," *Jewish Quarterly Review* 33 (1942-43) 497-499.

Schalit, Abraham. *Namenwörterbuch zu Flavius Josephus*. Ed. and intro. by Karl H. Rengstorf. Darmstadt, 1970.

Schmidt, Guilelmus. *De Flavii Iosephi Elocutione Observationes Criticae*. Leipzig, 1893.

Schreckenberg, Heinz. *Bibliographie zu Flavius Josephus*. Arbeiten zur Literatur und Geschichte des Hellenistischen Judentums, I. Leiden, 1968.

Schwartz, Emanuel. *Die syrische Uebersetzung des ersten Buches Samuelis*. Berlin, 1897.

Sevenster, J. N. *Do You Know Greek? How Much Greek Could the First Jewish Christians Have Known?* NTS, XIX. Leiden, 1968.

Shenkel, James Donald. *Chronology and Recensional Development in the Greek Text of Kings*. Harvard Semitic Monographs, 1. Cambridge, Mass., 1968.

_____. "A Comparative Study of the Synoptic Parallels in I Paraleipomena and I-II Reigns," *HTR* 62 (1969) 63-85.

Shutt, R. J. H. "Biblical Names and Their Meanings in Josephus *Jewish Antiquities*, Books I and II, 1-200," *Journal for the Study of Judaism* 2 (1971) 167-182.

Skehan, Patrick W. "The Biblical Scrolls from Qumran and the Text of the Old Testament," *Biblical Archaeologist* 28 (1965) 87-100.

_____. "Exodus in the Samaritan Recension from Qumran," *JBL* 74 (1955) 182-187.

_____. "A Fragment of the 'Song of Moses' (Deut. 32) from Qumran," *BASOR* 136 (1954) 12-15.

_____. "The Qumran Manuscripts and Textual Criticism," *Volume du Congrès Strasbourg 1956*. Supplements to *V.T.*, IV. Leiden, 1957, pp. 148-160.

Smith, Henry Preserved. *The Books of Samuel*. ICC. Edinburgh, 1899.

Sperber, Alexander. "How to Edit the Septuagint," *Harry Austryn Wolfson Jubilee Volume*. Jerusalem, 1965, pp. 751-773.

Stockmayer, Theodor. "Hat Lucian zu seiner Septuagintarevision die Peschito benützt?" *ZAW* 12 (1892) 218-223.

Strack, H. L. *Introduction to the Talmud and Midrash*. Rev. from the 5th German ed. New York, 1959.

Sutcliffe, E. F. "The κοινή 'diversa' or 'dispersa'? St. Jerome PL 24, 548 B," *Biblica* 36 (1955) 213-222.

Swete, Henry Barclay. *An Introduction to the Old Testament in Greek*. Rev. ed. R. R. Ottley. New York, 1968.

Talmon, Shemaryahu. "Aspects of the Textual Transmission of the Bible in the Light of Qumran Manuscripts," *Textus* 4 (1964) 95-132.

_____. "Double Readings in the Masoretic Text," *Textus* 1 (1960) 144-185.

_____. "Synonymous Readings in the Textual Traditions of the Old Testament," *Scripta Hierosolymitana* 8 (1961) 335-383.

Thackeray, H. St J. *A Grammar of the Old Testament in Greek*. Cambridge, 1909.

_____. *Josephus: The Man and the Historian*. New York, 1929.

_____. *The Septuagint and Jewish Worship*. London, 1921.

_____. *Some Aspects of the Greek Old Testament*. London, 1927.

_____, and R. Marcus. *A Lexicon to Josephus*, Parts I-IV: Α-εμφι.... Paris, 1930.

Thenius, Otto. *Die Bücher Samuels*. 3rd ed., Max Löhr. Leipzig, 1898.

Theodoret. *Opera Omnia*. Ed. J. Schulze. Halae, 1769.

Thornhill, Raymond. "Six or Seven Nations: A Pointer to the Lucianic Text in the Heptateuch, with special reference to the Old Latin Version," *JTS*, n.s. 10 (1959) 233-246.

Tiktin, H. *Kritische Untersuchungen zu den Büchern Samuelis*. Göttingen, 1922.

Tov, Emanuel. "Lucian and Proto-Lucian--Toward a New Solution of the Problem," *Revue Biblique* 79 (1972) 101-113.

_____. "The State of the Question: Problems and Proposed Solutions," *1972 Proceedings: IOSCS and Pseudepigrapha*. Ed. Robert A. Kraft. Missoula, 1972, pp. 3-15.

_____. "Transliterations of Hebrew Words in the Greek Versions of the O. T.--A Further Characteristic of the *kaige*-Th Revision?" *Textus* 8 (1972) 78-92.

Ulrich, Eugene C. "4QSam^a and Septuagintal Research," *Bulletin of the International Organization for Septuagint and Cognate Studies* 8 (1975) 24-39.

Vaccari, Alberto. "The Hesychian Recension of the Septuagint," *Biblica* 46 (1965) 60-66.

Veijola, Timo. *Die Ewige Dynastie*. Helsinki, 1975.

Walters, Peter (formerly Katz). *The Text of the Septuagint*. Ed. D. W. Gooding. Cambridge, 1973.

Wellhausen, Julius. *Der Text der Bücher Samuelis*. Göttingen, 1871.

Wevers, John W. "Exegetical Principles Underlying the Greek Text of 2 Sam. 11:2--1 Kings 2:11," *CBQ* 15 (1953) 30-45.

_____. "Exegetical Principles Underlying the Septuagint Text of 1 Kings 2:12--21:43," *Oudtestamentische Studiën* 8 (1950) 300-332.

_____. "Principles of Interpretation Guiding the Fourth Translator of the Book of the Kingdoms," *CBQ* 14 (1952) 40-56.

_____. "Proto-Septuagint Studies," *The Seed of Wisdom: Essays in Honour of T. J. Meek.* Ed. W. S. McCullough. Toronto, 1964, pp. 58-77.

Würthwein, Ernst. *The Text of the Old Testament.* Tr. Peter Ackroyd. Oxford, 1957.

Ziegler, Joseph. "Hat Lukian den Griechischen Sirach rezensiert?" *Biblica* 40 (1959) 210-229.

LIST OF 4QSam[a] FRAGMENTS

1 S		2 S
1:11-13, 22-28		2:5-16, 25-27, 29-32
2:1-6, 8-11, 13-36		3:1-8, 23-39
3:1-4, 18-20		4:1-4, 9-12
4:9-12		5:1-16 (om 5:4-5)
5:8-12		6:2-9, 12-18
6:1-7, 12-13, 16-18, 20-21		7:23-29
7:1		8:2-8
8:9-20		10:4-7, 18-19
9:6-8, 11-12, 16-24		11:2-12, 16-20
10:3-18, 25-27		12:4-5, 8-9, 13-20, 30-31
11:1, 7-12		13:1-6, 13-34, 36-39
12:7-8, 14-19		14:1-3, 18-19
14:24-25, 28-34, 47-51		15:1-6, 27-31
15:24-32		16:1-2, 11-13, 17-18, 21-23
17:3-6		18:2-7, 9-11
24:4-5, 8-9, 14-23		19:7-12
25:3-12, 20-21, 25-26, 39-40		20:2-3, 9-14, 23-26
26:10-12, 21-23		21:1-2, 4-6, 15-17
27:8-12		22:30-51
28:1-2, 22-25		23:1-6
30:28-31		24:16-20
31:2-4		

271

LIST OF CHRONICLES PARALLELS TO SAMUEL AND 4QSam[a]

Samuel	Parallel in Chronicles	4QSam[a] Fragments
1 S 31:1-13	1 C 10:1-12	1 S 31:2-4
2 S 1:6-10	10:1-4	
3:2-5	3:1-4	2 S 3:2-5
5:1-3	11:1-3	5:1-3
5:4-5	3:4	5:4-5 (om)
5:6-10	11:4-9	5:6-10
5:11-12	14:1-2	5:11-12
5:13-16	14:3-7 (= 3:5-9)	5:13-16
5:17-25	14:8-17	
6:1-11	13:1-14	6:2-9
6:12-19	15:25--16:3	6:12-18
7:1-29	17:1-27	7:23-29
8:1-14	18:1-13	8:2-8
8:15-18	18:14-17	
10:1-19	19:1-19	10:4-7,18-19
12:26-31	20:1-3	12:30-31
21:18-22	20:4-8	
23:8-39	11:10-41	
24:1-25	21:1-27	24:16-20

(2 S 22:2-51 = Ps 18[17]:2-50; hab 22:30-51 4Q)

273